Skintight

Skintight

An Anatomy of Cosmetic Surgery

Meredith Jones

Oxford • New York

First published in 2008 by
Berg
Editorial offices:
1st Floor, Angel Court, 81 St Clements Street, Oxford, OX4 1AW, UK
175 Fifth Avenue, New York, NY 10010, USA

Berg is the imprint of Oxford International Publishers Ltd.

Library of Congress Cataloguing-in-Publication Data
Jones, Meredith (Meredith Rachael), 1965-
  Skintight : an anatomy of cosmetic surgery / Meredith Jones.
    p. cm.
  Includes bibliographical references and index.
  ISBN-13: 978-1-84520-668-0 (cloth)
  ISBN-10: 1-84520-668-1 (cloth)
  ISBN-13: 978-1-84520-669-7 (pbk.)
  ISBN-10: 1-84520-669-X (pbk.)
  1. Skin—Surgery. 2. Surgery, Plastic. I. Title.

  RD520.J58 2008
  617.4'77—dc22

                                                    2007043766

British Library Cataloguing-in-Publication Data
A catalogue record for this book is available from the British Library.

ISBN 978 1 84520 668 0 (Cloth)
     978 1 84520 669 7 (Paper)

Typeset by JS Typesetting Ltd, Porthcawl, Mid Glamorgan
Printed in the United Kingdom by Biddles Ltd, King's Lynn

www.bergpublishers.com

For Ruby-Rose O'Halloran

Contents

Illustrations

Acknowledgements

My biggest debt of gratitude is to my dear friend and mentor Zoë Sofoulis, who showed constant interest and pleasure in this project and was endlessly generous with her diverse body of knowledge, her personal library, and her profound insights. Thanks also go to the colleagues at my former workplace, the Centre for Cultural Research at the University of Western Sydney, especially Reena Dobson, Bob Hodge (for telling me when to stop), Elaine Lally, Maree O'Neill and Greg Noble. I have many supportive colleagues at my current workplace, the Institute for Interactive Media and Learning at the University of Technology, Sydney. In particular I would like to acknowledge Shirley Alexander, Maher Berro, Linda Leung, Grant Matthews, and Jo McKenzie. The book would not exist in this form without the conversations I've been privileged to have with my sparkling friend, philosopher Cressida Heyes, about her analyses of cosmetic surgery. Thanks to Catherina Landström for helping me understand Actor Network Theory and to Leigh Blackmore for doing the final proof-read. My family supported me through a grave illness while I was working on this book – love to Richard, Betty, David, Gareth, Dorian, Laura, Hugh, Julia, Helen, Ruby, Chris, Griffin, and Sailor.

The book of course would not have been possible without the people who consented to be interviewed. Although they must remain anonymous I thank them deeply for coming forward and being so candid and honest about intensely personal issues.

An earlier version of Chapter 4 was published in 2004 as 'Mutton Cut Up as Lamb: Mothers, Daughters and Cosmetic Surgery' in *Continuum: Journal of Media and Cultural Studies*, Volume 18, Number 4, pp. 525–539. Parts of Chapters 2 and 8 were published in 2004 as 'Architecture of the Body: Cosmetic Surgery and Postmodern Space' in *Space and Culture: International Journal of Social Spaces*, Volume 7, Issue 1, pp. 90–101.

Every effort has been made to secure permission to reproduce the images in this book. If there has been any oversight, please contact the publisher.

Introduction

Instances of cosmetic surgery have risen[1] and our perceptions of it have changed dramatically in the past decade. No longer a bizarre indulgence for the rich, famous or narcissistic, cosmetic surgery has become an everyday practice that popular media tell us we 'deserve'. It is even presented as something that will enable our 'true selves' to emerge. For some, it is an aesthetic and cultural imperative. Television programmes like the USA's *Extreme Makeover* and the UK's *Ten Years Younger* go so far as to present it as an activity that requires bravery and courage: cosmetic surgery in these contexts is an indication of self-determination and triumph over physical misfortune or signs of ageing. So connected has cosmetic surgery become to notions of mental well-being that one critic calls it 'scalpel psychiatry' (Jordan, 2004: 333). One of the characters (a cosmetic surgeon) in the hugely successful television drama *Nip/Tuck* declares that 'sometimes giving a person a nose job changes their life in more profound ways than a lifetime of mood controllers' (Christian, Episode 3, Series 1). Recently there have been profound shifts in how we see cosmetic surgery – the aim of this book is to examine them.

People in poorer parts of the globe are not immune to the lure and effects of cosmetic surgery. Late in 2005 Nigeria went into national mourning because Stella Obasanjo, the 59-year-old wife of the president, died after a cosmetic surgery operation in Spain. In 2004, 22-year-old Feng Qian won a national competition in Beijing and was crowned the world's first 'Miss Artificial Beauty' – far from being a bimbo she is now studying to be a plastic surgeon. In Iran the Grand Ayatollah Saanei informs Shi'ite Muslims via an advisory website that if a specialist says that breast implants and liposuction are not harmful to the patient then they are permitted within Islamic law.

Cosmetic surgery is more than surgical technology, more than medical discipline. It has deep symbolic meaning and rich cultural connotations; throughout this book I argue that it is a vital part of what I call 'makeover culture'. Broadly, I suggest that in makeover culture the process of *becoming something better* is more important than achieving a static point of completion. 'Good citizens' of makeover culture publicly enact urgent and never-ending renovations of themselves. I argue that cosmetic surgery is makeover culture's quintessential expression.

I use many discursive and concrete examples to explore the cultural aspects of cosmetic surgery; most are examined using feminist and cultural studies approaches. This book also includes philosophy, psychoanalysis, media studies and actor-network theory. The texts drawn upon include popular women's magazines, websites, celebrity

1

lives, myth, specialised cosmetic surgery magazines, television programmes, fairy stories and medical journals. The world of cosmetic surgery includes face-to-face interactions so a further level of analysis is offered via interviews with cosmetic surgery recipients and surgeons. I conducted formal interviews with sixteen cosmetic surgery recipients between 2002 and 2005. They all lived and worked along the Eastern seaboard of Australia, mostly in Sydney but also in Melbourne, Brisbane and on Queensland's Sunshine Coast. Some answered an advertisement I placed in Sydney local newspapers *Wentworth Courier* and *North Shore Times*. I connected with others using the 'snowball approach' where, for example, someone would put me in contact with her aunt or friend. Some had already had their surgery, some I spoke to both before and after their surgery, and one decided not to go ahead with her planned facelift. In addition to the sixteen interviewees, some of my friends and acquaintances had cosmetic surgery while I was doing this research. Most happily gave me in-depth interviews about their motivations, desires and the surgical experience. An old friend revealed a secret: both she and her male partner had cosmetic surgery a decade ago. Only one person I approached through the grapevine refused to speak with me about her cosmetic surgery. All interviews were based on a predetermined set of questions but many became free-flowing and turned into conversations. As some of them were with friends and acquaintances, they dovetailed with other interactions and occasionally happened in unexpected places like cars and on the telephone. Most were taped and transcribed but impromptu sessions had to rely on my note taking. All names have been changed to ensure anonymity. I also spoke with four surgeons in their consulting rooms, approached directly by letter and phone. Two were plastic surgeons and two were cosmetic surgeons (an important distinction, which I discuss in Chapter 3).

All the interviewees were Australian but much of the media analysed originates in the UK and USA (although it was reprinted in Australia). The ubiquity of UK and US images and stories about cosmetic surgery in Australian magazines, television and cinema shows how cosmetic surgery is closely connected to accelerating processes of globalisation. In Chapter 2, I explore cosmetic surgery as a simultaneously local and global practice.

Many feminist researchers and writers do not hesitate to position themselves as part of what they study – I am no exception. I am not objective but rather part of what I analyse. Theoretically and physically connected to the cosmetic surgery world, I absorb advertisements, compare celebrities' smoothed faces to my own and thrill at cosmetic surgery horror stories. I am part of makeover culture and make no pretence of being immune to its pressures and pleasures. For these reasons this piece of writing can only be utterly situated and never objective. It is bound up inside the social structures, discourses, profit margins, power plays and evolving techniques that make up the borderless site of cosmetic surgery. Susan Stewart writes, 'we are surrounded by the image of the woman's face, the obsession of the portrait and the cover girl alike. The face is what belongs to the other; it is unavailable to the woman herself' (1993: 125). The idea that in a sense our faces (and bodies) don't belong to us but are rather part of a wider mediascape is a powerful underlying theme throughout this book.

We love to talk about cosmetic surgery – we are fascinated by scandals and successes alike. Listening to me through the din at parties, people sometimes thought I was training to be a cosmetic surgeon and would ask advice about droopy eyelids or large thighs. It seems that many of us have a list of body-alterations we would 'need' to become perfect. Once upon a time we fantasised about which movie star would play us in the story of our life; now we wonder what cosmetic surgery we could have in order to be a movie star ourselves. As Virginia Blum writes, 'little by little, we are all becoming movie stars – internally framed by a camera eye' (2003: 288).

Cosmetic surgery is increasingly widespread, available, desirable and normalised. It affects us all, whether we choose to have it or not. It is here to stay. We need to understand where it comes from and what its cultural significance is. We need to find new ways to address it. Feminists especially need a full understanding of how it manifests in order to create a vocabulary with which to deal with it. I critically examine it as part of everyday life: as a titillating, scandalous, contradictory, seductive and embedded part of our cultural landscape.

Cosmetic, Plastic, Reconstructive and Aesthetic Surgeries

'Plastic', 'cosmetic', 'reconstructive' and 'aesthetic' are used somewhat inter-changeably to describe cosmetic surgery. 'Plastic surgery' generally covers the entire field. 'Reconstructive surgery' treats deformity due to disease, congenital defect or injury. 'Cosmetic surgery' (and the lesser-used 'aesthetic surgery') refers to elective and anti-ageing procedures. Cosmetic surgery is sometimes represented as the 'bastard child of plastic and reconstructive surgeries, held in contempt by "real" surgeons who believe they are fixing "real" problems...' (Brownell, 2005: 137). The distinction between plastic and cosmetic surgery is a value-laden and sometimes moral one, not necessarily connected to actual procedures that are similar if not identical across the disciplines. Cosmetic surgery and plastic surgery both work with skin grafts, implants, removal of 'excess' flesh and minimisation of scar tissue. My focus is mainly on cosmetic surgery, which consists of operations not related to birth defects, burns, disease, injury or mastectomy; operations conducted on bodies that are generally accepted as undamaged except by time and age; and operations that aim to minimise or eradicate signs of ageing such as drooping, wrinkles, loss of skin lustre and 'middle age spread'. Although I argue that borders between elective and non-elective surgeries are increasingly blurred, for the purposes of keeping this book under control I have to draw a line somewhere. This is why, for example, I do not discuss female or male circumcisions, or sex-change operations – these are deeply complex topics that deserve their own volumes.

Elective, anti-ageing facial cosmetic surgery is often referred to as 'facelift' surgery, which implies a single operation but is usually a collection of procedures (often done simultaneously under one anaesthetic), such as 'S' lift, browlift and blepharoplasty. Elective anti-ageing cosmetic surgery can include many procedures. A basic list would include:

- 'S' lifts or rhytidectomy, where the skin and muscles of the jaw and neck are lifted and tightened after cutting an 'S' shape around the ear (rhytidectomy alone is sometimes referred to as a facelift, especially in Britain. See British Association of Aesthetic Plastic Surgeons, http://www.baaps.org.uk/, for a full explanation of this procedure);
- browlifts/forehead lifts, conducted via line incisions or endoscopic (keyhole) surgery where stab incisions are made above the hairline in order to cut and raise the muscles of the brow;
- blepharoplasty, where skin and fat are removed from the upper and/or lower eyelids;
- 'injectables' such as Botox® and collagen that 'freeze' muscles and 'plump up' wrinkles and lines respectively;
- lip surgeries, where products such as Restylane® or the patient's own tissue or fat – for example, that removed during an abdominoplasty ('tummy tuck') – is injected, and/or vermilion advancement, where the mucosa on the inner lip is turned out to create a fuller look;
- liposuction, where cannulas are inserted between the skin and the muscle, then connected to a suction machine, and fat cells from localised areas are removed;
- dermabrasion, laser, or acid peel treatments that 'resurface' the skin by removing dermis mechanically or chemically so that new skin must grow;
- mammoplasty (breast augmentation or reduction), performed either by inserting sacs of silicone or saline or by removing breast tissue via insertions in breast, nipple, armpit or navel;
- rhinoplasty (nose jobs), where the nose is reshaped via bone and cartilage reduction or manipulation; and
- malar (cheekbone) and chin augmentation or reduction, where small implants are placed under the skin or where bones are filed down.

I use the generic term 'cosmetic surgery' to refer to various compilations of these procedures and their aesthetics in relation to both individuals and collectives. For example, I might discuss a certain person's look and how it has been surgically modified, or I might analyse a more generalised 'surgical aesthetic' that is not confined to a single individual.

Chapters

Chapter 1 situates cosmetic surgery in history and outlines the most important feminist writings in the area. It introduces makeover culture as a contemporary paradigm that is rich, varied and contradictory. The cultural logics embedded in and around the 'before/after' model, a dominant trope in the representation of cosmetic surgery, are examined. The famous *Awful Plastic Surgery* website (awfulplasticsurgery.com) is closely analysed as a microcosm of makeover culture. This website embodies some common paradoxical stances – in it cosmetic surgery is advertised, glorified and condemned all at once. I suggest that a productive study of contradiction is possible within a framework built around the notion of 'ideological complexes' (Hodge and Kress, 1988).

Chapter 2 shows how cosmetic surgery is part of globalisation. It gives a world-view of cosmetic surgery and argues that while it is a global practice it can never be separated from its local environments. Two very specific sites are analysed with this in mind. One is a concrete, architectural space where bodies actually exist – the Bonaventure Hotel – the other is a television and web-based space – *Extreme Makeover*. The Bonaventure is analysed somewhat metaphorically – via Fredric Jameson's famous reading – in relation to before/after and 'older' cultural logics around cosmetic surgery. *Extreme Makeover*, a striking part of the contemporary global mediascape, is offered as a quintessential example of the new cultural logics of makeover culture at work.

Many narratives and critiques situate the surgeon/patient relationship at the heart of the cosmetic surgery matrix. I prefer to see him[2] as one interdependent part of the makeover culture network. He is analysed in Chapter 3 as part of an entanglement, an assemblage of actors that includes cosmetic surgery recipients and non-human actors such as Botox®. I figure the surgeon as central to the materialisation of cosmetic surgery but also as a conduit by which non-human and human cosmetic surgery actors come together. Doctors, recipients and strange creatures such as Botox® form an intertwined and codependent collection at the hub of cosmetic surgery culture. This chapter deploys the Pygmalion myth to examine agency in this recipient/surgeon/product assemblage: who is the provocateur, who or what has power, and how is power determined?

The concept of the 'stretched middle age' is crucial to contemporary cosmetic surgery. Chapter 4 introduces the term and explains how it relates to anti-ageing and the youth paradigm. I argue that anti-ageing cosmetic surgery allows subjects to perform conscious presentations of the self and is about designing, not denying ageing. The chapter looks at how cosmetic surgery is able to upset and undermine traditional connections between chronology and appearance, and the ways that these 'disruptions' of temporality are represented in various media. It especially focuses on my interviews and one sub-genre: the mother/daughter cosmetic surgery article.

I offer an alternative deployment and reading of anti-ageing cosmetic surgery that suggests that although generational tensions are highlighted by mainstream cosmetic surgery discourse it may offer opportunities for new connections between mothers and daughters, both literal and figurative.

As cosmetic surgery becomes popular and commonplace it is necessary to look at how concepts of 'normal' are negotiated and renegotiated within makeover culture. Chapter 5 argues that, once cosmetic surgery has been chosen, the manner in which it is carried out and its display are subject to continual and obsessive scrutiny. Individuals who use cosmetic surgery operations to perform the work of makeover culture must negotiate some complex boundaries: having cosmetic surgery does not guarantee benefits and can be a distinct disadvantage. 'Going too far' or 'going wrong' is possible in many subtle ways: cosmetic surgery is a difficult and complicated arena in which to be an active consumer. To demonstrate this I analyse a selection of damning reports and speculations about cosmetic surgery 'freaks'. Using feminist explanations of monstrosity I show how cosmetic surgery is a tool in the regulation, definition and policing of 'normality'.

I show throughout this book how makeover culture is utterly tied up with post-modern values of consumption, revision and the importance of surface. However, it also has mythical and richly metaphoric elements. Chapter 6 examines an extreme practitioner of cosmetic surgery, Lolo Ferrari. Her famous breast augmentations and her lesser-known statements about loving the state of anaesthesia are analysed in order to highlight some of makeover culture's fantasies. In line with my aim of examining cosmetic surgery in ways that augment the traditional feminist areas of interest – agency, control and ethics – I offer this interpretation to show how its aims and desires are rooted in legend and are abundantly symbolic.

Not all cosmetic surgery is used for anti-ageing, for looking 'normal' or for attaining 'beauty'. Some is deliberately excessive or grotesque. Chapter 7 engages closely with Orlan and Michael Jackson. Their intensely public relationships with cosmetic surgery are scrutinised in terms of the boundaries they cross, their chosen monstrousness and their foci on always-becoming. I argue that they have each become a living work of art through cosmetic surgery. They exemplify a delinquent makeover citizenry – dramatically combining the horrors and desires of cosmetic surgery. Whether they are successful artists or spectacular failures is irrelevant: their extreme embodiments and excessive relationships with cosmetic surgery herald carnivalesque and radical possibilities.

The concluding chapter speculates about alternative cosmetic surgery aesthetics. A controversial urban development – Melbourne's Federation Square – is used as a template for imagining 'designer monstrosities' that would be self-consciously grotesque, blurring lines between radical body modification practices and cosmetic surgery. Crucially, this chapter suggests that actively remaining cosmetic-surgery-free may well become a brave and rebellious act.

Before/After

From Heresy to Makeover Culture

A little rhinoplasty can always make the pretty look prettier

AwfulPlasticSurgery.com

The history of cosmetic surgery is fascinating and complex, closely tied to war and migration, to developments in medicine and surgery, and to cultural changes in perceptions of what it means to be a fulfilled human being. Cosmetic surgery operations date from at least as early as 600BC when Indian surgeons were making new noses from flaps of skin brought down from the forehead or across from the cheek for people (usually men) who had lost them through disease or injury. Chinese records from the tenth century AD tell of surgeries designed to fix harelips (Gilman, 2005: 65). There are records of nose reconstructions performed in Europe from the 1400s, especially in Italy, to recreate noses sliced off during swordfights (Haiken, 1997: 5) or rotted away by syphilis (Gilman, 2005: 66). The earliest record accompanied by pictures is the work of Gaspare Tagliacozzi, professor of surgery at the University of Bologna (1545–99). Significantly, Tagliacozzi's work was condemned by the powerful Roman Catholic Church. It was seen as a heretical 'unnatural and immoral science' (Jordan, 2004: 330) because it minimised evidence of divine retribution thought to be on the bodies of syphilis sufferers (Gilman, 2005: 66–72). Tagliacozzi was so hated by the Church that his corpse was exhumed and moved to unconsecrated ground. His surgical work was then ignored or forgotten for centuries.

The promise of pain- and infection-free surgery was probably the most important factor in the rise of cosmetic surgery through the nineteenth and early twentieth centuries. Before the developments of anaesthetic (1846) and antiseptic (1867), surgeries were performed, by modern standards, in filthy conditions accompanied by terrible pain. The risk of death through infection, blood loss or shock was high. Surgery was hugely dangerous, so it is no wonder that operations designed only for aesthetic purposes were rare. In this context historian of cosmetic surgery Sander Gilman notes 'it is a sign of the power of the stigma associated with the missing nose that patients were willing to risk such procedures' (2005: 82). Many contemporary cosmetic surgery procedures were only invented after anaesthesia became common

– the first tummy tuck (abdominoplasty) was recorded in 1899, the first facelift in 1901 and the first blepharoplasty (eye lift) in 1906 (Gilman, 2005: 83–8).

Elizabeth Haiken's excellent history *Venus Envy* (1997) traces the ways that cosmetic surgery changed during twentieth century America. She notes that early in the century 'cosmetic surgery appeared to contradict both the traditional American injunction against vanity and the Hippocratic injunction against doing harm ... "beauty surgery" was the province of quacks and charlatans' (1997: 1–2). But by the end of the century 'the stigma of narcissism that once attached to cosmetic surgery has largely vanished, leaving in its place the comfortable aura of American pragmatism, with a whiff of an optimistic commitment to self-improvement thrown in' (1997: 7). Haiken's foundational book links cosmetic surgery's rise to the development of psychology (in particular to the concept of 'self-esteem'), to the growth of consumer culture, to technological developments, and to straightforward increases in personal wealth. She identifies cosmetic surgery as a particularly American phenomenon: 'the surgical solution has allowed us to hold on to an idealised self-image ... [we are] bent on creating and recreating ourselves in the most modern of all possible ways' (1997: 15).

It was not until the First World War that plastic surgery became a powerful and fully recognised branch of medicine. This was due to three combined factors: shrapnel, which created horrible injuries including burns; trench warfare, in which often only heads and shoulders were exposed so that injuries disproportionately affected the face; and advances in medical and emergency treatments, which simply meant that more soldiers survived their injuries. Huge numbers of men with profound disfigurements returning from war necessitated urgent research and experimentation into techniques for rebuilding their faces. New Zealander Harold Delf Gillies (1882–1960), sometimes called the father of cosmetic surgery, invented many techniques during and after the First World War that are still used today. His work was groundbreaking and sometimes astonishingly adventurous. Figure 1 is of a wax model showing his technique of skin grafting using 'pedicule tubes' – pipes of the patient's own living tissue 'borrowed' from non-injured places on the body – to supply blood to aid skin grafting. Gillies is also famous for the aphorism that while reconstructive surgery is 'an attempt to return to normal' aesthetic surgery is 'an attempt to surpass the normal' (1935, quoted in Gilman, 2005: 98). The attempt to define 'normal' in relation to cosmetic surgery is a highly complex and contested one – by surgeons, recipients, health insurers, psychologists, philosophers and feminists – and is an issue revisited and examined throughout this book.

By the 1920s most cosmetic surgery operations were being done on women. Gillies and his colleagues had honed techniques and built respectable careers during the war, and turned to more 'aesthetic' surgeries in order to keep practising. Communications scholar John W. Jordan describes the move: 'The restored bodies of soldiers were a kind of *a fortiori* argument in more peaceful times and reversed the earlier proscriptions against vanity surgery: if plastic surgery could work wonders

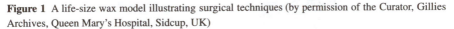

Figure 1 A life-size wax model illustrating surgical techniques (by permission of the Curator, Gillies Archives, Queen Mary's Hospital, Sidcup, UK)

on the horrible disfigurations of a wounded soldier, surely it could repair unsightly features on an otherwise healthy body' (2004: 332).

That cosmetic surgery's focus changed in the twentieth century from fixing war wounds to making people more beautiful is something that holds great interest for British sculptor Paddy Hartley, who told me:

> In civilian practice Gillies did the lot, nose jobs, breast reduction, sex changes, the lot. The surgeons who had honed their reconstructive surgical skills during the First World War essentially had no patients after servicemen were fixed up. Having all these skills and few patients to treat created the new field of aesthetic surgery. As well as a way of earning a living, it's this 'thing' built into anyone working in sciences – a compulsion to push the limits of their practice.
>
> Personally I think that if people contemplating cosmetic surgery knew what a lot of these facially-injured First World War chaps went through and the surgery they endured, they might think twice about that brow-lift or chin tuck. Maybe they wouldn't, but it's a part of history that still needs to be fully acknowledged (interview with the author, 2006).

Hartley is working on an artistic response, *Project Façade*, to the Gillies Archive, which is held at Queen Mary's Hospital, Sidcup, in Southern England. The project consists of modifying original First World War uniforms using cutting techniques, fabric manipulation and digital embroidery to reflect upon and recall the injuries that servicemen endured and the surgical treatments that Gillies devised (Figure 2). Hartley has presented his work at body modification conferences where he shares the platform with people talking about tattooing, piercing and contemporary cosmetic surgery. His work reminds us of the oft-forgotten links between reconstructive and cosmetic surgeries. An intriguing and sobering art practice, it prompts us to recall that cosmetic surgery has its roots in war and in sometimes agonising disfigurement.

Cosmetic surgery has always been a precarious practice fraught with controversy and contradiction – from the Renaissance Church's view that it was sinful to diminish the marks borne by syphilis sufferers, to the transitions Gillies made

Figure 2 Paddy Hartley, *William* (2007). British Army Officers Uniform and sculptural facial garment illustrating the rhinoplastic surgery of 2nd Lieut. William Spreckley. Embroidery details feature notes and sketches made by Sir Harold Gillies in the preparation of Williams's surgery and correspondence between the artist and Williams's granddaughter.

between reconstructive and 'beauty' surgery in the early twentieth century, to today, when the reconstructive versus elective debate is still potent. Hartley told me

> The difference between reconstructive and cosmetic surgery is – they're not the same things – the whole point of reconstruction is to get you back to what you were originally – people might see ageing as a traumatic event which happens to us all. Having part of your face torn off is an infinitely more traumatic and unique event to an individual (interview with the author, 2006).

His observation about ageing experienced by some as a trauma resulting in a body that needs reconstruction highlights the ways the borders between reconstructive and cosmetic surgeries are increasingly blurred in makeover culture. Feminist theorists of the body have grappled with these borders and definitions for decades – the most important of their discussions are outlined later in this chapter.

Makeover Culture

Originally this book was planned as a feminist analysis of interviews with women who had chosen to have cosmetic surgery. Inevitably though, I became attracted to narratives in women's magazines about cosmetic surgery 'disasters' or 'weirdos' – people like Farrah Fawcett, Cher, Michael Jackson, Joan Rivers and Pete Burns. The magazines mingled on my desk with my interview material. I began to take articles about people like Farrah Fawcett and Michael Jackson from sources like *NW* and *New Idea*[1] as seriously as I was, for example, taking Kathy Davis's socialist-feminist analyses of cosmetic surgery recipients in The Netherlands. Struggling with how to describe this miscellany, I sat down to procrastinate with Jerry Springer.[2] And suddenly a carnivalesque moment gave rise to the idea that we are living in a *makeover culture*. The programme was about friends and family telling their loved ones how embarrassing they are because they dress inappropriately. In most cases the problem was that an overweight middle-aged woman was dressing 'like a teenager'. An obese woman appeared on stage wearing a micro-mini frock and high heels. Her waiting family members shook their heads in disgust and the audience booed and jeered. But then Springer said she had recently lost 100 pounds. Instantly boos changed to cheers and the woman sat down proudly, ready to defend her right to wear skimpy outfits. Makeover culture was in force. The large woman was suddenly praiseworthy because she was undergoing transformation: she was no longer horribly fat but was now 'losing weight'. Negative judgements about her inappropriate dress sense became praise for being in the process of becoming slimmer. Thus we learn from the 'pedagogical voice of reality TV' (McCarthy, 2005) that a big woman can't wear sexy clothes but a woman who has lost 100 pounds can, even if those two women are exactly the same. This is because makeover culture valorises and rewards processes of working on the self. I show throughout this book how makeover culture is about the display of ongoing change and labour, and how cosmetic surgery is its quintessential example.

Makeover culture is a state where *becoming* is more desirable than *being*. It valorises the process of development rather than the point of completion. It is closely related to renovation and restoration, and includes elements of both, but where renovation and restoration imply achieving a final goal or a finished product, 'make-over' – used either as noun or verb – is in the present tense. Despite appearances then, makeover culture is not about the creation of finished products – whether houses, psyches, bodies or gardens – rather it is about showing subjects, objects and environments being worked upon and improved. This is why the large woman was applauded for losing weight: being in a process of self-improvement – being in makeover – overrode her inappropriate dress sense. Good citizens of makeover culture improve and transform themselves ceaselessly. For individuals the makeover paradigm rewards display of continual development and growth made via intellectual, emotional or aesthetic means. I argue that in makeover culture success is judged on the display of the never-ending renovation of the self.

Other scholars are also beginning to work around these ideas, for example media and cultural theorist Frances Bonner has identified 'makeover' as a new television genre (2003: 130–6; also see Brunsdon, 2003). Deborah Caslav Covino's book *Amending the Abject Body* (2004) uses the phrase 'makeover culture' almost unproblematically. Although never clearly explaining what the phrase means, Covino states that '"makeover" has become an increasingly popular name for the normalisation of the self around procedures and prospects that are tied up with body image and related forms of abjection' (2004: 14). The online journal *Flow: A Critical Forum on Television and Media Culture* has published several articles that analyse makeover television programmes alongside new economies of labour (McPherson, 2005), work ethics (Kim, 2004) and models of government (McCarthy, 2005). The phrase is becoming important in critical and academic feminist vocabularies but it needs explication and elaboration.

For the purposes of discussing how makeover culture intersects with cosmetic surgery, *labour revealed* is important. For example, the television programme *Extreme Makeover*, analysed in detail in Chapter 2, shows cosmetic surgery operations in ways they have never appeared on mainstream television before: surgeries are filmed, blood and gore are crucial parts of the show, and patients' excruciatingly painful recoveries are followed in detail. Media theorist Tara McPherson has suggested that on makeover television 'bodies become one with the bitstream, as easily morphed as a Photoshop file. Beauty is no longer a surface phenomenon, with the exterior reworked to match a "beautiful" interior through a careful consumption of products. The inside and outside now collapse and blur, all up for reconfiguring and all requiring hard work' (2005). *Hard work* is the key point: makeover culture is about industriousness and the display of labour. Programmes like *Extreme Makeover*, which are built around painful recovery periods, embarrassing consultations and vulnerable anaesthetised subjects, frame cosmetic surgery as tough. It becomes something that only the most motivated consider: it becomes an act of courage and bravery, part of the toil of makeover culture.

McPherson situates her observations about the labour revealed in makeover programmes inside wider changes connected to electronic culture. She suggests that just as electronic culture blurs boundaries between work and home, makeover television helps to define another new space for labour: the body. Television, as part of electronic culture, skills us 'for the new modes of living demanded by post-Fordist economies, modes that require a new relationship to our very corporeal selves' (McPherson, 2005). I argue that one of these new relationships is enacted via cosmetic surgery.

Makeover does not only refer to cosmetic surgery; it can describe many aspects of contemporary culture and resonates with other important trends. For example, makeover's visualising of the previously hidden is similar to the 'medi-porn' (Cadigan, 1991) that features in forensic police television like *CSI* and *CSI Miami* where internal organs, dead bodies and autopsies are shown in graphic detail, and in the *Visible Human Project*, a digital rendering of the entire human anatomy (Waldby, 2000). It is evident in the popularity of mediatised home renovation, interior decorating, choosing 'correct' clothing, 'confession' and 'self-improvement' shows like *Dr Phil* and *Oprah*, and practices such as lifelong learning. There is even a case to be made for the US fetish for rehabilitation being part of makeover culture.

Ideological Complexes: Contradictions in Makeover Culture

Makeover culture does not describe a neat and logical world. Its products and rhetoric are often illogical and hypocritical. Investigating makeover culture's 'logics' requires a theoretical or interpretative framework able to explain the contrasting elements and tendencies within it. So I begin from the standpoint that contradiction can work in the service of general discursive and cultural formations. Robert Hodge and Gunther Kress explain in *Social Semiotics* (1988) that 'forms of intercourse (*verkehr*: communication, systems of exchange) correspond to particular forms of social organization and are necessary to their very existence' (1988: 2–3). They argue that modes of social organisation such as contemporary capitalism (in and by which cosmetic surgery has been created) require particular types of discursive intercourse in order to survive and thrive, and, importantly, that contradiction is a characteristic of them. Contradiction can work to enhance and strengthen rather than to undermine:

> In order to sustain ... structures of domination the dominant groups attempt to represent the world in forms that reflect their own interests, the interests of their power. But they also need to sustain the bonds of solidarity that are the condition of their dominance.

Dominated groups are not always and everywhere blinded to the operations of these structures – as they have been portrayed in certain Marxist accounts. They in their turn attempt to resist the effects of domination, often succeeding, in countlessly many social encounters within social structures (Hodge and Kress, 1988: 3).

The interplay between discourses of domination and resistance and the countless grey areas between them creates what Hodge and Kress call 'ideological complexes'. The term expresses 'a functionally related set of contradictory versions of the world' (1988: 3) that are used by the dominant group to coerce or by the resistant group to subvert. It is important that they are theorised as *functionally* related. These contradictions operate together to create a functional and stable whole, working against dysfunction. The hypothesis suggests that contrasting viewpoints do not destabilise dominant cultural forms but can cross-hatch to create a solidly fused structure that is stronger precisely because it incorporates different paradigms.

Seeing makeover culture and cosmetic surgery as incorporated parts of a series of ideological complexes allows me to study contradictory, oppositional elements without posing them against each other. For example, in Chapter 3 I engage with surgical discourses and doctors' voices and in Chapter 6 I deploy the myths and biography of Lolo Ferrari, a pornography worker who had the largest breast implants in the world, while feminist voices resonate throughout the book. This multivocal strategy might seem full of opposing elements: feminist theorists are generally resistant to and critical of cosmetic surgery; surgeons form a dominant group that stands to gain much wealth and status from its widespread adoption; Ferrari's cosmetic surgery voice seems deeply submissive. But the framework of ideological complexity makes it possible to see these diverse strands – and many others – as interlocking, each adding to the strength of a dominant discourse, here theorised as makeover culture.

Awful Cosmetic Surgery

Sociologist Kathy Davis has observed that cosmetic surgery is not reducible to a single viewpoint but is 'problem and solution, oppression and liberation...' all in one (1995: 67). Even within single texts there may be many contradictory viewpoints (Fraser, 2003). For example, the website *Awful Plastic Surgery: the good, bad, and ugly of celebrity plastic surgery* (quoted at the beginning of this chapter) embraces diverse views on cosmetic surgery. It emphasises the dangers of cosmetic surgery and even has a section dedicated to cosmetic surgery deaths: 'Earlier this year, Micheline Charest, a co-founder of the CINAR animation company, died on April 14 from complications of plastic surgery. She was 51. Charest had cardiac arrest following a face-lift, breast-lift and liposuction' (November 15, 2004). It includes gleeful 'exposures' of cosmetic surgery deemed to be ugly or awful: 'yet another photo illustration of Meg Ryan's yucky plastic surgery. Wouldn't you rather have a few wrinkles than look like your face was made of plastic? Her lips are awful' (September 22, 2003). And yet it exhorts celebrities who are deemed to 'need' cosmetic surgery to quickly get some:

> Chris Noth[3] has really huge under eye bags; seriously, according to a makeup artist who worked on 'Sex and the City', they are so large you could get lost in them. Weirdly enough, Chris has not jumped on the celebrity plastic surgery bandwagon although he definitely could use an eye job; lets give him some encouragement by showing him these [airbrushed] before and after photos of what he could look like once he gets an eye job (September 30, 2003).

Further, the site celebrates 'good' cosmetic surgery:

> *Blue Crush* star (and Orlando Bloom girlfriend), Kate Bosworth, has made some barely perceptible changes to her nose in the past year. Her nose used to be much rounder and snub. Now, her profile is stronger and her nose tip is more defined (December 28, 2003).

In addition to these seemingly oppositional views of cosmetic surgery *Awful Plastic Surgery* includes advertisements for cosmetic surgery. An article mocking someone's over-inflated lips will have a link to a product that promises 'luscious lips without injections!' A posting about lopsided breast implants will have a link to a cosmetic surgeon who specialises in mammoplasty. The 'crimes' that the website uncovers are committed by vain celebrities who 'go too far', or by greedy or incompetent doctors: 'someone sent us a photo of Bree Walker's huge lips. And they are massive, rivaling both Lisa Rinna's and Melanie Griffith's huge pairs of trout lips. Whoever is giving her lip collagen injections should be arrested for malpractice' (November 2, 2004).

Ideological complexes neatly describe what is going on here: a series of inversions and revisions, congratulations and condemnations, all working to convey a cultural dominant. In many ways *Awful Plastic Surgery* is a microcosm of the world of cosmetic surgery wherein subversive, critical viewpoints dovetail with ones that support the dominant culture. Hodge and Kress assert that 'an ideological complex exists to sustain relationships of both power and solidarity, and it represents the social order as simultaneously serving the interest of both dominant and subordinate' (1988: 3). The 'social order' that I am addressing here is what I call 'makeover culture'. Voices within it may be resistant, conservative, compliant, angry, manipulative, old and new; they may contest and dispute each other but nevertheless construct together a cultural form that is sturdy and growing.

Ideological complexes cannot operate alone: by themselves they would fail to function because of how they exploit contradictions. Hodge and Kress suggest that 'the different halves of their contradictions would cancel each other out' (1988: 4). They rely on a vital layer of meaning-creators that Hodge and Kress call 'logonomic systems'. Logonomic systems regulate ideological complexes: 'A logonomic system is a set of rules prescribing the conditions for production and reception of meanings, which specify who can claim to initiate (produce, communicate) or know (receive, understand) meanings about what topics under what circumstances and which what modalities (how, when, why)' (1988: 4).

There are many logonomic systems that support and police the ideological complexes of cosmetic surgery within makeover culture. For example the doctors' voices examined in Chapter 3 operate within logonomic systems of medical discourse, scientific expertise and sometimes artistic sensibilities. The women's magazine discourses examined in Chapters 4 and 5 work within logonomic systems that perpetuate and define specific notions of beauty and normality. The 'body-text' of artist Orlan in Chapter 7 works within a logonomic system of subversive and controversial art practice. Despite having different rules and different intended recipients or audiences these systems interlock to support makeover culture. Further, within most discourses there are residual older traditions implicated in newly emerging ones. My own part in creating discourse is an example of this: I see cosmetic surgery as too complicated a practice to be analysed in terms of agency or victimhood, the two most common feminist angles on the technology, yet these modes of engagement are never left out of the picture of networks, industries, narratives and desires that I paint.

Before/After

One of the ways that makeover culture elaborates cosmetic surgery is within a framework that carefully shows the gruesome work of modification. This is a recent change. Prior to programmes like *Extreme Makeover* cosmetic surgery was popularly represented in terms of before/after (see Figure 3). The before/after trope is discussed extensively in this book. It has been subsumed by makeover culture but still plays a complex and crucial role in how cosmetic surgery is represented. Put simply, before/after is a mode of representation where cosmetic surgery's labour and pain is hidden. The before/after hermeneutic framework typically contrasts two photos of a body part, one before surgery and one after recovery is complete. 'Before' shots are usually placed to the left of 'after' shots, adhering to a visual grammar where left-becomes-right. Often the 'after' shots are better lit and framed and the subjects are smiling or wearing more flattering make-up. The images give an impression of seamless and painless change.

The most important aspect of before/after is that 'during' is obfuscated. The processes of creation are obscured in order to portray a hermeneutic 'magic' – signs of labour are eliminated. This has caused concern for feminists – and also

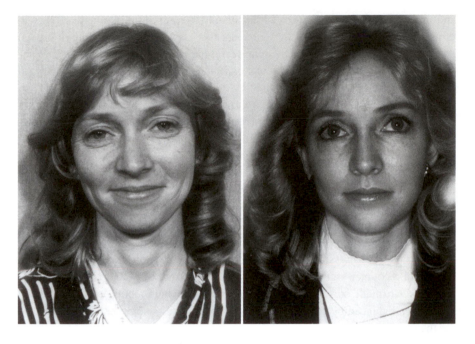

Figure 3 Before/After (facelift, upper and lower lid blepharoplasties and a chin implant), photos courtesy Dr Darryl Hodgkinson, http://www.drhodgkinson.com

for some surgeons – because cosmetic surgery usually involves major surgery that is neither simple nor undemanding, and such magical representations promote a potentially harmful practice as trouble-free and inviting, on a par with putting on lipstick. Most importantly, before/after implies transformation, or more correctly, transmogrification (magical transformation or conversion). It expresses surgical change without pain or recovery time.

Susan Bordo has analysed the written narratives that often accompany before/after images: 'the transportation of fat from one part of the body to another is described as breezily as changing hats might be' (1993: 246). Vivian Sobchack points out that before/after feeds the mythology of the 'quick fix' and she calls this tendency the 'morphological imagination'. She says that 'what you simply have is transformation without necessarily the notion of development' (quoted in Muller, n.d.). Change and transition are elided by the before/after slash. Time and space are compressed: the strict duality of before/after folds away the space-time where operations and recoveries happen.

Hiding the labour of cosmetic surgery and linking it with supposedly uncomplicated transformations is something that has equated it with danger and mystery. Common sense tells us that behind the scenes – hidden in the slash between before/after – real and intensely painful experiences are happening. Representing cosmetic surgery in terms of trouble-free change may fool some but it also creates a feeling of hidden danger: the sense that there is something secret happening.

Before/after can also apply to actual experiences. Nobody returns to work with their nose in plaster, two black sutured eyes and weeping skin. Instead people 'go on holiday' to have their operations, returning mysteriously 'refreshed'. Cultural silences around the actual process of cosmetic surgery mirror the logic of before/ after, meaning that the substantial emotional and physical pain, risk and suffering involved in the transformative methods are disavowed.

Before/after shots create a stasis: the viewer must call on a suspension of disbelief to accommodate the silent space between them. Feminists, artists and many journalists have tried in the last few decades to expose the 'during' between before/ after by describing or demonstrating how operations are done. The commonest case against cosmetic surgery has been that it is a hazardous, agonising process pursued by only the most narcissistic. And until recently, danger, vanity and narcissism have been strong counter-arguments used to offset the magic of before/after's powerful rhetorics. Cosmetic surgery as transmogrification – where labour is not articulated – has been balanced by the counter-claim that it is a gruesome practice conducted for the worst reasons.

However, in the last few years popular discourse around cosmetic surgery has undergone an important change. As if ingesting anti-cosmetic surgery discourse, where 'labour exposed' is paramount, spatial and temporal moments between, before and after have been increasingly revealed. Importantly, 'between' moments have been uncovered not only by feminists or people who are anti-cosmetic surgery, but by the very industries that stand to gain from a widespread acceptance of the technology as part of everyday life. The television programmes *Extreme Makeover*, *I Want a Famous Face*, *The Swan* and *10 Years Younger* show operations in progress yet aim to promote cosmetic surgery. And ironically, in making public the gory facts of operations and recovery periods, the technology has been demystified and has become increasingly widespread. 'Between' images – so carefully hidden only a few years ago – are now commonplace. The often gruesome narratives and pictures appearing regularly in various media serve to desensitise and initiate a formerly surgical-virgin audience so that cosmetic surgery is no longer associated with danger but instead becomes an everyday mediatised occurrence. What was recently unwatchable is now on television at dinnertime.

Feminist Perspectives on Cosmetic Surgery

Suzanne Fraser's book *Cosmetic Surgery, Gender and Culture* (2003) is a useful starting-point for a discussion about various feminist discourses and cosmetic surgery. Fraser eschews the path that asks why women choose cosmetic surgery, or whether it is a 'good' or 'bad' practice. She instead examines discourse about cosmetic surgery: discourse that she finds powerful in the construction of gender, particularly femininity. She asserts that 'what is said about cosmetic surgery and how it is said indicates a great deal about how femininity and masculinity are configured in contemporary culture' (2003: 3–4). And as 'what is said about cosmetic surgery' includes what feminists say, Fraser holds the same analytical lens to feminist discourse that she holds to medical, magazine and legal discourses. Indeed, she argues that texts making significantly different arguments (for example pro-cosmetic surgery advertisements and anti-cosmetic surgery feminist journal articles) often express the same underlying beliefs and assumptions about nature, vanity and agency. Thus she finds that 'the status of texts as either for or against cosmetic surgery is often irrelevant to their role in reproducing traditional notions such as the value of the natural' (2003: 71). While this is an example of ideological complexes in action, Fraser's most interesting and provocative findings are the strong similarities she identifies between women's magazine discourse, where positive attitudes towards cosmetic surgery are far more prevalent than negative ones, and academic feminist discourse, which is largely anti-cosmetic surgery.

Fraser argues that although academic feminism is critical of cosmetic surgery it constructs a 'logical and positive relationship between women and the surgical pursuit of "beauty" or "normality"'. And further, that 'feminism ... produces femininity and cosmetic surgery as fundamentally compatible' (2003: 98). Specifically, Fraser finds that some feminist discussions of cosmetic surgery problematically appeal to 'nature' as an essential category while others, in positioning women as agents rather than victims, ignore how 'agency itself is constructed in culture' (2003: 112). For example she shows how Kathryn Pauly Morgan (1991) vacillates between using 'natural' (in inverted commas) to highlight its problems as a category and natural (without inverted commas) 'for establishing the value of the non-surgical body' (2003: 101). Similarly Naomi Wolf (1991) is shown to move between an awareness of the constructedness of 'nature' and her own use of the notion to adhere 'to the nature/culture divide in criticising cosmetic surgery' (2003: 104). Susan Bordo's look at cosmetic surgery in *Unbearable Weight* (1993) also comes under close scrutiny. Fraser finds that in using the Foucauldian model of body-as-surface inscribed by culture, Bordo suggests that there is a body before culture: 'although Bordo makes it clear that no body can exist that is not touched by culture, the repertoire she uses constructs a body that at least for some initial moment, exists beyond culture; before the imprint' (2003: 106).

Carole Spitzack, whose classic article 'The Confession Mirror: Plastic Images for Surgery' (1988) is discussed in detail in Chapter 3, is no exception to Fraser's observations: while acknowledging her own complicity and effacement in the system of beauty, and clearly sympathetic to women who have had cosmetic surgery, Spitzack describes them damningly. The receptionist in the surgeon's office she visits is 'a beautiful featureless woman', the faces of the women in the waiting room are 'streaked by man-made colour', while the women themselves are 'objects before me, seemingly pure surface' (1988: 42). While acknowledging the important legacy of feminist writings like Spitzack's that are 'anti'-cosmetic surgery I also take Fraser's point – that much feminist writing about cosmetic surgery perpetuates the idea of the female body as raw material waiting to be worked upon – to heart. This idea adds another dimension to my reading of feminist analyses of cosmetic surgery and shapes my own arguments: I use it to try to ensure that the voices of my interviewees are respected and the appearances of those who have had mainstream cosmetic surgery are not belittled.

Fraser notes how feminist academic writing often describes cosmetic surgery recipients as complicit in and effaced by a repressive system (2003: 97–121). She argues that this further positions women as weak and malleable and therefore ideally suited to surgical intervention. Her fine critique makes it clear that cosmetic surgery and cosmetic surgery discourse are ubiquitous. She points out, quoting Donna Haraway, that discourse has important material effects – 'we inhabit these narratives, and they inhabit us' (2003: 185). So discourse about cosmetic surgery is everywhere; we are all – at least metaphorically – cosmetic surgery recipients; and feminists are as guilty as anyone of seeing the female body as raw 'natural' material ready to be moulded.

Before/after has been a huge influence on feminists who engage with repres-entations of cosmetic surgery. Feminist analyses of cosmetic surgery have also, until recently, worked with the fact that cosmetic surgery was practically and discursively unusual. Both these bases have altered. Cosmetic surgery has become common and widespread, and the previously uncrossable gap between before/after and the bleak realities of surgery has been broached within makeover culture. The glamour and transmogrification implied by before/after and the blood and gore of surgery are now co-joined, a change graphically demonstrated by reality television cosmetic surgery. Thus, critiques that demonstrate the contradictions between the promises of the glossy 'after' images and the concealed realities of the gruesome slash between before/after no longer paint a full picture of the cosmetic surgery paradigm. Dramatic cultural shifts mean that feminist arguments based on analysis of what before/after obfuscates are no longer enough. Appraisals of cosmetic surgery within makeover culture need to recognise that inconsistencies, denials and contradictions form part of its strength. The notion of ideological complexes is again useful: contradictions here do not undermine makeover culture but make it more potent. Inconsistencies in makeover culture, like the one that maintains the fantasy of before/after while revealing the 'between' are integral parts of its logic. They provide discursive intercourse and allow the culture to survive and thrive. It is clear then, that newly adaptive ways of looking at and theorising cosmetic surgery from feminist viewpoints are needed.

Feminist literature about cosmetic surgery can be fitted into some broad categories. I outline these below and introduce some of the main protagonists of each, while keeping in mind that the writers I mention fit into multiple categories. My aim is not to place particular writers inside certain set viewpoints but rather to flag the main wide and overlapping feminist approaches to cosmetic surgery.

'Just Say No'

This approach criticises cosmetic surgery as essentially commercial, repressive, demeaning and hazardous. Naomi Wolf's bestselling book *The Beauty Myth* (1991) exemplifies this stance. She argues that 'cosmetic surgery processes the bodies of women, who make up the vast majority of its pool, into man-made women' (Wolf, 1991: 220; also see Baird, 2004; Bordo, 1993; Greer, 1999; Lakoff and Scherr, 1984). Although never condoning cosmetic surgery, this stance is sometimes sympathetic to the needs and desires of women who choose it. It does this by positioning them as victims of two increasingly repressive and interlocking cultures: one that glorifies the body-beautiful, and one where medical discourse is a vital part of the patriarchal machine, upholding and promoting the notion that women's bodies are inherently sick, disabled and lacking. This medico-beauty paradigm invents terms like 'hypomastia' or 'micromastia' (medical descriptions for small breasts); it redefines aesthetic characteristics as disease and links them to psychological ailments. Gilman quotes H. O. Barnes, a doctor writing in 1950: 'hypomastia causes psychological rather than physical distress. Its correction has been receiving increased interest only since our "cult of the body beautiful" has revealed its existence in rather large numbers' (1999: 238). In other words, when it comes to cosmetic surgery, misogynistic culture and medicine have been intertwined in the 'discovery' of both diseases and cures (Fraser, 2003a; Jacobson, 2000; Zimmerman, 1998).

Dystopic scenarios are never far away from 'Just don't do it' views of cosmetic surgery. Susan Bordo tells the story of a *Twilight Zone* episode where people of the future choose from a limited number of body models (1997: 9–12) and argues that cosmetic surgery wants to make all women look the same: 'with created images setting the standard, we are becoming habituated to the glossy and gleaming, the smooth and shining, the ageless and sagless and wrinkleless. We are learning to find any "defect" repellent, unacceptable … [for example] we expect real breasts to be as round and firm as implants' (1997: 3; see also Balsamo, 1996: 71 and Padmore, 1998).

These standards particularly relate to female celebrities, whose high visibility in the public sphere is tolerated only so long as they allow men (movie directors, fashion photographers, cosmetic surgeons) to frame, position and remake their bodies. Importantly, in this scenario it is mainly men who are able to define and create female beauty, and if women's agency is recognised or acknowledged it is only as a willing pawn disabling herself in order to embody a beauty norm. It is not surprising then that dystopic writings about cosmetic surgery call for women to resist at all costs: the rhetoric is much like 'Just Say No' drug campaigns. Cosmetic surgery is identified as a destructive practice for individuals and for women as a whole, who all suffer from scrutiny and discrimination that circulates around their appearances (Gagné and McGaughey, 2002: 814). The solution to this strand of argument is struggle: to work daily to embrace and keep our differences and wrinkles, to argue constantly against the repressive structures that uphold cosmetic surgery as a solution for imaginary diseases, and to hope that cosmetic surgeons will eventually go out of business for lack of patients. At its blackest, this mode of cosmetic surgery examination successfully and logically argues that a ban on genital mutilation (such as that in force in the UK) should also mean a ban on cosmetic surgery, and vice versa (Jeffreys, 2000; Sheldon and Wilkinson, 1998; Winter, Thompson and Jeffreys, 2002).

For many feminists though, struggle and resistance in terms of plain refusal is too simplistic. Any body, whether practising actual cosmetic surgery or not, is embedded in mainstream beauty culture: a culture formed by a myriad of disciplines including cosmetic surgery. Virginia Blum's book *Flesh Wounds* (2003) argues that it is unconstructive for feminists to be polarised in their critiques of cosmetic surgery:

> Let's be clear about what is happening here so we don't continue to harass one another about the relationship between our politics and our bodies. *No one* who wants surgery 'resists' it. In many ways the wanting is partly the doing, inasmuch as you've already said yes to a whole host of surgery-related activities – that you would go that far, that you have already pictured your surgically reconstructed body part. Those who urge us to resist are never tantalized by a surgical solution in the first place, so they aren't resisting much of anything. Hence, there is no difference really between the 'good' feminists who resist the seduction and the 'bad' feminists who capitulate. (2003: 63)

Blum rightly notes that 'sometimes capitulation and resistance happen in the same arena' (2003: 64; also see Radner, 1995: 172).

The second and third broad areas of feminist cosmetic surgery analysis are more localised, focused on individuals who have had procedures. Kathy Davis's distinguished work spans these two areas (1991, 1995, 1996, 1998, 2003). Below I introduce her arguments and weave them with some of Susan Bordo's responses.

'I Did it For Myself' and 'I Just Want to be Normal'

Sensitivity to the narratives of individual cosmetic surgery recipients often interacts with a strand of justification for cosmetic surgery put forward by patients and surgeons: that cosmetic surgery is a way for the 'outer' and 'inner' selves to become aligned. Even while problematising the essentialism inherent in the belief in a true inner self, feminists looking at cosmetic surgery through this lens focus on the agency of recipients and recognise that cosmetic surgery can provide psychological and social benefits. While locating cosmetic surgery as a practice rooted in the discourse of feminine inferiority they acknowledge and examine how it is sometimes described as a form of liberation. For example, Davis's book *Reshaping the Female Body: The Dilemma of Cosmetic Surgery* (1995) begins with a concern for 'the horrors being perpetrated on women's bodies by the medical system' (1995: 1). Her initial sociological research into cosmetic surgery came about because she 'disliked the concomitant tendency among feminists to treat the recipients as nothing more than misguided or deluded victims' (1997: 168). Davis interviewed women in The Netherlands who had undergone or were planning cosmetic surgery and found that their decisions were far from frivolous or unconsidered. She showed that they were not mindlessly adhering to patriarchal imperatives but rather actively and consciously engaging with them. She describes agents rather than victims: women working within a repressive system in deeply considered ways.

Susan Bordo is highly critical of this approach: '*I'm doing it for me* ... In these constructions "me" is imagined as a pure and precious inner space, an "authentic" and personal reference point untouched by external values and demands. A place where we live free and won't be pushed around' (1998: 193, her italics). Bordo asserts that Davis's privileging of cosmetic surgery recipients' 'agency' ignores the cultural pressures that lead to the 'need' for surgical intervention: 'In focusing on narratives of individual "empowerment", Davis – like Oprah's guests who claim they did it "for themselves" – overlooks the fact that the norms that encouraged these individuals to see themselves as defective are enmeshed in the practice and institution of cosmetic surgery itself. And so is individual behaviour' (1998: 202).

Davis finds that choosing cosmetic surgery is not about trying to be beautiful but rather about becoming 'normal'. The women she interviewed described their pre-surgery selves as abnormal, even deformed. They said they did not seek to stand out as attractive but rather to blend in (see also Gimlin, 2000). They described emotional, psychological and social suffering related to their appearance and said that ongoing distress led to their decision to have cosmetic surgery. In this light, cosmetic surgery is a treatment that can fix psychologically disabling 'abnormalities' and thus is not only understandable but, for some individuals, unavoidable (Davis, 1995: 74; 1997: 169). Davis argues that in deciding to have cosmetic surgery women may initiate dramatic change and become agents in the transformation of their own bodies and lives (1996). She argues that for some, cosmetic surgery is the only possible solution to a long-term 'biographical' problem (1995, also see Goodman, 1994). She comes to the complex conclusion that cosmetic surgery can be an act of empowerment even while it is a symptom of oppression, and describes her position as a 'balancing act' that finds 'a way to be critical of the practice which is dangerous, demeaning, or oppressive – without uncritically undermining the women who see it as their best, and, in some cases, only option for alleviating suffering which has gone beyond the point of endurance' (1998: 131).

Bordo – in a beautiful academic narrative that contrasts the films *Braveheart* and *Babe* in order to discuss the many cultural imperatives that create our bodies

– responds that Davis's findings are 'typical of a certain contemporary preference for the rhetoric of "agency" over close analysis of social context and cultural reality' (1998: 196). And further, that the idea of 'agency' adds nothing beyond 'rhetorical cheerleading concerning how we, not the images, are "in charge"' (1998: 197). She asserts that Davis's models of empowerment obscure social and cultural realities:

> there is a consumer system operating here that depends on our perceiving ourselves as defective and that will continually find new ways to do this. That system – and others connected to it, generating new technologies and areas of expertise organised around the diagnosis and correction of 'defect' – is masked by the rhetoric of personal empowerment. (1998: 201)

Davis herself sums up Bordo's critique of her work nicely: 'in her view, any cultural analysis worth its salt has to provide a "picture of the landscape" and not just "individual snapshots"' (2003: 11). My stance combines these two scholarly approaches. Throughout this book I describe and analyse how cosmetic surgery occurs in various physical and media landscapes, from specific nations, to buildings, to magazines. But there are also many 'individual snapshots' dotted throughout and (like Davis) I take each person's voice and statements at 'face value' (2003: 10), keeping in mind that 'every competent actor has a wide-ranging, but intimate and subtle, knowledge of the society of which he or she is a member' (Giddens, quoted in Davis, 2003: 12). I show how most cosmetic surgery recipients are 'competent actors' who have carefully weighed up how to position themselves in relation to social and cultural imperatives and opportunities.

Like Bordo, Suzanne Fraser sees similarities between Davis's thesis and discourses that seek to promote cosmetic surgery – both advocate that strength is needed to undertake it. She argues that because Davis's 'active agent' approach exalts women who choose cosmetic surgery, it subtly denigrates women who do not. Fraser sees an important parallel between feminist descriptions of women who choose cosmetic surgery as battlers who overcome great adversity and cosmetic surgery promotional material:

> The emphasis on battle, courage and heroism appears in both popular and internal medical material, and ties in closely with other repertoires that emphasise women's activeness and strength of will in undertaking surgery. At the same time, it implies that women who don't choose to have surgery have surrendered; that they lack the necessary moral fibre to obtain or maintain appearances. (2003a: 39)

The parallels are clear but there is an important difference between Davis's idea of strength and choice and cosmetic surgery advertising's depiction of those qualities. Davis and Fraser are talking about different stages in the growth and normalisation of cosmetic surgery. Cosmetic surgery advertising seeks to convince a broad audience of 'normal' women to buy a product. Davis has begun with the belief (gained from her interviewees) that women who have cosmetic surgery see themselves as abnormal. Fortitude in this instance is connected to being an outsider, taking drastic steps to integrate oneself. The fortitude that Fraser observes, in advertising's stories about women being strong enough to keep themselves nice, is all about *staying inside* society, not being rejected because of age or ugliness, remaining in the centre. The subtle difference is between fixing what has never been perceived as 'right' (Davis) and maintaining or enhancing what is acceptable (Fraser).

The suffering that Davis's interviewees expressed must also be considered alongside the fact that cosmetic surgery was available at small cost under The Netherlands' national health scheme, but crucially, only if deemed psychologically necessary (Davis, 1995). Hence, it is no surprise that her interviewees spoke about their desires to have cosmetic surgery in terms of fixing deformity, because deformity and its psychological effects are accepted as serious medical conditions. I am not suggesting that Davis's interviewees were manipulative but rather that they had ingested the values of a particular logonomic system – something like 'if you really need cosmetic surgery, you must be deformed or abnormal, or at least strongly believe that you are'. They were operating in an environment where cosmetic surgery was only acceptable if couched in terms of mental anguish. An interesting study would be to re-interview Davis's subjects in light of makeover culture. Would they still describe themselves as having been abnormal or deformed before surgery? And if they were now considering more cosmetic surgery, would they explain their current desires using different language?

From the mid 1990s cosmetic surgery began to be repositioned as something 'normal' people could have, something you didn't have to be psychologically compromised to desire (Brooks, 2004). One woman I interviewed straddled this divide and her story shows how much the scene has changed.

Nearly twenty-five years ago Ellen got breast implants. She had slightly asymmetric breasts because of heart surgery as a child and the difference between them increased after she breastfed her children. Her husband was cruel: '[he was] constantly reminding me of the fact that my breasts "aren't right, they're not normal" to the point where it was not uncommon for me to be the brunt of the joke in front of other people ... because my breasts weren't 100% as he put it'. Ellen internalised his criticisms and saw herself as deformed. To have cosmetic surgery – like the women Davis interviewed – she needed a psychiatric referral:

in those days you actually had to go to a psychiatrist to get referred to have a breast enlargement done and I actually didn't have any problems there because of the fact that it was a medical thing and it really was affecting me mentally ... [it cost] very little because I got most of it back. I got almost all of the money back [from the health care fund]. I had four young children and money was an issue with me. I couldn't have afforded to pay for it.

A quarter of a century later, having long divorced the abusive husband, Ellen (now in her sixties) was considering a facelift at the time of interview but with quite a different attitude:

> I'd have no qualms about having plastic surgery done on my face, and I am seriously thinking about it … to me it's part of looking after yourself and if it's an essential part of looking after yourself then so be it. At least I'm taking the pride in myself to make me want to look better, and that's got to make me a better person… If I won Lotto I'd have a facelift tomorrow. It's just a matter of the money.

Just as her approach in the late 1970s had mirrored the societal and medical beliefs of the time, in the early 2000s Ellen had adopted the rhetoric of cosmetic surgery being part of 'looking after yourself'. Her early cosmetic surgery needed to be justified psychologically and medically but her later cosmetic surgery was seen as self-development: part of the being a good citizen of makeover culture. Sociologist Abigail Brooks has observed that contemporary cosmetic surgery is still sometimes occasionally presented in the popular media as a 'cure' for psychological ill-health but with a scary inversion: 'saying "no" to cosmetic technologies, increasingly accessible and easy to use, may risk ill health and irrationality' (2004: 225).

The links Ellen made between cosmetic surgery and money are important too: her early 'necessary' cosmetic surgery was paid for by the Australian government health system; twenty-five years later she must save her own money (or win Lotto) for 'optional' cosmetic surgery. Cosmetic surgery is now a purchase, characterised by rhetorics of fashion, consumerism and self-presentation rather than medical or psychological necessity. The women Davis interviewed were similar in attitude to Ellen's younger self, while most of the discourses that I examine are closer to those that Ellen aligns herself with now. Cressida Heyes describes the change wittily: 'Botox parties are the *reductio ad absurdum* example here: the image of the woman who saunters over to the syringe-wielding doctor for a quick jab between the eyebrows hardly conforms to the agonized and anguished subject Davis describes' (2007: 106; also see Fraser, 2003: 3).

Feminist Cosmetic Surgery?

Many feminists see cosmetic surgery as 'unalterably opposed' to feminist values and goals (Haiken, 1997: 275) or as 'almost by definition, "bad news" for women' (Davis, 2003: 21). However, a small but important collection of researchers devote some time to the idea that feminist cosmetic surgery *may* be possible. For example, Davis wrote a favourable chapter about Dr Suzanne Noël, a French feminist and pioneer of cosmetic surgery practising in the early twentieth century (2003). Noël not only reached the top of a male-dominated field but also invented new surgical techniques, published her findings, and operated on women firmly believing she was improving their lives, mainly by expanding their career prospects. Rather than judge Noël by contemporary feminist standards, Davis situates her in her own time period and notes that:

> As [a] feminist, Noël belonged to a woman's organisation which was concerned, first and foremost, with gaining access to work, particularly work in the professions ... She was convinced that cosmetic surgery alleviated suffering and was a useful tool for helping women – to be sure, affluent, professional women – to achieve financial independence and social recognition. (2003: 36)

She concludes:

> we should look for Madame Noël's feminist contribution – not in her attempts to empower individual women through face-lifts, but rather in the kind of professionality which she represented. While this may not be enough for a feminist cosmetic surgery, it is an ingredient which a feminist critique of cosmetic surgery should not ignore. (2003: 37)

Davis conditionally recognises the contributions of a feminist surgeon and sees via her interviews that having cosmetic surgery can be an act of courage and empowerment rather than a capitulation. What she doesn't consider is how *recipients* of cosmetic surgery might be enacting feminist values. Anna Kirkland and Rosemarie Tong have argued in their promisingly titled 'Working within Contradiction: The Possibility of Feminist Cosmetic Surgery' that although cosmetic surgery exists because of socially constructed demands it is nevertheless possible to choose it for personal 'legitimate' reasons that are 'not necessarily damaging to feminism' (1996: 151). They suggest counselling in order for patients and doctors to uncover the 'true reason' for wanting surgery. This approach is naïve, ignoring the facts that cosmetic surgeons are not psychologists, are keen to do surgery fast and often, and most cosmetic surgery recipients are quite sane and know exactly what they want and why. Further, actions that are 'not necessarily damaging to feminism' are rhetorically somehow outside it, or neutral: in this schema cosmetic surgery is only viable if it is (impossibly) separated from – and has no effect on – feminism.

Anne Balsamo, Kathryn Pauly Morgan and the artist Orlan have ventured into more complex arguments for feminist cosmetic surgery, suggesting collectively that 'it is not the surgery itself that is oppressive but the ends it serves, particularly when those ends reify cultural hegemony' (Gagné and McGaughey, 2002: 818). Balsamo and Morgan make strong stands against cosmetic surgery as it is currently deployed but also consider how it might be inverted or reappropriated under feminist terms. For Balsamo, if cosmetic surgery were to be open rather than secretive about its own histories and labours then the constructed and artificial nature of beauty would be highlighted. She suggests that if the body's history and labour were to be revealed then surgically altered bodies would bear their scars and alterations proudly. Thus cosmetic surgery would not necessarily be about eradicating indications of life and experience as is especially the case with 'anti-ageing' cosmetic surgery. Instead, if conceptually separated from normative femininity, cosmetic surgery could be 'a vehicle for staging cultural identities' (Balsamo 1996: 78–9). In the next chapter I show how Balsamo's call for the industriousness of cosmetic surgery to be revealed has indeed occurred, but has not been accompanied by a distancing from notions of normative beauty. Texts like *Extreme Makeover* show the history and labour of cosmetic surgery but only in order to reposition cosmetic surgery as a necessary part of being a good citizen of the makeover culture, not as a way to open possibilities for staging alternative cultural identities.

In her foundational article 'Women and the Knife: Cosmetic Surgery and the Colonization of Women's Bodies' (1991), Kathryn Pauly Morgan, following Judith Butler, suggests two 'performance-oriented forms of revolt', both of which include *having* cosmetic surgery. The first valorises 'ugliness' and thus destabilises the beautiful, exposing its 'technologically and culturally constitutive origin and its political consequences' (1991: 45). In this cosmetic surgery utopia women might *choose* to have wrinkles scored on, breasts pulled down with weights and hair dyed grey (1991: 46). Her second suggested form of revolt imagines the 'commodification aspect' of cosmetic surgery: commercial boutiques where an array of body-altering technologies, products and implants are openly for sale, where purchase of larger or smaller breasts is like purchase of a new pair of shoes (1991: 45–7). Ironically this demystification of cosmetic surgery has actually happened in the years since Morgan wrote her piece. In a landscape of commercial democratisation of cosmetic surgery there are now adjustable breast implants[4] and shopping centres with 'day spas' or clinics that offer Botox® and other 'injectables'. But Morgan's speculative array of non-normative differences is as far off as ever – instead of widespread cosmetic surgery leading to a plethora of modifications it has resulted in increased normalisation and aesthetic homogeneity.

Orlan, a French artist whose 'Carnal Art' consists of having 'live' cosmetic surgeries performed on herself, uses cosmetic surgery to disrupt dominant beauty norms. She says 'my work is not a stand against cosmetic surgery, but against the standards of beauty, against the dictates of a dominant ideology that impresses itself more and more on feminine (and masculine) flesh' (quoted in McCorquodale 1996: 91). Her engagements with cosmetic surgery are complex and rich, and are dealt with in detail in Chapter 7. Orlan explores Balsamo's assertion that feminists 'need to understand how technologies get employed to serve certain agendas, and start to figure out how they may be deployed to serve other agendas' (interview with Muller, n.d.).

Cressida Heyes proposes a feminist approach to cosmetic surgery that recognises how pervasive the rhetoric of 'working on the self' is: 'Control and self-determination are fetishised in Western cultures at the same time as we lack feminist contexts in which these qualities can find an alternative purchase. Simply refusing to have cosmetic surgery cannot therefore be an adequate form of resistance' (2007: 110). She suggests that 'we need to substitute a new solution for the psychic needs that cosmetic surgery both generates and claims to meet' (2007: 110).

The ageing body, especially the ageing female body, is often posited by feminists as a 'natural' antidote for the culturally dominant and mandatory forms of youthful femininity and mainstream beauty. However, I argue that the two need not be at odds. Alternative cosmetic surgery might be a joiner of opposites, a uniting force. Not by making everyone look the same, that common dystopic refrain, but by making everyone 'surgical' to use Blum's (negative) phrase. I argue throughout this book that alternative and subversive adoptions of cosmetic surgery are possible and are happening, not just with 'extreme practitioners' like Orlan and Lolo Ferrari, but also with people who use cosmetic surgery to design, rather than deny age, to call into question traditional intergenerational relationships, and to challenge surgeons' traditional monopoly over provision and acceptable aesthetics of cosmetic surgery.

Conclusion

Most feminist engagements with cosmetic surgery have been necessarily largely influenced by the dominant before/after model, and by the fact that cosmetic surgery has until recently been relatively unusual. But before/after is transformed in makeover culture and cosmetic surgery is now much more common. New ways of seeing and theorising cosmetic surgery from feminist viewpoints are called for. Rather than rally in opposition to a powerful set of discourses and practices, feminists need to engage with them imaginatively. This does not mean condescendingly offering 'understanding' to cosmetic surgery recipients (implying that they are dupes of the beauty myth) but instead accepting that cosmetic surgery is now a meaningful part of our world: metaphorically, we are all cosmetic surgery recipients, we are all makeover citizens, and we must find ways to constructively understand, examine, and live with this fact.

Space and Place

Globalisation and Mediascapes

I saw all the mirrors on earth and none of them reflected me...

Jorge Luis Borges

When the only physical beauty is created by plastic surgery, the only urban beauty by landscape surgery...

Jean Paul Baudrillard

Feminists and cultural scholars have long recognised that examining bodies, behaviours or objects outside of their everyday environments can result in strangely disembodied findings (Gatens, 1996; Grosz, 1994). For example, Bronwyn Davies points out that 'theoretical writing about the body generally constitutes the body in isolation from the physical spaces in which it exists' (2000: 13). To redress this she writes about 'bodies in landscape, bodies as landscape, and landscapes as extensions of bodies, all being worked and reworked, scribed and reinscribed' (2000: 249). With Davies's *modus operandi* in mind I consider cosmetic surgery and place. This chapter looks at cosmetic surgery as part of the global mediascape, as part of politics and values that are peculiar to certain nations, and in the context of a specific urban space.

Cosmetic Surgery and Globalisation

Undergoing cosmetic surgery is 'acting globally' at several levels. Being penetrated by material that has been created on the other side of the planet makes a locally situated body an international body in a very physical sense. Having cosmetic surgery can have both local and global significance: an Australian who has an 'S' lift, liposuction or breast augmentation might travel to Thailand or South Africa to have her operation cheaply and away from curious family and friends. She may immediately feel different in her local environment and cosmetic surgery also initiates her into a glamorous globalised mediascape, a world where she may be aesthetically positioned alongside a movie star who lives in Beverly Hills. Conversely, her surgery may place her globally in terms of disfigurement, illness, medical controversy, ongoing court battles, legal findings and perhaps eventual compensation. Cosmetic surgery is also a practice dominated by 'transnational elites' – that is, surgeons who are internationally mobile, who publish in and read international medical journals, and who are often trained in the West. Like many medical techniques cosmetic surgery expertise often comes about via 'study abroad, conferences, visiting experts, medical journals and textbooks, and [international] personal friendships' (Brownell, 2005: 142). It is a practice embedded in the 'scapes' of global culture.

Globalisation is best described as a series of 'flows'. In 1990 Arjun Appadurai proposed five terms with which to explore its dimensions: 'ethnoscapes', 'technoscapes', 'finanscapes', 'mediascapes' and 'ideoscapes'.[1] I am mainly interested in mediascapes and ideoscapes, both of which describe the 'landscape of images' (Appadurai, 1990a: 298). Mediascapes are created by the spread of electronic media across the world and the images and discourses proliferated by those media. They provide

> large and complex repertoires of images, narratives and ethnoscapes to viewers throughout the world, in which the world of commodities and the world of news and politics are profoundly mixed. What this means is that many audiences throughout the world experiences themselves as a complicated and interconnected repertoire of print, celluloid, electronic screens and billboards. (Appadurai 1990: 9)

Ideoscapes refer to 'concatenations of images' (Appadurai, 1990a: 299) but are more likely to be political. As an example Appadurai suggests 'democracy' which he says is a 'master-term' that has spread all over the world (1990a: 298). Importantly, he points out that while master-terms have global meaning, they vary significantly according to local context.

I propose that 'beauty' is another master-term. Like democracy, it has a global meaning that is somewhat homogeneous. It also has important heterogeneous – or local – aspects that vary according to context. Perhaps a Claudia-Schiffer-style beauty is close to something perpetuated as a global ideal: long legs, large breasts, thin body, fair hair and skin, delicate features, big blue eyes. People from Poland to Pakistan may well be sufficiently versed with global mediascapes and ideoscapes to recognise and accept Schiffer as a 'universal beauty'. But attractiveness is also inflected and varied according to local contexts. Global culture may flow everywhere but its morphology varies depending on its host. As Appadurai says, 'globalisation involves the use of a variety of instruments of homogenisation ... which are absorbed into local political and cultural economies, only to be repatriated as heterogeneous dialogues' (1990a: 307).

Homogeneity is often characterised as 'Americanisation' – a global cultural force dominated by the politics, economics and media of the USA. There is an underlying assumption in a reading of globalisation as a homogenous Americanising process that it suffocates the societies it infiltrates, leaving a wasteland littered with

Coca-Cola cans and McDonalds signs where there were once diverse local cultural practices. Mike Featherstone has called this approach 'monological', saying it misses 'not only the cultural variability of non-Western nation-states and civilisations, but the specificity of the cultural complex of Western modernity' (1995: 102). Here I review some of the research that has been done into specific groups of people and their cosmetic surgery in order to show how Western modernity's version of 'beauty' is further complicated when realised in non-Western contexts and analysed as part of the flows of globalisation.

'Ethnic' Cosmetic Surgery

Before reviewing cosmetic surgery in non-Western contexts it is crucial to note that race is also important for cosmetic surgery in the West. 'Ethnic cosmetic surgery' is a growing phenomenon, especially in the USA, where surgeons may declare special expertise in certain groups such as African Americans, Hispanics or Asians. Cosmetic surgery for these groups is on the rise.[2] Lists of popular procedures for various groups show that ethnic cosmetic surgery usually aims to Aryanise features to some extent. Wide noses are narrowed, flat noses are raised, cheekbones are heightened, thick lips are thinned, slanted eyes are rounded. 'Race- and ethnicity-based surgery is always focused on the most identifiable, and most caricatured, features: for Jews, noses; for Asians, eyes; for African Americans, noses and lips' (Haiken, 1997: 176). A journalist who spent a day in a Los Angeles cosmetic surgery clinic waiting room noted 'it seems clear that a lessening of ethnic characteristics (rather than a "refining"—whatever that means) is what is going on' (Wilentz, 2006). The clinic actually called some of its nose jobs 'westernisation rhinoplasties' although most surgeons take care to appear more politically correct than this. Despite a seeming diversity of procedures across ethnic groups the end results often aim for homogeneity that fits a 'whiter' ideal.

Migration and transnational flows of people have been linked to ethnic cosmetic surgery for more than a century. Sander Gilman has written about how Irish 'pug noses' and 'bat ears' were 'Americanised' in the late 1800s so that Celts could pass as Anglo-Saxons (2005a: 112–13). The Irish were thought to be degenerate and suffered numerous discriminations; minimising signs of one's Irishness was a way to smooth social and career pathways and slip into the mainstream. Similarly, throughout the 1900s, German surgeons worked on changing noses and ears that were considered 'too Jewish': 'Jewish males generally could enter into the world of masculine endeavours as long as they were not too evidently Jewish' (Gilman, 2005a: 118–19). And of course for some European Jews in the first half of the twentieth century the desire for alteration of 'Jewish' appearance may well have been for the purpose of survival itself. Looking 'too Jewish' is a notion that survives strongly today. Virginia Blum's book *Flesh Wounds* (2003) is testament to this – it tells how as a teenager she underwent a rhinoplasty, arranged by her mother, partly designed to make her look less Jewish. She notes numerous other incidents of the practice in the contemporary USA.

Using cosmetic surgery to minimise Asianness works in much the same way, as Eugenia Kaw's research into Asian double eyelid surgery in the USA shows. Double eyelid surgery is an operation to create a fold in the upper eyelid. Most surgeons heartily deny that it has anything to do with looking more Western. For example, one advertising website declares:

> While approximately half of all Asian people are born with an upper eyelid crease, that crease is different from an Occidental crease in important ways, most notably in height, shape, and depth. Some natural Asian creases are almost rudimentary and may be highly variable in their expression day to day. Of those born without a crease or with a very low or weak crease who later seek double eyelid surgery, very few are trying to look Western. (http://www.drmeronk.com/asian/asian-overview.html)

The language here is telling – pre-surgical creases are 'rudimentary', 'low' or 'weak' – by association their owners share these characteristics. Kaw rejects the idea that double eyelid surgery is a simple aesthetic choice: 'for the women in my study, the decision to undergo cosmetic surgery was never purely or mainly for aesthetic purposes, but almost always for improving their social stature as women who are racial minorities' (1993: 78). Another 'Westernisation' happens when Middle Easterners who live in the West have nose jobs to distinguish their faces from the stereotypical 'Islamic fundamentalist' face that is often linked to terrorism in mass media (Gilman, 2005a: 133–5).

Import of captured Africans to be sold as slaves in America and those people's later emancipation is also connected to the history of cosmetic surgery. Many people of African heritage choose to try to 'pass' as white for social and economic reasons. After the civil war some surgeons published papers about how to 'correct' the 'negroid nose' or 'mulatto' complexion. Interestingly, Gilman points out that 'no reputable surgeon in the United States wanted to be seen as facilitating crossing the colour bar' (2005a: 119). This meant that such operations were only discussed in terms of fixing whites with the misfortune to have a coincidentally 'black' feature, rather than in terms of operations that would allow blacks to pass as white. The anxieties around cosmetic surgery, blackness and passing in America are equally fraught with angst today. I discuss some of their complexities in Chapter 7 in relation to Michael Jackson and an *Extreme Makeover* recipient.

Cosmetic Surgery Tourism

Historical flows of people *to* the West (part of Appadurai's 'ethnoscapes') are connected to certain kinds of cosmetic surgery, just as flows of images and information *from* the West (part of his 'mediascapes') are. The two are intertwined in a fascinating and rapidly expanding area that is severely under-researched: cosmetic surgery tourism, where operations are packaged with tourist experiences. South Africa offers 'Surgeon and Safari: Privacy in Paradise' (http://www.surgeon-and-safari.co.za/). Thailand's Samui Clinic in Koh Samui promises 'the highest level of medical care and attention at prices far below that of the western world' along with luxury beachside accommodation (http://www.cosmeticsurgerythailand.com). A cosmetic surgery company located in Rio de Janeiro suggests you take in the sights of Christ the Redeemer, the Burle Marx botanical gardens and the Jardim Botânico after having your surgery (http://www.cosmeticvacations.com/).

James Willis travelled to South Africa from Britain to have a facelift and go on safari. He told the Australian radio programme *PM*:

> I just felt as though I needed something in my life, which was going to cheer me up a little bit. I've had a lot of ups and downs the last five years and nearly got married but didn't. So that was another experience in life, and so I thought it's time for me now to take some time out and come to terms where I am and do something nice for myself for a change.
>
> I'm doing it for me I think. This is a new experience for me, so that's really why I'm here. It's a new experience. (http://www.abc.net.au/pm/stories/s300362.htm)

Do his comments refer to the holiday or the surgery? They conflate the tourist experience with the surgical one and connect them both to personal growth and rejuvenation. Certainly, a major motivation for having cosmetic surgery offshore is financial – procedures can be up to a quarter of the at-home price – but there is much more to say about this topic. As I show throughout this book, cosmetic surgery is far more than a medical procedure. Because it is connected to ideas about self-love, body-maintenance and psychological well-being it is more easily coupled with holidays and indulgence than, say, a hip replacement operation. In makeover culture travelling to Thailand for a luxury spa holiday and a facelift is a logical combination, as is visiting South Africa for some liposuction and a safari.

Surgeons' professional associations frequently express horror at cosmetic surgery tourism, citing the likelihoods of unqualified practitioners, infections and the costs to taxpayers at home when revisions are required. But I've found no statistics to support such claims. I suspect that medical dangers to do with cosmetic surgery tourism may be more connected to long-haul flights soon after surgery than to the surgeries themselves, which are often conducted in world-class hospitals by internationally trained surgeons. Nor is cosmetic surgery tourism limited to cheap places. The website advertising Dr Craig Layt's practice, located on the Australian Gold Coast, features pictures of waterfalls, beaches, people learning to surf and sunny café scenes. The text informs us that 'patients of all ages come from overseas, interstate and locally in search of cosmetic surgery, plastic surgery and anti-aging treatments to improve their physical appearance and, for many, their quality of life and self-esteem' (http://www.drlayt.com/). Physical and mental health have been associated with a change of scene for centuries and medical tourism in the form of visiting places thought to have rejuvenating water or air is an ancient practice. Perhaps there is nothing really different about cosmetic surgery tourism at all. It needs to be examined as a new phenomenon but also as part of a continuum.

Non-Western Cosmetic Surgery

A comprehensive worldview of cosmetic surgery is difficult because in most countries statistics simply don't exist. 'Western influence' is equally hard to determine. In the Middle East, for example, statistics are rare although journalists report on increases in cosmetic surgery. Their interviews with local cosmetic surgeons and cosmetic surgery recipients offer some insights. A Lebanese surgeon notes a direct correlation between demands for smaller noses and the infiltration of the Western press: 'I think that the Lebanese population tends to be very fashion oriented. People want to look as good as possible. They're influenced by Western aesthetic norms and by magazines and TV' (quoted in Renahan, 1999). As with noses that are 'too Jewish', 'too Asian' or 'too Negroid', noses that are 'too Middle Eastern' are shaved down to more Western dimensions, often to display their owners' cosmopolitanism. In contrast an Egyptian model who had her nose 'made better' said that Egyptian women weren't imitating or aspiring to Western notions of beauty: 'they just want to look better. They are now more conscious about their beauty and this is a good trend that we should encourage. Egyptian women want to look smart, not Western' (quoted in Kamel, 2004). In Saudi Arabia a distinctly local practice, the Jamiah,[3] is sometimes used to raise money for cosmetic surgery (Hatrash, 2006), and in Iran nose bandages after rhinoplasties are worn proudly in public as status symbols (McGeogh, 2006: 23).

Brazilian Cosmetic Surgery – Plástica

In Brazil profound social inequalities exist alongside free cosmetic surgery (plástica) that is part of the national health scheme. Plástica is immensely popular.[4] Copacabana hosted the world's largest cosmetic surgery conference in 2006, attended by 2,400 surgeons from nearly 80 different countries. There are various explanations for the immense status of plástica, including climate (Brazilians live on the beach and are thought to be more body-conscious as a result), legislation (the national health scheme), Brazil's 'superstar' cosmetic surgeon Ivo Pitanguy (discussed below) and the Brazilian 'open attitude' (plástica is far from taboo and is rarely kept secret). One surgeon said: 'The mentality of the Brazilian people ... is a very open kind of mentality compared with that of the Europeans. Brazilians have a much greater ease in seeking out plastic surgery. It is a tropical country, where people enjoy exposing their bodies. This helps stimulate people to have surgery' (quoted in Phillips, 2006).

The illuminating work of Australian anthropologist Alex Edmunds on cosmetic surgery in Brazil (unpublished) helps to complicate these simplistic explanations. Edmunds argues that plástica cannot be attributed to something inherent in the 'Brazilian mentality' and that it is too easy to see it as an extension of the West and a product of globalisation. He reminds us that the developing world has different class and cultural bases to those in the West and encourages us to see plástica 'as a social practice grounded in a local context of meaning' (unpublished). When the global beauty-medico system meets Brazil's particular political and social characteristics, Edmunds notes that 'anxieties surrounding new markets of work and sex mingle with fantasies of social mobility, glamour, and modernity' (unpublished).

Sander Gilman's research into Brazil's attitudes towards cosmetic surgery comes to slightly more straightforward conclusions. He says that plástica once had largely domestic significance but has in the last decade been influenced by global images of beauty. He explains that the country's large African population meant that the question of blackness played an important role in the early uptake of cosmetic surgery, particularly breast surgery. It was thought that the 'black breast' was bigger and more pendulous than the 'white breast', so because whites were socially and financially dominant in Brazil, women opted – until the mid 1990s – for breast reductions. Even those with middling sized breasts would choose reductions in order to minimise signs of 'blackness'. In the early 1990s globalisation prompted changes in Brazilian notions of beauty and women began asking for augmentations rather than reductions. Gilman suggests that 'now, in an age of globalised notion of the erotic, breast augmentation is the procedure of choice rather than an emphasis on correcting the appearance of race' (2005a: 120).

Brazil is distinguished by Ivo Pitanguy, the world's most famous cosmetic surgeon. He is a living legend and a national hero, surpassed only by Pelé the soccer player. The hugely wealthy octogenarian (he owns a large island off Rio) is lauded at national festivals and has reportedly operated on everyone from Leni Riefenstahl to Candice Bergen. Something of a philosopher, he refuses to differentiate between reconstructive and aesthetic surgeries: 'in both instances I perceive human pain. I don't draw a line between medical and aesthetical indications of suffering. To be happy with yourself is by no means a superficial desire. My operations are not just for my patients' bodies, they are also for their souls' (quoted in Karcher, 2005: 174).

His influence has no doubt influenced the country's emphasis on free plástica and everyone's right to surgery, even the very poor – there are reportedly plástica clinics opening in shantytowns (Phillips, 2006). Perhaps Pitanguy really is the hugely talented surgeon that he purports to be. Certainly, doctors from all over the world travel to study under him (Gilman, 2005). However, this may be less to do with Pitanguy's talents and more to do with the hands-on experience that can be gained by working in the Brazilian health care system. In exchange for her free cosmetic surgery, the Brazilian woman must spend months or years on long waiting lists, and even physically queue (some lines stretch overnight) to have her operation. She will also be denied the privacy she would have had at a private clinic, and must be prepared to be exhibited and discussed in front of up to forty surgeons, partially disrobed, for educational purposes (Edmunds, unpublished). Edmunds points out that 'plastic surgery wards in public hospitals provide unique "opportunities" ... for residents in surgery' (unpublished). A European resident told him he had performed ninety-six surgeries in a year, and 90 per cent of them were cosmetic: 'There is nowhere else in the world ... [where] I could have gotten that kind of experience in so short a time' (unpublished).

Plástica plays an important role in the global world of cosmetic surgery. It attracts residents from all over the world who want practical experience. These residents also facilitate plástica's continuation, performing many of the operations without getting paid. They often use the experience gained practising on Brazil's poor to make their fortunes in US private clinics. It could be said that some of the world's most expensive cosmetic surgery is subsidised by the Brazilian maids, housewives and shop assistants who queue for their right to plástica, even as they are denied other rights such as decent pay and working conditions. As Edmunds says, 'those who cannot fully achieve the status of citizen-consumer can through the tools of medicine estética remake themselves as aesthetic and sexual subjects in a new regime of health' (unpublished).

One English medical student wrote about going to Brazil to study under Pitanguy, highlighting the seeming mismatches between terrible working conditions and plástica:

> SlimMed is the largest implant factory in Latin America and often encourages surgeons at the Pitanguy clinics to visit their factory, which is located in one of the shanty towns, Favelas, on the outskirts of Rio ... Entrance to the factory was through a secret false wall, which retracted revealing a small underground city of people in spacesuits making breast, buttock, chin, and penis implants. The temperature in my spacesuit was stifling and there was little air conditioning. I was drenched with sweat on leaving (Sheldon Lloyd, 2005).

The false wall is necessary because the favelas are overrun with drug lords who regularly target and rob visitors to the factory. SlimMed implants are used all over the world so this is another instance of Brazil's cheap labour force fuelling a world economy of cosmetic surgery.

Edmunds argues that in Brazil cosmetic surgery is less about 'becoming normal' and more about being competitive and aspirational. Rather than plástica working through a 'negative logic of pathologisation' it is 'positive incitement' that creates demand. Part of this 'positive incitement' is to participate in a global economy of beauty, even while participation in other global economies is extremely limited. In makeover culture health is not an absence of disease but rather a state that must be continually worked towards through social, aesthetic, emotional, educational, psychological and surgical projects. This is a global phenomenon, and Edmunds (although he doesn't use the term makeover culture) observes that

> in Brazil it takes on a pronounced, localised form in a context where reproduction, family relationships, and sexual norms are being 'modernised' in a collapsed time frame. The growth of biomedicine in twentieth century Brazil has been intricately bound up with the hopes and anxieties of the project of modernisation. (Edmunds, unpublished)

Chinese Cosmetic Surgery – from Bourgeois to Everyday

The Evercare Medical Institution in Beijing performed more than twelve operations on 24-year-old Lulu (sometimes called Lucy) Hao in 2003, including double eyelid surgery, breast implants and nose heightening, all designed to create a Eurasian look. Hao then became a 'living billboard' and spokeswoman for cosmetic surgery in China. The purpose was to promote Chinese cosmetic surgery and to stop citizens going overseas for their operations (Weaver, 2003). Solid Chinese statistics are hard to come by but cosmetic surgery is certainly on a steep trajectory there. More than 10,000 institutions in the country offer cosmetic surgery operations; industry profits are rising by up to 30 per cent per year; 200,000 malpractice lawsuits have been filed in the last ten years by unhappy cosmetic surgery recipients; around a million Chinese had facelifts in 2002, and the Shanghai Ninth People's Hospital alone reported an increase of 300 per cent for overall cosmetic surgery from 1991 to 2002. Leg lengthening operations are popular in China and there is an entire hospital – the Beijing Institute of External Skeletal Fixation Technology – devoted to the procedures. These are painful, time-consuming operations where bones are broken then fitted with steel pins connected to external metal braces that are gradually stretched to create ten to fifteen extra centimetres in height. The procedure is practised in the West but seems to have a special importance in China where height is very socially important. For example, the foreign ministry requires male applicants to be over five foot seven and women over five foot three. In some provinces people under five foot three cannot get driver's licences, and even some university law schools have height requirements (Watts, 2003).

Anthropologist Susan Brownell describes how globalisation has influenced Chinese body practices, something she believes is revealed in the uptake of cosmetic surgery (2005). She shows that double eyelid surgery is indeed a transnational practice informed by global beauty standards but insists it is still filled with local meaning. Her fascinating research shows how cosmetic surgery has been appropriated and accepted in different ways at different historical and political moments as a local practice in China.

The history of cosmetic surgery in China is a process of oscillation and negotiation between international or global processes and values, and specifically Chinese
ideology and politics: 'because of its identification with "bourgeois" vanity,
[cosmetic surgery's] practitioners were attacked and denounced in socialist China
from the 1950s until the 1980s' (Brownell, 2005: 135). As with Western cosmetic
surgery, it was the wounds induced by modern warfare that facilitated modern
cosmetic surgery's development. In the early 1940s, during the Anti-Japanese War,
the government realised that plastic surgeons were needed to treat the ruined faces
of returned soldiers. So in 1943 Dr Song Ruyao was selected to travel to the USA
to study at the University of Pennsylvania Medical School (ironically, he then spent
1951–6 treating Chinese soldiers who had been wounded by American artillery
in the course of the Korean War). It was not just wounds but also global flows of
people during wartime that created desires for cosmetic surgery – Elizabeth Haiken
describes how in the years after the Second World War ended 'American films,
magazines, and soldiers familiarised Asians with western models of beauty, and
surgeons began to explore what they called "revision" of the "Oriental eye"'(1997:
201).

The differences between plastic and cosmetic surgery in China were politicised in
the 1950s by a government that valued function over form. Dr Song paraphrases the
instructions he received at the time, noting that rhetorics of class struggle had been
applied to cosmetic surgery: 'Emphasising form is a capitalist style of treatment; a
proletarian ought to emphasise the recovery of function' (quoted in Brownell, 2005:
138). Song, who had been officially invited to open a plastic surgery hospital in
1957, endured repeated attacks during the Cultural Revolution for his 'bourgeois'
aesthetics, culminating with all his staff being sent to Jiangxi for 'labor reform'
in 1969. So although cosmetic surgery arrived in China with some of its Western
meanings intact those meanings took on new significance in light of China's political
scene, especially its Cultural Revolution:

> Cosmetic surgery was associated with the bourgeois pursuit of beauty then, and it still
> is. The difference is that within China the pursuit of beauty was formerly attacked and
> denounced, but after the end of Maoism it was glorified as a natural expression of human
> nature, of the personal freedom and individuality that had been suppressed under Mao.
> (Brownell, 2005: 142)

From the 1980s onwards China's radically changing domestic politics and
international relations contributed to what Brownell calls the 'neutralisation, naturalisation, and acceptance' of cosmetic surgery (2005: 142). The notion of naturalisation
is particularly interesting. It is a process by which previously Western ideas and
practices come to have their own meanings in a new context. It is achieved via a sort
of appropriation, where for example Japanese women can have skin that is 'better
than white', and Chinese cosmetic surgeons can take particular pride in fixing the

mistakes of their Western peers (Brownell, 2005: 143). In the 1990s Dr Song was finally asked to establish the Beijing Badachu Plastic Surgery Hospital, currently the biggest plastic surgery hospital in the world.

Double eyelid surgery can easily be analysed as an attempt to look Western, but this is not necessarily always the case. Brownell points out that double eyelids exist in 30–50 per cent of the Chinese population anyway (also see Haiken, 1997: 202, 208), and indeed that the creation of a double eyelid does not equal a non-Chinese eye shape. Surgeons and patients alike are divided about whether the aim of this surgery is to look more Western. This is an example of a hybrid practice that takes some of its values from the West and some from the East. Gilman suggests that the demands for nose augmentations, double eyelid surgery, and even leg extensions are a way for 'the new Chinese capitalist [to look like] the Westerner – and therefore [to be] a better citizen of his or her new country' (2005a: 130). But for Brownell, the double eyelid surgery is 'a transnational form that has been reinvested with uniquely Chinese meanings' (2005: 149).

Japanese Cosmetic Surgery – Whiter than White

Skin-whitening is a worldwide phenomenon but particularly prevalent in Japan. Double eyelid surgery and whitening creams are advertised in most Japanese women's magazines (Darling-Wolf, 2003: 166). Sales of face-whitening chemicals in Japan have been high since the late 1980s and face-whitening is very common (Ashikari, 2005). Rather than being about emulating Western colouring the Japanese preference for paleness may be rooted in the country's own history and aesthetics. The Japanese middle class has long valued whiteness as a symbol of *Japaneseness itself* – that is, as a marker of being different and more 'refined' than other Asian 'races' (Ashikari, 2005). Indeed, many Japanese women insist that white Japanese skin is superior in texture and tone to white non-Japanese skin, which they say ages badly and looks rough (Ashikari, 2005). Of course Japanese women are also subject to 'universal' or 'master-term' versions of so-called 'Caucasian' beauty (Darling-Wolf, 2003: 166). But their preference for whiteness comes with a history based in Japaneseness, and it can be argued that theirs is 'a Japanese form of whiteness' (Ashikari, 2005: 89). Gilman writes that Japanese skin-whitening, double eyelid surgery, and breast and nose augmentations indicate a wish to look more Western. However, he suggests these modifications are not for the purposes of 'passing' in the West but in order to be more accepted in Japan, as a 'modern' Japanese. They are influenced by global (Western) notions of beauty but have a distinct Japanese flavour. Like manga comics and anime films, which are very Japanese but were originally inspired by American cartoons (and which interestingly feature characters with huge round eyes), Japanese cosmetic surgery is a Japan–West hybrid with its own distinct features.

Another interesting Japan–West hybrid concerns breasts. Laura Miller notes that large breasts are increasingly valued in Japan but rates of breast implantation lag far behind those in the West. She suggests that this is partly because of Confucian beliefs about the body being an inheritance from ancestors: to alter it is disrespectful. So rather than surgery, many Japanese opt for the very popular *basuto appu* procedures offered by 'Aesthetic Salons'. These are topical treatments intended to increase bust size using mudpacks, massage, manipulation by mechanical devices and suction. They are, importantly, not surgical, and are therefore not seen to be at odds with Confucian codes (Miller, 2003: 283–4).

Global media perpetrate global ideas of beauty and project 'master-terms' that most people who choose cosmetic surgery are aware of and influenced by. Each person is also part of a local culture that has its own more specific ideas of what is beautiful and which physical attributes are important. While 'beauty' works globally it is never interpreted uniformly. Designing cosmetic surgery then, is partly an act of negotiation between these two factors. Absorbing cultural and social norms perpetuated by global media makes us all, to some degree, citizens of the world. Perhaps cosmetic surgery helps us to be part of a global culture as well as citizens of a particular nation. But cosmetic surgery in any geographic context is also subject to local economic, social and political factors, to 'upwardly mobile' class aspirations and to definitions of national and domestic identity. It may be denounced in political terms, as it was in China during the Cultural Revolution, or celebrated as a nationalistic practice as it is in Brazil. Globalisation may prompt behaviours that manifest in local as much as international or transnational forms (Appadurai, 2001) because every culture has its own negotiations with flows of information, practices and images.

Cosmetic Surgery and Architecture

As well as happening on a world stage and at national levels, cosmetic surgery occurs in specific local environments. It manifests in malls, supermarkets and on television and cinema screens. In this section I review changes in cosmetic surgery over the last two decades by zooming in to examine two 'sites' created twenty years apart. The first is a building, the Westin Bonaventure Hotel in downtown Los Angeles, famously analysed by Fredric Jameson in 1984 (see Figure 4). I show how cosmetic surgery is part of the postmodernism that Jameson describes – sharing its homogeneous, alienating, glossy and superficial aesthetics – particularly when considered in context of the powerful before/after trope. The second is a global 'mediascape', *Extreme Makeover*, a US reality television show and website (also seen on British, Canadian and Australian television) where operations are shown in gory detail. *Extreme Makeover* is analysed and explained as a quintessential

Figure 4 Westin Bonaventure Hotel, Los Angeles, photo courtesy Yves Rubin, rubinphoto.com

example of cosmetic surgery at work inside makeover culture, in which before/after has taken on significant new meaning.

As I explained in Chapter 1, popular discourse around cosmetic surgery is dominated by before/after representations that make cosmetic surgery seem almost magical by hiding moments of 'during'. Jameson's famous 1984 description of the Bonaventure hotel resonates with my observations about before/after and cosmetic surgery (Jones, 2004).

For Jameson, postmodernism and postmodern objects are exemplary expressions of global capitalism (2001). He states that postmodernism is not merely a style but rather a 'cultural dominant' encompassing genres, diverse features, and preoccupations that exist simultaneously. And he suggests that 'in the realm of architecture ... modifications in aesthetic production are most dramatically visible' (2001: 551). The Bonaventure Hotel is the acme of postmodernity: a 'full-blown postmodern building ... [offering] some very striking lessons about the originality of postmodernist space' (2001: 575). Cosmetic surgery can be theorised as one of the diverse features of postmodernism. It shares cultural logics with postmodern architecture and springs from similar capitalist values. In a piece that I examine more closely in my final chapter, architect Rem Koolhaas asks, 'is each of us a mini-construction site?' (2001: 421).

It is especially fitting that the Bonaventure is located downtown in Los Angeles, the world capital of cosmetic surgery. In fact one cosmetic surgery reality television programme, *Dr 90210*, directly capitalises on this (90210 is the Beverly Hills post-code): 'this show is based in Beverly Hills, California, the epicenter of the plastic surgery world' (http://www.ienhance.com/dr90210/dr90210-premiere.asp). I suggest that the aesthetics produced and valued by traditional, mainstream cosmetic surgery – especially when expressed in terms of before/after – align with those that Jameson saw in the Bonaventure: this building and mainstream cosmetic surgery share a system of cultural logics that derive from the same source values.

Entrances and Orifices

Jameson describes how the Bonaventure's entrances are almost invisible and do not behave like traditional hotel doorways. Rather than clearly marking transitions from streetscape to interior the doorways are strangely placed. They position visitors in unlikely and inconvenient spots, funnelling them onto floors lacking lobbies or reception areas. He analyses the incongruous placement of entrances as the building's anthropomorphic desire to be

> a total space, a complete world, a kind of miniature city. In this sense, then, ideally the minicity of Portman's Bonaventure ought not to have entrances at all, since the entryway is always the seam that links the building to the rest of the city that surrounds it: for it does not wish to be a part of the city but rather its equivalent and replacement or substitute. (2001: 577)

Cosmetic surgery and before/after parallel this reading of postmodern aesthetics in several ways. In the Bonaventure the notion of gradual change – from outside to inside – is problematised. Similarly, before/after pictures of cosmetic surgery operations obliterate moments of transition, implying instantaneous change. On a corporeal level cosmetic surgery mirrors the Bonaventure's lack of openings: many cosmetic surgery operations diminish the body's openings: nostrils become smaller, ears are pinned back and cut down, even labia minora are reduced to make the vaginal entrance seem smaller (Weil Davis, 2002). And procedures that make eyes wider and lips bigger (blepharoplasty, lip enhancement) leave them metaphorically closed and less flexible. Removal of 'hooded lids' creates a doll-like stare while collagen-fattened lips and implanted breasts construct barriers between the body and its surroundings. 'Before' photos show mobile faces that have moved over time, skin around eyes drooping, lips thinning and blending with the face. 'After' photos show features controlled and immobile: the entrances to the body have become stand-ardised and somewhat inaccessible. So cosmetic surgery, both materially and when enmeshed in the logics of before/after, zips up the openings to the body. Just like the Bonaventure, cosmetic surgery bodies in this schema aim to be 'total spaces', 'complete worlds' that are seemingly unaffected by their environments.

Façades and Faces

The Bonaventure's outer membrane is all gilded mirrored panels. Jameson analyses it as a

> great reflective glass skin [that] repels the city outside... In a similar way, the glass skin achieves a peculiar and placeless dissociation of the Bonaventure from its neighbourhood: it is not even an exterior, inasmuch as when you seek to look at the hotel's outer walls you cannot see the hotel itself but only the distorted images of everything that surrounds it (2001: 577; also see Soja, 1994: 158).

The poreless lustre of the Bonaventure's 'skin' parallels the results of facelifts, laser dermabrasions and chemical peels. These procedures seek to minimise pore size and blemishes and thus make the body's surface seem impenetrable, securely separating inside from outside. They appear to repel outside forces like gravity, time and sun. However, while the hotel's façade declares its separateness from the world, the sparkling, mirrored mask also reflects that world – city, sun and sky. Likewise cosmetic surgery is a reflection of 'outside events' because the surgical face is a compilation of concentrated codes that replicate or mimic what is considered beautiful: flawless skin, streamlined nose, almond eyes, cupid-bow lips, defined jawline – these heterogeneous elements that rarely manifest on a single face are all 'captured' by cosmetic surgery and presented as a homogenous whole.

Gravity-Defying Elevators and Face Lifts

The lifts of the Bonaventure are not hidden inside shafts but run along its outer walls. More than mere functional or engineering components, Jameson suggests they 'henceforth replace movement but also, and above all, designate themselves as new reflexive signs and emblems of movement proper ... this is a dialectical intensification of the autoreferentiality of all modern culture, which tends to turn upon itself and designate its own cultural production as its content' (2001: 578).

The externalisation of a previously hidden form of labour (the lifts) foreshadows makeover culture, where displays of process are valorised. In the mid 1980s the 'work' of the building was externalised and became an entertainment spectacle – now in the early twenty-first century the 'work' of cosmetic surgery has come out from the space between before/after and is likewise an entertainment spectacle within texts like *Extreme Makeover*. More speculatively, the lifts create movement on the immaculate surface of the Bonaventure that is stilted in the same way that Botoxed® eyes still blink and mouths still open on tightened faces. Cosmetic surgery exalts pristine skin and immobilised facial muscles, allowing only strictly regimented busyness to remain.

The elevators are self-referential, making their own cultural production their content. Cosmetic surgery turns in on itself in a similar manner: no matter what the intentions of its recipients the end effect is often that they share a similar look. An extension of this is that the 'origins' of beauty have changed because of cosmetic surgery: people now have cosmetic surgery in order to look like other people who have had cosmetic surgery. One example is Cindy Jackson, the 'living Barbie' who has had 'Eye lifts, Nose jobs, Cheek implants, Lip enhancement, Cosmetic Dentistry, Chin reduction, Jaw reshaped, Facelifts, Breast implants in, Breast implants out, Dermabrasion, Chemical peels, Fat transfers, Liposuction, Filler injections, Laser treatment, And much more...' (http://www.cindyjackson.com/my_cosmetic_surgery2.php). Jackson takes the normative, heterosexual aims of cosmetic surgery to their logical ends, perfecting homogenised beauty so effectively that it becomes a standard, one she is happy to share. She gives advice (for a price) on how others can do the same: 'the features I have now aren't my own; they are a kind of uniform, specifically tailored according to scientific principles to make me look as appealing as possible to men. Why should I mind if other women want to achieve the same results?' (http://www.cindyjackson.com)

Beauty becomes surgical, defined by cosmetic surgery: wide-open eyes, exalted breasts, fattened lips, small noses, prominent cheekbones, all atop a superslim body. As cosmetic surgery is increasingly commoditised it becomes desirable to have it for its own sake. Virginia Blum has noted that when Jewish women have their noses reshaped to fit a 'gentile ideal' the new nose may look peculiarly out of place, but 'it didn't matter. The nose itself was the mark of a coveted cultural assimilation' (Blum, 2003: 39).

A fashionable nose at the moment is one that is 'sculptured' at the tip to create a vertical dent. Teenage pop star Avril Levine sported one when she visited Australia in 2004; rock star and lesbian pin-up Melissa Etheridge wears a more extreme version. The nose-dent is a form of cleavage, mirroring pressed-together breasts (and the 'new cleavage' made famous by Paris Hilton in the first series of *The Simple Life*. In Australia it is known as 'plumber's crack'). This fashion in women's noses is imitated in men's chin augmentations that sometimes feature a 'dimple' à la Kurt Cobain's (non-augmented) chin. For men and women, the creation of some 'face cleavage' on either nose or chin sexualises the face by raising vulva, buttocks and breasts, with their symmetry and their centre parting. There is no need to undress anymore; the body is all above the neck.

Architecture of the Body

I have suggested how cosmetic surgery works at aesthetically bringing bodies into line with glistening, high-tech architectures like the Bonaventure. If we imagine two bodies in a Bonaventure elevator – one wrinkled and saggy, the other lifted and stretched – it is clear how mainstream cosmetic surgery's aesthetics are also 'full blown' examples of postmodernism; they parallel postmodernism's aesthetics and fit within its architecture.

Jameson declares that humans have not 'kept pace' with the 'mutation in built space itself' that postmodern architecture has created. 'The newer architecture ... stands as something like an imperative to grow new organs, to expand our sensorium and our body to some new, as yet unimaginable, perhaps ultimately impossible, dimensions' (2001: 576). It is possible to follow Anne Balsamo's lead and stretch this alignment to imagine a 'matrix of forms of technological embodiment' (1996: 233) possible within the Bonaventure and other structures. Along these lines I take Jameson's imperative to 'grow new organs' literally. Imagine a compass on a stick, grown like a phallus, to help navigate the spaces that so confuse Jameson; or eyes in the backs and sides of our heads with which to negotiate the vast indoor spaces; or wings to fly about massive atriums such as the Bonaventure's lobby; or monkey-like tails for swinging between its artificial trees, or customised escalator-implants that extend and retract from the soles of our feet.

These dream-like scenarios are not as far-fetched as they may seem: Joe Rosen, a celebrated North American plastic and reconstruction surgeon, promised to be able to graft wings onto humans by 2007: 'Human wings will be here. Mark my words' (Hari, 2002). Although unassisted human flight won't be possible with this model, the wings will be made of flesh and bone and will enjoy full sensation: depending on the style chosen the wings could resemble those of angels or large bats.

Here we have a surgeon jumping the border between 'acceptable' cosmetic surgery and radical or subversive body modifications. Rosen pushes beauty-bound youth-mimicking cosmetic surgery up against practices like tattooing, piercing, branding and corseting. By refusing to stay within the range of traditional procedures he confronts both cosmetic surgery and therapeutic prosthetic surgery. By going beyond simple beautification via normalisation, and by hijacking prosthetics traditionally used for repair, Rosen designs a whole new area of potential human etymology.

While many practitioners of New Age body modifications see procedures such as tattooing, scarification and piercing as tribal, connected to the cosmos and deriving from ancient rituals, cosmetic surgery is usually characterised as consumerist, suppressive and misogynist. The two areas – body modification and cosmetic surgery – even tend to have their own sets of specialised academics and analysts, with body modifications usually written about by psychologists and sociologists, while cosmetic surgery is most often critiqued by feminist philosophers and cultural theorists. A woman with breast implants is rarely compared to a person with a pierced tongue, a facelift is seen as significantly different from a tattoo, and the corporeal results have wildly different connotations and public receptions. Rosen's attempts to suture these very different attitudes gains him harsh criticism from his colleagues: '[he's] way too far out, totally beyond mainstream medicine or mainstream cosmetic surgery. No plastic surgeon I know would do anything of this sort, and nor should he' (John Hugill quoted in Hari, 2002). But Rosen does my rhetorical work for me here: he told detractors in 2001: 'why do we only value the average? Why are plastic surgeons dedicated only to restoring our current notions of the conventional, as opposed to letting people explore, if they want, the possibilities?' (Hari, 2002) Most cosmetic surgeons, as I will show in Chapter 3, work hard to be accepted into the medical mainstream as respected specialists. Perhaps because he comes from the luxury of a stellar profile as a reconstructive surgeon, Rosen is able to have a different project. His visions point to a future where cosmetic surgery, body modification and prosthetics may merge and lead to operative wings: a drastic thought, but one that redefines the average facelift as a hopelessly bland deployment of available technologies.

In order for cosmetic surgery to move from its current narrow homogeneity to being a celebration of the radically modified or even 'the grotesque' it would have to display its assorted effects without embarrassment, embracing both heterogeneity within its own realm and its overlaps with prosthetics and other body modifications. There are many conservative binaries and attitudes currently embraced in the world of cosmetic surgery: it strongly upholds gender, racial and class divides as well as more abstract differences between the 'normal' and the 'monstrous'. But if we follow Rosen's imaginative lead its future could be rich with chosen mutations.

A Marriage Made in Melbourne

While the Bonaventure is an unwitting subject of postmodern theory and my place-ment of cosmetic surgery bodies in it is deliberately contrived, a more recent building actively makes the parallel between postmodern architecture and cosmetic surgery. Figure 5 shows what is known as the 'Sam Newman/Pamela Anderson' house.[5] Sam Newman is an Australian footballer and television celebrity who in 2000 commissioned architect Cassandra Fahey to design his house in Melbourne's St Kilda. Pamela Anderson was a star of the US television series *Baywatch*, a huge hit in the 1990s and the first ever American programme to air in China. Some say that it was Anderson's implanted breasts and tiny red swimsuits that were the real stars of the show; she is also known for her silicone-enhanced lips and very blonde hair. Although it was Fahey's first commission the only requirements were that the house be 'exotic' and provide both light and privacy. The façade is a huge panelled mural of Anderson's face. Entry is via her mouth, which flips up with the garage door.[6] The image is printed on highly polished Perspex so that from some angles we see only reflections of ourselves, the streetscape and the sky. This house embodies my parallel between the Bonaventure's reflective surface and the 'reflectivity' of the beauty that mainstream cosmetic surgery creates: in its mirrored façade we see ourselves and/or a 'perfect' surgically altered face, and the two become confused. It literally conjoins a surgically altered body with a piece of postmodern architecture.

Figure 5 *White Noise*, Melbourne, photo courtesy David Gabriel-Jones

The gigantic image remarks on Anderson's status as a pop-culture icon and her chosen gigantism – her breast implants. Newman told a reporter 'the Pamela Anderson thing has been blown out of all proportion ... for which I blame her plastic surgeon, but never mind' (Peterson, 2005). The face is the size it would be on a cinema screen – where it would be unremarkable – but on the street its proportions shock. Fahey's building confronts drivers and pedestrians with a glossy, flat, pixelated image instead of a three-dimensional house. The house has views of the park, a lap pool and large light rooms, but from outside nothing is revealed of its internal shapes – there are only two dimensions. It comments on the manufactured nature of identity in contemporary culture and conflates notions of self and environment.

In her discussion of cosmetic surgeons' use of technological imaging devices to predict how patients might look post-surgery Anne Balsamo suggests 'it is not so much the inner or essential woman that is visualised; her interior story has no truth of its own. Both her surface and her interiority are flattened and dispersed' (1996: 58). In this structure Anderson's pixelated face is literally flattened and dispersed, and while it incongruously suggests that there is nothing 'inside' it also holds a certain unsettling power. Laura Mulvey has famously suggested that woman's image in film is 'an indispensable element of spectacle … yet her visual presence tends to work against the development of a story-line, to freeze the flow of action' (1989: 19). This disembodied façade demonstrates this power to interrupt: cars slow down, pedestrians are startled. The house wears its image like a mask; both it and Anderson are 'all front' although Fahey denies the audience access to Anderson's defining feature, her breasts. The face-alone nature of the work ensures that this building *stares back*, turning objectification around on itself. It plays with themes of superficiality, manufactured identity, celebrity, 'internal' and 'external' subjective spaces, and the commoditisation of everyday life.

There are resonances between cosmetic surgery and certain architectural spaces, specifically in relation to the trope of before/after. The next section deals with a media space, *Extreme Makeover*, showing how before/after has been embraced and deployed by makeover culture. *Extreme Makeover* is as much about surfaces as are the Bonaventure and the Pamela Anderson house. It also shows makeover culture in action, opening the temporal and physical spaces between before and after.

Makeover Culture and *Extreme Makeover*

If you have always dreamed of having an extreme makeover, which includes multiple plastic surgeries, this is your opportunity!

All candidates must be US citizens and in good physical health. If selected, we will give you a truly Cinderella-like experience by changing your looks completely in an effort to transform your life and destiny, and to make your dreams come true. This is all accomplished through the skills of an 'Extreme Team', which includes the country's finest plastic surgeons, eye surgeons and cosmetic dentists, along with a talented team of hair and makeup artists, stylists and personal trainers. (*Extreme Makeover* website)

The Bonaventure agitated Jameson with its autoreferentiality and denial of connection to the world. Before/after has concerned and infuriated feminists – and some surgeons – for similar reasons. Its representational framework shrouds cosmetic surgery in deceit and secrecy – it makes major surgery look easy. It also keeps cosmetic surgery recipients silent – within it they are merely fragmented body parts. As I have explained, a cultural shift has occurred in the last few years around the before/after trope. What happens *between* before and after is increasingly being shown … not by radical artists but on mainstream television shows like *Extreme Makeover*.

Extreme Makeover is a product of makeover culture and also an excellent example of cosmetic surgery at work in this new arena. The show recruits members of the public and gives them cosmetic surgery overhauls that most could never afford. Money is presented as the only barrier to cosmetic surgery in this schema that never questions the necessity or desirability of cosmetic surgery. Vicky Mayer writes about sitting next to a potential recipient of an extreme makeover on a plane and learning how for 'Sue Ellen' this wasn't a luxury but rather a chance for basic health care. Having spent all her life suffering from terrible teeth, and completely unable to pay for the dental work required, the nervous first-time plane traveller told Mayer that

> she would be a likely candidate for a nose and boob job, eye tucks, and a face peel – 'the one where they scrub your skin off.' She said she didn't care about all the rest. 'As long as my teeth get done, they can do whatever… If I had good health insurance, I wouldn't be doing this.' (Mayer, 2005)

The fairy godmother aspect of shows like *Extreme Makeover* is quite real, touching people who have been left behind by the brutal US health system. Most recipients are women and most are lower or lower-middle class. Cressida Heyes, in a fine Foucauldian analysis of the programme, says that in it 'disability and working class status are represented as hierarchies that must be flattened without overt comment' (2007: 97).

Most of the show's participants receive major surgical and dental work, usually between five and ten major operations each. Surgeons who donate their services enjoy celebrity status; being on the programme is probably much more lucrative than any form of advertising. The *Extreme Makeover* website lists contact details for the 'Extreme Team' for each makeover, including beauticians, fashion consultants, dermatologists, dentists and even the caterer. Each programme features two or three individuals, usually white women, who are introduced to the audience as deserving and interesting.

The rhetoric of vanity is pushed as far from the fore in these programmes as possible. *Extreme Makeover* explicitly mobilises the *Cinderella* makeover story. Just like Cinderella, who is beautiful underneath the grime of her unwashed face and suffers in cruel circumstances, the programme's subjects are not vain but instead worthy because of having suffered hardship. Participants are selected on the basis of their physical 'flaws' and their willingness to share painful intimacies.

They are often the meritorious poor, seeking physical transformation as a method of self-improvement and a way of expressing their 'true selves'. Blum suggests that 'according to the makeover story of modern female culture, the after is always construed as the real you that was just itching to assert her identity, to reveal her real face' (2003: 191). People wanting to have their 'real selves' revealed include a 'church choir singer', a 'dedicated mother [who has] worked hard to make everyone else happy', a man who has endured 'the loss of his wife, his job and his savings all in a short period of time', and a woman who 'worked the land as a rancher, surviving the hardest elements' (*Extreme Makeover* website). Acceptance on to the show is highly competitive and open auditions attract thousands.

After being accepted, at which they usually cry and thank God, beneficiaries are video-documented through months of consultations, operations, recovery, exercise, dieting and grooming. The culmination of each programme is a dramatic 'Reveal' ceremony where they present their new bodies and faces to their children, partners, friends and an international audience. Importantly, the transformations themselves occur away from friends and family, out of the context of patients' normal lives. This means that despite the heavy documentation of the painful procedures, before/after remains secure as a key structuring trope. The audience follows the recipient on a 'secret' and 'private' transformative process via the space of the television screen.

Screens render transformation familiar, making it everyday. The violent processes of cosmetic surgery (sawing away of nose cartilage, strenuously forcing implants up under breast muscle) become acceptable via the screen. Two powerful transformative devices – the television screen and the scalpel – are bonded on *Extreme Makeover*, making cosmetic surgery palatable and positioning all viewers as potential participants. The programme's official website includes links to 'Makeover Experts' in your town, and also features an 'apply for finance' link. 'Inner selves' are also eviscerated, exhibited and improved for public consumption on *Extreme Makeover*. Many of the recipients express private insecurities, from terror of rejection to feelings of sibling rivalry and inadequacy. The makeovers are presented as portals through which they gain confidence, become the people they 'really are' and fulfil themselves in careers and romance.

Banishing Vanity

The producers police a fine line in choosing recipients: they must be deserving, like Jeff, who has heroically 'lost 200 pounds on his own in only one year with a rigid diet and exercise regimen' and Tammy, who 'feels as if she's been living in perpetual adolescence. Her self-esteem, personal relationships and love life have been scarred by the severe acne she's suffered from all her life' (*Extreme Makeover* website).

The recipients often have a 'dream': Jeff wants an 'extended body tuck' to remove the great flaps of skin that were stretched and lost elasticity when he was obese. We are told that 'the procedure is his once-in-a-lifetime chance to live the normal life he's always desired, a dream he desperately wants to see come true'. Tammy also has a dream: '[as] the oldest dancer in her dance school, her dream is to perform in front of the chorus line – if only she were confident enough to be in the spotlight' (*Extreme Makeover* website). As well as being deserving and having a dream, both of which fulfil classic narrative trajectories and provide easy fairytale-type storylines, *Extreme Makeover* recipients also include a selection of individuals whom the audience relates to on the level of everyday concerns: 'after two decades on the job, Peggy, a 48-year-old crime scene investigation detective from Colorado, wants to look 20 years younger at her upcoming work anniversary party. She is transformed from looking dead tired to drop dead gorgeous' (*Extreme Makeover* website).

These stories are presented in the same way as the ones that feature people like DeShante, 'a 22-year-old church choir singer from Pittsburg, California, [who] feels that her life has been marred by her cleft palate and lip. Called "harelip" by kids when she was young, DeShante underwent four operations until her parents' money ran out. Consequently, the congenital deformity has never been corrected – until now' (*Extreme Makeover* website). DeShante's problem is apparently nothing to do with a user-pays health system or her black family's poverty. While the space between before/after may be opened up for inspection, elisions to do with class and race continue. By setting common concerns such as ageing against more unusual concerns like post-mastectomy implants and harelip reconstructions, cosmetic surgery is presented as an antidote equally applicable to everyone. By paralleling anxieties that once fell into the category of vanity with deformities, each becomes as valid as the other. The suffering of the woman with droopy breasts becomes as deserving of intervention as the suffering of the cancer survivor with only one breast. Most people can probably relate to at least one of the recipients on *Extreme Makeover*. Every disappointing physical attribute can now be medicalised and linked with psychological hardship, and cosmetic surgery is presented as a panacea for all manner of psychosocial problems and crises of confidence.

Labour Revealed

The majority of each programme features footage and discussion about consultations, procedures, operations and recoveries. These processes are not presented as messy moments to be endured on the pathway to better selves, but rather as almost enjoyable, in and of themselves. Rhetorics of care are emphasised, with anaesthetists figuring in every programme and nurses hovering post-operatively. Transformations continue post-surgery with hair stylists, make-up artists and fitness trainers. The episodes are about processes of becoming – processes that begin during surgery and then continue through recovery, grooming and further 'personal growth' in everyday life.

The operations on *Extreme Makeover* take up to ten hours but are televisually condensed into a few minutes. Time is compressed but repeated close-ups of clocks during the operations are a reminder that there is nothing instant about this process. As I suggested earlier, this opening of the time and space between before/after has, counter-intuitively, contributed to cosmetic surgery becoming increasingly mainstream and fashionable. The simple explanation for this is that gruesome scenes desensitise and initiate a surgical-virgin audience. Surgery becomes an everyday media event. In this sense television is a cultural anaesthetic through which we experience virtual surgery, making that small step to real surgery a little bit easier. But the connection is more complex: it is to do with showing *labour revealed* within a very specific framework. When painful recovery periods, embarrassing consultations and vulnerable, anaesthetised subjects are displayed, cosmetic surgery becomes associated with hard work and sacrifice. It is removed from vanity and narcissism and becomes something that requires motivation, something that tough and hardy people with a strong ethic of self-improvement consider: it becomes an act of courage, bravery and self-determination.

So rather than being presented as vain, subjects on *Extreme Makeover* are presented as commendable. Witnessing someone go through suffering and distress in order to reach their target is an ancient narrative that enlists barracking: we want the protagonist to achieve her goal. The bleeding and bruised cosmetic surgery recipient is a kind of Cinderella, just as the show's producers suggest, and the audience identifies with her, especially if she's been presented as deserving to begin with.

The before/after will for magical transformation is still a strong theme in texts like *Extreme Makeover*, but the between stages, the moments of becoming, are now just as important, if not more important, than achieving an end result. In fact, what makeover culture most validates is a ceaseless, stretched, *period of becoming*, rather than a finale that displays a completely transformed self. Transformation becomes a temporal and spatial *mode of being*, replacing a static end result: makeover culture is not a means to an end but a continuing lifestyle. Cosmetic surgery recipients as shown on shows like *Extreme Makeover* epitomise these new ideals: they are not simply transformed but are engaged in active becoming.

Little Pedagogies

As I have already indicated, makeover culture relates to practices, trends and desires other than cosmetic surgery. For example, the 'knowledge economy' is theorised as a new paradigm where adaptation and potential are important. When it comes to employment in the knowledge economy, *flexibility* is more desirable than permanence or fidelity. In this environment the working-learning self must be constantly mobile. Nikolas Rose suggests that identity is now a 'project' (1996: 160) and that contemporary life is about making identities via practices like lifestyle shopping and homemaking. Further, he writes that citizen formation no longer happens according to external morals and obligations. Ethical selves are now created via active self-fabrication. Contemporary moral life is taught in what he calls the 'little pedagogies' of talk shows and soap operas (1999: 164) – and I would add, now, makeover shows. *Extreme Makeover* is in this sense a site for teaching and learning, a site for ethical formation, a site where we learn to be flexible and changeable. Subjects on *Extreme Makeover* in this way are the role models of makeover culture.

Magic Reinstated

At the end of each *Extreme Makeover* programme, after the Reveal, the before/after rhetoric is strongly restated. This is done using a device where the screen is divided in two, with the left side showing the 'before' body while the right side shows the 'after' body, with a voice-over describing the work done. The two digital bodies rotate so they are viewable from 360° and are haloed by a series of glowing rings.[7] Despite all the blood and gore then, final bodies on *Extreme Makeover* are presented as digital statues: as virtual figures incapable of pain and on permanent display. In the before/after model this was about showing magic at work, but in makeover culture it is also about the display of hard-won achievement: the 'old you' is not abandoned in makeover culture but is repurposed as a ghost-twin, an emblem of how far you've come. The twin digital images mean that 'after' bodies are presented as *always linked* to their 'befores'. Carole Spitzack has suggested that no matter how much we may cut, tuck, suck and lift, the shadow of our 'diseased' pre-operative selves will always lurk within our 'improved' bodies. 'After' bodies simply cover over the impure, uncut body parts that remain 'flawed and pathological' (1988: 52). Jordan Crandall, in an article about gym-work and mirrors, puts it this way:

> it is nearly impossible to assess where one stands in the spectrum: the 'real' body is always shuffled into the deck. Image and corporeality, present and future, are enmeshed in an oscillation that beats to the rhythm of routine… It seems that wherever there is an image there is an incomplete body running after it, endeavouring to catch it or interpolate itself into it. (1997)

Makeover culture opens up the space between before and after and situates 'running' inside that space as the most productive and worthy activity for its citizens. Makeover culture does not abandon before/after, it merely makes the transition between before and after never complete. 'Afters' in this schema are never permanent, in fact in makeover culture the 'after' is the new 'before', simply heralding the next portion of labour. Efrat Tseëlon writes that 'beauty, for the woman, is an identity claim, except that it is a conditionally spoiled identity. It is only through *hard work* that the woman can avoid being shown up as ugly' (1995: 80, my italics). The hard work of makeover culture is a way to ensure constant running from the 'incomplete body' that Crandall invokes. Both the magic and the horrors of before/after remain intact inside makeover culture: they are merely transformed via a new set of indicators.

A will for simple transformation remains a very strong theme in texts like *Extreme Makeover*. In addition to this I argue that the *between stages*, the moments of becoming, are now more important than achieving an end result. In fact, what is most desirable now is a ceaseless, stretched, *period of becoming*, rather than a finale that displays a new body. Transformation becomes a temporal and spatial mode of being rather than a static end result. I use the word 'becoming' rather than 'transformation' because they are subtly different: transformation brings to mind a quick change, a definitive before and after, whereas becoming connotes growth and slower change. Becoming can be explained as a mode of living whereas transformation implies rupture and a stop-start action foreign to daily life. The cosmetic surgery recipient is not simply transformed: rather, she displays herself as a person manufacturing her own becoming.

Transformation and Makeover

The body that shows its becoming-process is enacting 'makeover' while the one whose labour is hidden – especially via before/after – merely shows 'transformation'. Makeover and transformation are closely related but vary in some significant ways, as shown in Table 1. Cosmetic surgery is no longer hidden: its corporeal processes have been opened up and now our knowledges of it are better. But these knowledges are often gruesome and repulsive, so why is cosmetic surgery more desirable than ever? I suggest that the articulated makeover does not replace magical transformative

Table 1 Transformation and makeover compared

Transformation	*Makeover*
Result achieved by magic.	Result achieved by work.
Labour hidden.	Labour displayed.
Time is conflated or diminished.	Time is shown more chronologically.
Cosmetic surgery is painless: pain is barely mentioned.	Cosmetic surgery is painful: pain is a rite of passage.
Patient and doctor are the only actors shown.	Many more actors are shown: beauticians, fitness trainers, nurses and psychologists.
'Becoming' is hidden in the slash between before/after.	'Becoming' is integral to process of transformation.
The temporal story is contained in the before/after; cosmetic surgery is all there is.	The temporal story is stretched. Recipients speak of childhoods and post-cosmetic surgery lives. Cosmetic surgery is positioned as part of the lifespan.
The action-space is confined to the recipient's body, which is removed from everyday life for the period of hidden change and later reintegrated.	The action-space includes operating theatres, surgeries, other cities, other practitioners' spaces: beauticians, fashionistas, hairdressers, personal trainers.
The body is presented as closed and finished once surgery is complete.	The body is presented as open and malleable, always ready for more work.
Cosmetic surgery results try to be indistinguishable and 'natural'.	Cosmetic surgery results may boast themselves.
Cosmetic surgery, while necessary for some, is essentially a shameful practice.	Cosmetic surgery is a reward, something earned, and is potentially available to all.

discourse but works cleverly in conjunction with it: together, makeover and magic create a powerful set of rhetorics. We could easily assume that makeover has replaced transformation; on the contrary, it adds another layer to cosmetic surgery discourse. Fantasies of transformation remain dominant, now accompanied by a new and potent ally. Rhetorics of magic and labour combine to create makeover culture.

Pleasure and Pain

In the paradigm of makeover culture and becoming-transformed there is little to distinguish between the pleasures and pains of cosmetic surgery. Pain is a rite of passage, an industriousness undertaken to achieve a pleasurable result. Cosmetic surgery used to be presented as the 'easy way out.' For example, liposuction was popularly thought to be for the faint-hearted who were too lazy to exercise or wanted slim bodies too soon. Now it is more likely to be presented as an endeavour requiring great effort and self-control, much like dieting and gym-work. Pain can give validity to the feeling of 'deserving' to look better after cosmetic surgery and may operate as a corporeal marker of an important life-transition.

The neutralisation of blood and pain via our screens and other everyday media means that cosmetic surgery has been distanced from vanity, frivolity and narcissism. It is now seen as a means to improving mental well-being, and as part of the continuing development of the self. The opening up of the processes between before and after is happening synchronously with the re-framing of the rationales for having cosmetic surgery. Paradoxically, exposing the ugliest elements of cosmetic surgery has made it more desirable.

Conclusion

Makeover culture combines postmodern notions of a fluid, malleable self with modernist notions of self-creation and self-improvement. These values are gaining global currency. The idea of the self as a transformable construct is not new but the difference is that in makeover culture the transformation of the self is *imperative*. Self-renovation by whatever means is compulsory and never-ending. Self-improvement is something that makeover culture insists *everyone* needs: it is a continuing enterprise that may be realised via home renovation, lifelong learning, career enhancement or body-work such as cosmetic surgery. Good citizens in makeover culture are in a permanent state of becoming something better. In modernity we are entrepreneurs of our own selves (Rose 1999), in postmodernity we have many selves to choose from (Poster, 2001; Turkle, 1996). In makeover culture it is not who we choose to become that is important as much as the *display* of our ongoing improvement: the visible act of labouring to acquire one's choices, the public performance of moving from one self to another.

The Bonaventure is a building that perfectly houses and mirrors madeover and groomed bodies. In the model of before/after, they are bodies that have been transformed *elsewhere* and only reveal themselves once they're perfectly healed. In contrast, makeover culture 'surfaces' or 'outs' labour: bodies in permanent transition are its goal. Texts like *Extreme Makeover* exemplify this change. In them the spatial and temporal moments between before and after are increasingly documented: not by people who are anti-cosmetic surgery or making radical statements like Orlan, but by the very industries that stand to gain from a widespread acceptance of the technology as part of everyday life. These programmes show the surgeries themselves, they dwell on the miserable healing periods, and cosmetic surgery recipients suddenly have voices and personalities. Texts like *Extreme Makeover* still definitely privilege transformation, before/after and magic, but they also show what used to be invisible: they have opened up what happens between and made it desirable. They are forming makeover culture whilst also reflecting it.

–3–

Morphing Industries
Surgeons, Patients and Consumers

We are neither audience nor actors, residing in neither the amphitheatre nor on the stage: rather we are 'in the panoptic machine, invested by its effects of power, which we bring to ourselves since we are part of its mechanism'.

Foucault, *Discipline and Punish*

I don't regard appearance as terribly important anyway. It's what the society wants that I'm reacting to.

Dr Young, interviewee

Agency in the Makeover Network

When it comes to cosmetic surgery, agency is constituted and distributed in diverse ways. The relatively new actor-network theory (ANT) is a useful tool for thinking about this.[1] The 'actors' in ANT are heterogeneous agents, which may be human or non-human, organic or artificial, visible or hidden, located in the past, present or future. The 'network' in the theory's name is a way of recognising that any entity or process is made up of many interconnected actors. Networks are formed and reformed by 'a series of transformations – translations, transductions' and are always in motion (Latour, 1997). Using ANT we see that while doctor and patient are clearly agents inside the cosmetic surgery network, so are professional organisations, hospitals, advertisements, consulting rooms, syringes, Botox®, implants, anaesthetics, etc. ANT argues that networks are constructions made by dynamic and intertwined collectives of non-human and human actors. Importantly, humans are not necessarily at the centre of these networks, nor are they placed in opposition to non-humans (Pile and Thrift, 1995: 36). In ANT traditional dichotomies like nature/culture and natural/artificial are problematised as a matter of course: 'the observer must abandon all *a priori* distinctions between natural and social events' (Callon, 1986: 200; also see Pile and Thrift, 1995: 35–7). Not only is agency credited to non-humans but objects may also *intersect* with humans, 'exchanging properties' with them (Latour, 1994: 46; Sofoulis, 1998: 4) – a particularly important idea when considering implants.

While accounting for many actors, ANT does not position them as equal or symmetrical. Rather it shows how powerful positions are defined during 'negotiations' and are created when certain actors enlist texts, artefacts, and processes as 'enrolled' or 'allied' players (Callon, 1991). Michel Callon writes that rather than trying to identify who holds power we should look at how actors

> define their respective identities, their mutual margins of manoeuvre and the range of choices that are open to them ... the capacity of certain actors to get other actors – whether they be human beings, institutions or natural entities – to comply with them depends upon a complex web of interrelations in which Society and Nature are intertwined. (1986: 201)

I trace some of these interrelations in this chapter to point out how surgeons seek compliance from other actors, how they sometimes fail in this endeavour and how their positions are being recalibrated inside makeover culture.

Cosmetic Surgeons and Plastic Surgeons

> ...all collectives are different from one another in the way they divide up beings, in the properties they attribute to them, in the mobilisation they consider acceptable. (Latour, quoted in Pile and Thrift, 1995: 36)

Plastic surgeons and cosmetic surgeons form two entangled and occasionally warring collectives. The plastic surgeons I interviewed were at pains to point out the differences between themselves and cosmetic surgeons in Australia. They were keen to tell me that although they *practise* cosmetic surgery, they are not *solely* cosmetic surgeons: for them, cosmetic surgery is just one category of plastic surgery. Plastic surgery might involve work on skin that is burned or scarred, face and hand reconstructions, skin cancers and many other surgeries that are not primarily 'aesthetic'. The Australian Society of Plastic Surgeons (ASPS) certifies doctors as plastic surgeons after at least eight years of specialist plastic surgery training. However, any medical doctor in Australia can hang a sign and print business cards calling himself a cosmetic surgeon. In the UK the rules are similar: plastic surgery is one of only nine medical specialities recognised by The Royal College of Surgeons; plastic surgeons are not registered until they have trained in plastic surgery, usually for six years after qualifying as a doctor. As in Australia 'cosmetic surgeons may be highly skilled and capable but there are not currently any regulations covering their training' (Royal College of Surgeons, England, http://www.rcseng.ac.uk/). In the USA board-certified plastic surgeons complete approximately seven years after medical school training in order to specialise in plastic surgery (American Board of Plastic Surgery, Inc., http://www.abplsurg.org/index.htm). However, as in England and Australia, any medical doctor with minimum qualifications can legally call himself a 'cosmetic surgeon'.

Plastic surgeons reside in closed collectives, well established in history and protocol. They tend to denigrate the qualifications and expertise of doctors who call themselves cosmetic surgeons – one I interviewed referred to their training with contempt as a mere 'weekend workshop'. Another plastic surgeon described the situation to me in terms of a battle:

> we spend a lot of time attempting to convince government that they must stop this nonsense of allowing unqualified people to call themselves cosmetic surgeons. We are winning. We will only win when ultimately the rest of Australia adopts the Queensland policy of having what we call vocational registration, that is, a doctor has to register his speciality to be allowed to practise in that speciality. And cosmetic surgeons will not be able to call themselves surgeons because they're not (Dr Fred).

This may be so, but cosmetic surgeons insist that their work is as good as or better than that of plastic surgeons and insist that plastic surgeons are merely lobbying for a monopoly on a highly lucrative market (see Daniel Fleming in *Buyer of Beauty, Beware*, 2006). Libby Harkness, in her well-researched consumer's guide to cosmetic surgery in Australia, writes that 'some procedures, such as liposuction, breast reconstruction and chemical peels, were not initially the province of plastic surgeons' (1994, republished in 2004: 28). Although plastic surgeons claim historical ownership of most cosmetic surgery procedures there are many other specialists doing cosmetic surgery. For example, ear, nose and throat specialists might do rhinoplasties and otoplasties (pinning back ears), ophthalmic surgeons might perform blepharoplasties (eye lifts), surgical oncologists might reconstruct breasts and dermatologists might carry out peels and dermabrasions. It is not inconceivable that some of these 'non-plastic surgeons' are actually better at performing those particular surgeries than some plastic surgeons might be because they have more intimate knowledge of particular areas of the body and more practice in operating on those areas.

Added to this web of specialisations, qualifications and expertise is the difference between hospitals and clinics. Cosmetic surgery operations can be performed in major public hospitals, in private hospitals, in small or large private clinics and in theatres attached to consulting rooms. In Australia, for example, public hospital boards usually only allow certified plastic surgeons to practise cosmetic surgery while any doctor can set up his own surgical clinic or private hospital. This can be confusing: one woman I interviewed had a consultation with a cosmetic surgeon who told her that her blepharoplasty would be performed 'upstairs', above his small suburban consulting room. She was surprised that the operation could take place outside of a hospital and decided to seek a plastic surgeon instead. 'It was unprofessional, it was like "oh we'll just whiz you upstairs and get it over and done with." It made me just want to leave and run out of there' (Kelly).

So if you visit a cosmetic surgeon he may be a plastic surgeon who calls himself a cosmetic surgeon because he mostly does aesthetic surgery; he may be some other sort of specialist like a dermatologist; or he may be simply a general practitioner or MD who has *probably* completed some sort of short course about cosmetic surgery.

Even within the ranks of plastic surgeons there are arguments about who can 'belong', and being a highly trained plastic surgeon doesn't guarantee being officially recognised by peers. A former president of the ASPS told me that one very high profile Sydney plastic surgeon – someone who is constantly in the media talking about cosmetic surgery – had been denied admittance to the society because his *image* is disapproved of:

> [He's] a properly trained plastic surgeon, and he does cosmetic surgery, and his surgery is as good and bad as everyone else's … [But] he is prepared to be regarded as being unacceptably commercial by the vast majority of his medical colleagues and laugh all the way to the bank, basically is how I see it. I value my reputation with my professional colleagues extremely highly, and I wouldn't do anything to threaten that, like doing what [he] does… He made an unsuccessful attempt at joining the Australian Society of Plastic Surgeons and he was rejected purely on that ground alone. His qualifications and training were perfectly adequate. (Dr Fred)

The surgeon's crime is that he is unashamedly commercial, working on developing a high media profile upon which to build a lucrative practice. In ANT terms, aspects of his mobilisation were deemed unacceptable by the collective to which he wanted entry. There are subtle issues to do with etiquette and upholding the delineations between plastic and cosmetic surgeons at stake here. Surgeons are enmeshed in webs of politics, infighting, labelling and disputes about territory, expertise and reputation. Medical, commercial and ethical imperatives fuel their debates as they compete for clients. Michel Callon says that 'understanding what sociologists generally call power relationships means describing a way in which actors are defined, associated and simultaneously obliged to remain faithful to their alliances' (1986: 224). What we see here is a constant tug for the power to speak and to represent; struggles for the authority to command a logonomic system. Within the changing landscape of cosmetic surgery in makeover culture surgeons' old alliances become problematised – below I look at some of the ways they deal with this.

Pygmalion's Many Faces

Ovid wrote his version of the Pygmalion story, 'Pygmalion and the Statue', around the time of the birth of Christ. A king is disillusioned with the sexual frivolity of the women around him. He is not merely disheartened by women, he loathes and abhors them:

Pygmalion loathing their lascivious Life,
Abhorred all Womankind, but most a Wife:
So single chose to live, and shunned to wed,
Well pleased to want a Consort of his Bed.

(Ovid: *Metamorphoses*, Book X)

To distract himself from sexual cravings he carves a statue of a woman. Unexpectedly he falls in love with it. He prays to Venus, the Goddess of Beauty, to bring the statue to life, and eventually she consents. The statue's name is Galatea and she becomes the perfect wife for Pygmalion.

The Pygmalion tale endures and has been famously reworked in art, plays, films and books. Paul Delvaux's famous surrealist painting (Figure 6) plays with some of its themes, depicting Venus embracing a lifeless statue of a male figure. The tale is also common in narratives about cosmetic surgery, where it is deployed as part of scholarly feminist critiques (Blum, 2003: 92–6; Davis, 1997: 31), by psychologists (Goin and Goin, 1981: 115), within journalism (Bankard, 2004) and in the websites of cosmetic surgeons who describe the 'Pygmalion complex' as 'the desire to create

Figure 6 Paul Delvaux, *Pygmalion* (1939). Oil on wood, Musées Royaux des Beaus-Arts de Belgique, Brussels. Photograph: IRPA

perfection, not out of marble but out of human flesh' (Talwar, 2002). One website says 'Just as a sculptor uses a mallet and chisel to render a 3-D human form, the plastic surgeon wields a cannula, or hollow tube, which is inserted through a small incision, to reconfigure stubborn fatty areas' (Manley, n.d.).

The Pygmalion myth is brought into play both positively and negatively in relation to cosmetic surgery: detractors easily and frequently couple it with the Frankenstein story to emphasise cosmetic surgery's 'unnaturalness' and monstrous implications. Supporters mobilise it to historicise and eternalise a contemporary practice, hoping to make cosmetic surgery appear more conservative by aligning it with Classical artistry.

Pygmalion is enlisted as an actor in order to define various positions – different viewpoints try to 'enrol' it to strengthen their own situations. I enlist it myself here to describe some of the roles that surgeons play in makeover culture and the ways they describe or 'sell' themselves and each other. They can be artist-sculptors, metaphorical fathers, lovers/husbands, charlatans and abusers.

Spitzack's Confession and Surgeon as Lover

In 1988, feminist communications scholar Carole Spitzack visited a cosmetic surgery clinic and underwent a 'diagnosis' and consultation. She describes the visit in detail with all its 'subtle splitting and jarring that prompts intense self-scrutiny, leading to an externalization and internalization of disease' (1988: 41). I have immense regard for this piece of scholarly 'life-writing' and consider it one of the foundation-stones of feminist analysis of cosmetic surgery. I do not endeavour to override or contradict any of Spitzack's observations but rather to show how they are now further problematised and complicated by makeover culture.

Spitzack's consultation moved beyond what she had expected: her enquiry about a rhinoplasty ended in unwanted advice about skin resurfacing. She experienced intense embarrassment when placed in front of three brightly lit mirrors and asked to describe her 'problem'. Once she had 'confessed' and her 'problems' had been identified – and she had accepted that two operations instead of one were necessary – the physician offered to help her deceive her insurance company by stating the operations were 'necessary' surgical procedures. Spitzack interprets this as: 'we will be cohorts in deception, like lovers committing a crime' (1988: 46–7). She describes how the surgeon sits close to her, 'no more than three feet away' and how he gently places his hand on her back to adjust her position (1988: 46). The 'love' situation she describes is similar to an unhealthy relationship where one party is controlling, working to destroy the self-confidence of the other in order to make them dependent. The doctor undermined her confidence, using the power of diagnostic language to make her 'realise' that her skin needed resurfacing. He then presented her with a 'solution' that was bound up in secrecy and codependence. The surgeon–patient relationship described here is one where woman is triple victim: of her own insecurities, of the surgeon's display of expertise and of his greed.

There are other ways in which the surgeon can be understood as lover. He has intimate access to the woman's naked body, he penetrates with scalpel and implants while she is prostrate, and he is her caregiver and confidante. Virginia Blum notes that 'insofar as conventional heterosexual male and female sexualities are experienced psychically and represented culturewide as the relationship between the one who penetrates and the one penetrated, surgical interventions can function as very eroticized versions of the sexual act' (Blum, 2003: 45).

The surgeon/lover connection also echoes through promotional rhetoric: 'I can easily push my 'aesthetic' button. It takes little for a male surgeon to appreciate female beauty. But to go beyond lust, to define physical beauty, and to struggle to bring it forth through operation, is a different matter, requiring study and training' (Robert Goldwyn, quoted in Adams, 1997: 60). For Goldwyn, artistic skill in surgery is tied to sexual attraction. He describes the surgeon–patient relationship in terms of sex and gender: the act of cosmetic surgery may go 'beyond lust' but it remains an extension of (hetero)sexual feelings. Thus cosmetic surgery is positioned as a 'natural' extension of 'natural' impulses; it is a surgical moment always tied to desire. Baudrillard has written, a little cryptically, that we are in an era of 'production of the Other ... romantic love is no longer about winning over a woman's heart, or about seducing her. It is rather a matter of creating her from inside [de l'interieur], of inventing her...' (1995). The dystopia he describes is close to makeover culture where love – of the self in particular – is created, worked for, deserved and won rather than simply given. In makeover culture, ideal people – those who are beautiful and lovable and worthy – have worked on themselves and/or paid others to work on them. Baudrillard asserts that contemporary love is figured via procedures such as cosmetic surgery: procedures that create lovable objects. His view is extreme but it resonates with the connections that makeover culture makes between creation and desire. We see these connections explicitly in cosmetic surgery where medicine and beauty, sex and surgery, and artistry and lust are all intertwined.

Spitzack's experience was psychically abusive and her interpretation of 'surgeon as lover' positioned him as a dishonest exploiter. I propose that the 'dirty' tactics she experienced are now more subtly manifested in makeover culture, where power relations around cosmetic surgery occur in an information-saturated mediascape. One of makeover culture's characteristics is an abundance of information – it has informed people about cosmetic surgery, particularly about what happens between 'before' and 'after'. Infotainments like *Extreme Makeover*, *I Want a Famous Face* or *Cosmetic Kids*, however absurd and problematic, do give lay people a previously unimaginable amount of knowledge about cosmetic surgery. An active potential consumer of cosmetic surgery would also be able to seek out more technical documentaries and hundreds or thousands of cosmetic surgery websites and chatrooms.

Crucially, there was very little of this kind of media available when Spitzack had her consultation. She was reliant on the surgeon as sole information provider, specialist and technician. His role was multiple and transcendent while hers was singular and passive. Furthermore she was expected to be grateful for his expertise. Now, while makeover culture may position cosmetic surgery as ubiquitous, even obligatory, the client is no longer entirely dependent on the surgeon for information about what she 'needs'. My interviews show that surgeons are now often the end-point of recipients' research about cosmetic surgery rather than the starting-point. In makeover culture the surgeon is more suitor than lover: he must woo his client, 'win her' and then hang on to her. Theirs is a relationship that must be negotiated and conducted within a mediascape that extends beyond the consulting room.

Surgeon as Slasher

The slash between before and after is frequently literal. Many cosmetic surgeries are violent. They do not require meticulous and intricate work. The precision and noetic concentration of the brain or heart surgeon is a far cry from the physical brutality of a breast augmentation or liposuction operation. Slits in the breast are prised apart and the implant is shoved up between fat and muscle: the surgeon exerts a fair amount of leverage and force. Liposuction cannulas look like long metal straws. They are jabbed in and then rotated rapidly, the surgeon moving his arms rhythmically as if he's stirring a big tin of paint.[2] Michelle Del Guercio's photograph (Figure 7) 'Liposuction' addresses the gore and violence of cosmetic surgery by simply focus-ing on the container of extracted bodily matter rather than on the surgeon or the operating theatre.

Ovid describes a textural, fleshy scene as Pygmalion molests Galatea into life:

But next his Hand on her hard Bosom lays:
Hard as it was, beginning to relent,
It seemed, the Breast beneath his Fingers bent;
He felt again, his Fingers made a Print,
'Twas Flesh, but Flesh so firm, it rose against the Dint:
The pleasing Task he fails not to renew;
Soft, and more soft at every Touch it grew;
Like pliant Wax, when chafing Hands reduce
The former Mass to Form, and frame for Use.

(Ovid: *Metamorphoses*, Book X)

Galatea morphs from ivory to wax to flesh under his probing fingers – her living flesh is his property. Although alive she remains one step away from wax and is 'pliant' and 'framed for use': thus the perfect woman is utterly malleable. Spitzack's

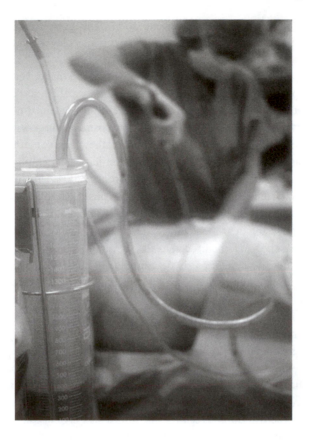

Figure 7 Michelle Del Guercio, 'Liposuction' *Plastic Surgery* series (http://www.mdmedicalphotography. com/), photo courtesy the artist

surgeon 'blandly' told her how he would dislocate or break her nose before carving it into a more 'feminine' shape. Horrified, she writes 'having one's nose broken calls forth violent imagery: physician as bodily harm, as villain' (1988: 46) and her subsequent analysis works partly as a cathartic retaliation.

Sometimes real-life Galateas fight back. Dr Franz Gsell, a well-known cosmetic surgeon who practised in Germany in the 1990s and early 2000s, transformed his much younger wife via multiple operations. Tanja and Franz enjoyed a high society life together for a decade until she left him to live with a young car dealer. Gsell continued to fund Tanja but finally threatened to cut her off financially. He was then killed with an axe after two masked men broke into his villa. Tanja was tried for conspiracy to murder, acquitted and inherited Gsell's fortune (Vasaga, 2003). The story was widely reported as a Pygmalion-gone-wrong scenario, where a man is misguided enough to attempt to create a perfect woman for himself only to have her turn against him (Alexander, 2002; Vasaga, 2003). This gory example shows again how the Pygmalion narrative can be rewritten by various players and is never clean-cut (so to speak).

The victim/abuser framework is problematised inside makeover culture simply because makeover culture repositions cosmetic surgery patient as 'client'. In order to become more desirable and widespread cosmetic surgery must not stigmatise its buyers. Thus we are seeing in makeover culture cosmetic surgery being gradually repositioned as a glamorous 'lifestyle choice' rather than something you 'need' because you are 'sick'. While this normalisation has many implications that are deeply disturbing for feminists (Heyes, 2007; Brooks, 2004; Brush 1998; Gillespie 1996) it also has some significant and possibly positive side effects. Instead of elective, aesthetic surgery being dressed up as 'psychologically necessary', and instead of doctors using their medical arsenals to bully women into having cosmetic surgery, they must now *sell* the procedures to discerning and knowledgeable clients. Redefining a patient as a client partly de-stigmatises the cosmetic surgery recipient. It replaces the diseased body that Spitzack was made to 'see' in her doctor's cruel three-sided mirror with a consumer-body: a body with spending power rather than one in need of intervention because of deformity.

Makeover culture encourages cosmetic surgery recipients to internalise the medical gaze and become their own 'surgeons'. And while media like *Extreme Makeover* give potential recipients the tools with which to 'diagnose' themselves they also, without doubt, encourage ordinary people to see their bodies as deficient. Further, as distinctions between normal and abnormal become ever more subtle these deficiencies are recognised in ever more insidious ways. Cressida Heyes describes this 'double, paradoxical effect' in Foucauldian terms: 'the very body that develops new capacities and skills also becomes the highly scrutinized subject of the minutest forms of manipulation' (2007a: 19).

When patients self-diagnose, doctors become a means to an end rather than arbiters of beauty and normality; he acts as the scalpel while she is the all-important expert eye. Surgeons are sometimes surprisingly keen to acknowledge that their patients are 'experts'. An editorial of the *International Journal of Cosmetic Surgery and Aesthetic Dermatology* – written by a cosmetic surgeon for a readership of cosmetic surgeons – strikingly places agency, expertise and responsibility away from the surgeon and with the recipient: 'beauty is in the eye of the beholder. The patient undergoing cosmetic surgery is the beholder in determining his or her own beauty and as such, determines what procedures are to be done and by what means' (Hernandez-Perez and Khawaja, 2003: 207). In this scenario the surgeon is the servant of the patient: his expertise is in providing a service rather than determining need. Later the writer advises, 'the satisfied patient results in other patients being referred, so the physician should pay attention to the patient's own desires' (2003: 234), making clear the economic imperatives behind this view. The doctor is selling a product and the customer always comes first. There are two competing logonomic systems here, a doctor/patient model where the doctor's expertise wields authority and a provider/consumer model where the customer's choices hold the most power.

Pygmalion Becoming Galatea

In makeover culture surgeons are certainly Pygmalion figures but they are also Galateas themselves, subject to their own and their patients' judgemental scrutiny. One plastic surgeon I interviewed spoke about possible surgery for himself in the future:

> if the need arises I will, if my brows come down or I get a lot of jowling. It depends how long I stay in the game. My boss is about sixty, and had a blepharoplasty – cosmetic surgeons have to look good themselves, and I'm currently sought as a young surgeon, because I'm not a fuddy-duddy. People don't want to have someone operating on them who hasn't bothered with himself. You'd have to ask, why hasn't he done something about those eyelids or that double chin or whatever? (Dr Young)

So to further complicate the new set of imperatives in makeover culture, doctors now become patients: this surgeon positions himself as part of makeover culture and sees the presentation of a 'becoming' self as interconnected with remaining vital – not being a 'fuddy-duddy' – and maintaining a good business. He is a walking self-advertisement and part of the general validation and normalisation of cosmetic surgery.

In 1998 I analysed several cosmetic surgery websites as part of another project. Most photos of surgeons then showed non-surgical faces, something that jarred for me as it positioned them as always whole and perfect while the women in the sites – shown only via before/after – were flawed and segmented. In stark contrast to this the celebrity cosmetic surgeons on *Extreme Makeover* have clearly all had work themselves, and photos of surgeons on websites now appear increasingly surgical. Surgeons' bodies are beginning to 'perform' – although nowhere near as much as the bodies they wish to operate upon. With the media selling the procedures now, and in some ways having taken over the marketing of cosmetic surgery itself, doctors are left in an increasingly competitive environment with the need to sell themselves. Websites are becoming more elaborate: many include sections about surgeons' 'philosophies' of cosmetic surgery:

> My philosophy regarding cosmetic surgery is to provide a natural change that is in harmony with the patient's features. Each patient that presents to my office is treated courteously, professionally, and with great attention to individual detail. (http://www.drmosharrafa.com/)

> Plastic Surgery is both an art and science, and can not be practiced with a cookbook. No two patients are the same, and my main goal is to sit down with every patient and

individualize their care. This practice philosophy allows both my office staff and me to give our patients optimal care. (http://www.dr-adams.com/)

Here Pygmalion as lover comes to the fore: the surgeon is primarily a carer, someone who 'puts you first'. This rhetoric is also found in relation to less-than-perfect cosmetic surgery:

if there is a problem, that's when the doctor-patient relationship needs to be strongest. Some patients you have big relationships with are the ones who had little problems. We [have to] be partners, go through it together... Some problems have to be fine-tuned. That's when it's important to have a good relationship with your doctor. You have to stick together, and if a revision is needed for the final result, be prepared to go for it. (Dr Michael Powell quoted in Lerche Davis, 2003)

The doctor's voice portrays the doctor–patient relationship like a marriage where couples must 'stick together' through difficult times. The aim of this manipulative rhetoric is to discourage unhappy patients from seeking compensation or making formal complaint, and rather to return to seek further treatments. It sternly enlists the patient's courage and audacity – 'be prepared to go for it' – and her ability to maintain strong relationships. But alongside the calculating language there is an important acknowledgement of the cosmetic surgery recipient as a 'partner' or in ANT terms an implicated and influential 'actant'. This rhetoric acknowledges patient and doctor as collaborators rather than as active creator and passive receiver. It may have been cynically written to minimise lawsuits but in doing so it highlights the woman's powerful position as a critical and potentially litigious consumer. The patient is seen as something of an avid shopper: only willing to commit to a 'purchase' after perusing all options. It is the potential promiscuity of the shopper that the surgeon wishes to counteract: he wants loyalty and commitment – monogamy – while she wants to choose, to leave her options open and to litigate if the project fails to live up to its promises. As one surgeon said, '[we] sit down with patients in consultation, but we're both obviously interviewing each other' (quoted in Rosen, 2004: 5).

Consultations are negotiations between surgeon and recipient. She is patient, client and expert; he is technician, doctor and expert. Most of the women I spoke to had done in-depth research about procedures they thought were appropriate and had shopped around for a surgeon, sometimes for many months. The meeting with the surgeon was the end of a process of gaining knowledge rather than the beginning of it.

Surgeon as Artist,[3] Patient as Impostor

I asked a plastic surgeon how he learned the aesthetic (rather than medical) skills necessary to change faces:

All plastic surgery is about that. ... And you train in it. That's what training's all about, it's not picked up like cosmetic surgeons at a 'weekend workshop' [said with contempt, making quote marks in the air] or observing someone, it is actually working with [an experienced specialist] in hospitals, seeing the patients before the surgery, being operated on, doing the operations, seeing them in an outpatient clinic, and eventually doing your training, being examined in it – you've gotta learn aesthetic proportions, its all been done for thousands of years. (Dr Young)

My interpretation of this wordy answer is simply that there is no training or exam-ination for surgeons in terms of artistic skills. It is picked up on the job, by watching others, through experience and the intriguing 'thousands of years' of aesthetics. It is very much a cultural training then, based upon social judgements, individual taste and popular media. Haiken notes that

if the phenomenon of plastic surgery is shaped by culture as well as by medicine, it seems logical that its practitioners would be as well ... plastic surgeons shape and are shaped by the specific culture they inhabit – in this case, the visual culture (movies, magazines, models) of the United States in the twentieth century. (2000: 91)

Foucault shows how visual culture and contemporary medicine are inter-twined: 'the great break in the history of Western medicine dates precisely from the moment clinical experience became the anatomo-clinical gaze' (1973: 146). In this philosophical schema cosmetic surgery is not a branch of clinical practice on the outer edge of 'real medicine', nor does it embody a newer set of surgical preoccupations than do other surgical specialities. Rather, its linking of vision and aesthetics with surgery places it at the heart of what surgery is and how it developed. In pre-modernity surgery was linked to grooming and artistry as well as to science and medicine. In the Middle Ages physicians might 'advise venesection but would rarely think of actually performing it' (Lyons and Petrucelli, 1978: 362). The people who actually performed surgeries were barbers. 'It is difficult for us today to fathom the wide range of concerns allocated to barbers in the past – not just the care of locks and beard but also tooth-pulling, minor operations, the setting of bones and the like' (Lyons and Petrucelli, 1978: 362). Contemporary cosmetic surgery is an echo of this early linking of surgery and beauty, of medical practice 'on the street' and of client-based surgery-on-demand.

The Artistic Gift

Cosmetic surgeons learn their aesthetics not only through the mythical 'thousands of years' of history but also through the beauty values of the visual culture they are part of. In the next chapter I show how cosmetic surgery recipients must negotiate versions of beauty that are never entirely stable. Similarly, surgeons' understandings of desirable aesthetics are always based in contemporary ideas of beauty – ideas that are malleable and shifting. In makeover culture this creates uneasiness and tension because, unlike medical expertise, artistic skill is difficult to measure. Surgeons can easily advertise medical and surgical training by listing qualifications, memberships, etc.; it is harder to advertise artistic sensibilities.

> Dr. Palmer can help you achieve the look that you've always desired through a combination of surgical mastery with a blending of artistic vision and sound aesthetic judgement that's taken years to cull. But, aesthetic vision and expertise vary among surgeons – so be sure that you're in the hands of someone who is highly skilled, well experienced and aesthetically gifted ... like Dr. Palmer. (http://www.beverlyhillsplasticsur.com/procedures.html)

Despite its intangibility the 'aesthetic gift' is something that many cosmetic surgeons try to sell. Their websites range from simple pages with contact details to detailed textual and pictorial resources with hundreds of links. The grander sites have some interesting characteristics in common. There is often a self-professed devotion to 'good work', sometimes with a charity named after the doctor himself. There are usually some flattering portrait-style photos of the doctor. There are invariably before and after photos of his patients. But the most surprising change for me since 1998 is the propensity of cosmetic surgeons who now display their own works of art. It seems that cosmetic surgeons are also painters,[4] photographers,[5] sculptors[6] and even musicians.[7]

Many professionals have artistic hobbies, but why do cosmetic surgeons actively include theirs as part of their advertising? I suggest it is because loss of status as sole expert is compensated by the deployment of a new kind of artistic expertise. The most vivid claims about artistry that I've come across are on the website of Francis Rogers Palmer:

> Dr. Palmer has been Director of Facial Plastic Surgery for the Head and Neck Surgery Department at the University of Southern California School of Medicine since 1991. As an artist in watercolor, oil and acrylic mediums who's [*sic*] style can best be described as photorealism, he considers himself a modern day soft tissue sculptor adding his artistic flair to every aspect of his surgery. 'Plastic surgery is artistry', says Dr. Palmer ... 'Plastic surgery, in order to be inspired work, must incorporate both the art and science of beauty. The surgeon must have an aesthetic eye.' (http://www.beverlyhillsplasticsur.com/index2.html)

This 'aesthetic eye' was evident when Spitzack attended her consultation. She suggests, *pace* Foucault, that the eye/gaze of the surgeon is part of the powerful set of knowledges and disciplines that construct woman's body as pathological and a potential threat to the dominant order. Similarly Anne Balsamo writes that 'the cosmetic surgeon's gaze doesn't simply medicalize the female body, it actually redefines it as an object for technological reconstruction' (1996: 64). Spitzack felt inspected by a series of experts, most of them housed in the body of the doctor: 'all around me, one who does not know, the eyes of judgment, from persons who know' (1988: 43). But in makeover culture those visual experts are dispersed, no longer holding together in the figure of the doctor. I suggest this is why surgeons are so keen to emphasise their artistic expertise and sell their 'aesthetic eyes'. Their attempts to promote their own artistic skills are connected to having lost control over an area of cosmetic surgery that they once dominated. One plastic surgeon I interviewed was contemptuous of women doing their own research. He disagreed with their aesthetic choices and saw himself as an expert whose opinions were being ignored:

> some people are already fairly savvy, they're on the internet, they're scanning, they're looking at pre- and post- [surgical photographs], reading it, even younger people coming in, eighteen- or nineteen-year-old ladies, they're already onto it, they know what I'll tell them on statistics ... they're researched, and if they come to me I've usually got a letter from their GP saying 'Sharon wants to have her breasts augmented, I've suggested strongly against it but she still insists so please assess.' She'll come in and say, 'He's a schmuck, what's he know, I've got the right to vote, I live with my boyfriend, I'm nineteen, I'm going to uni next year, I want to go on vacation, what's wrong with having large breasts?' What can I say? What can I say? (Dr Young)

He felt bombarded by young women wanting breast implants that he thought were too large. He wasn't against implants per se – far from it – but he knew what looked good: 'someone who doesn't look like they're augmented, but rather just having nice breasts – perky – cleavage'. While Spitzack was fearful that she 'might not identify [her] problem correctly' (1988: 45), the women Dr Young described to me were confidently self-describing. They certainly didn't see the surgeon as an omniscient seer and knower but rather as a means to an end, as technician rather than aesthetic expert.

The surgeons I spoke to were worried about their loss of aesthetic power. Dr Young wasn't concerned about medical issues to do with large breast implants – for example he didn't mention that encapsulation (painful internal scarring that can make the breasts hard and lumpy) is more likely to occur with larger implants – but with aesthetic issues and matters of power. He was working with two conflicting sets of logonomic systems. He didn't like being treated like a mere service provider by a young woman armed with a lot of information and a set of aesthetics that didn't match his own. In fact, I got the strange impression that he viewed these new 'knowing' clients as impostors. The surgeon's status as expert and his role as artist, which at the time of Spitzack's writing were unquestionable, must in makeover culture be managed alongside clients' own self-determined needs, expectations, knowledges and aesthetics.

Another Impostor: Botox®

> Your social appointments are escalating as the festive season nears. End the year looking
> rejuvenated and fresh. *Smooth, Youthful, Beautiful.* Spend fifteen minutes having
> BOTOX® wrinkle treatment and reap the rewards through the party season and New
> Year. *Rejuvenate, Refresh, Revitalise.* (Botox® brochure, inVIVO communications,
> collected July 2004, italics in original)

Surgeons are not only under siege in makeover culture from each other and from
knowledgeable clients. They also have to learn to deal – on a cultural level – with
powerful products such as Botox®. Botox® is one brand name for a neuromuscular
blocking agent called botulinum toxin. Botulinum toxins paralyse or weaken muscles
they are injected into, and have been used since the 1960s to treat eye muscle
disorders such as uncontrollable blinking. Doctors noticed that the frown lines of
patients who had been treated for eye disorders were diminished or 'softened', and
by the 2000s the toxin was being aggressively marketed as a wrinkle treatment.

Although this widely distributed brochure states 'It's not magic, it's Botox®', there
is a strong idea of magic at work. Botox® is thus aligned with transmogrification and
offered as a medical wonder. It is even allied with penicillin, arguably the twentieth
century's real wonder drug: 'Botox® is a highly purified protein that is extracted
from bacteria, in a similar way that penicillin comes from a mould'. Just as *Extreme
Makeover* shows the miserable mundanity of having cosmetic surgery and the
recovery process while retaining the magic of before/after in the Reveal, Botox® is
here framed as magical and simultaneously as mundane as antibiotics. Connections
between magic, labour, miracles and mundanity are vital in makeover culture where
simple everyday life is meant to be transformative and ever-improving.

The main protagonist in this brochure is Botox®: 'to ... ensure a safe and
effective treatment, ask for Botox® by name'. And in fact the product is alive: it is a
living toxin made from the same bacteria that causes the food-poisoning botulism.[8]
According to this brochure Botox® is the star, cosmetic surgery recipients are both
audience and stage, and doctors play mere supporting roles. Botox® is not the
only product that sets out to define itself in this way. Inamed Aesthetics, one of the
world's largest suppliers of breast implants, has a website that shows pictures of
the saline- or silicone-filled objects strangely disembodied from surgery and bodies
(http://www.inamed.com). They are reminiscent of flying saucers, Tupperware
containers, flowers and sea-creatures, and are represented as anything but 'medical'.
The objects are presented as beautiful in themselves, whole and self-contained, even
living (one has a streak behind it, denoting prior movement, one is surrounded by
rippling water). How long will it be before the brand name of breast implants is part
of their appeal?

The back page of the Botox® brochure advises 'to find out if Botox® might work
well for you, please consult a cosmetic specialist who is a trained professional and

can judge the optimum treatment to enhance your appearance'. The procedure, the decision, the recipient and the doctor take second place to the registered, branded, marketed product. A surgeon told me:

> the various plastic surgical supply companies, [the suppliers of] prostheses, or the suppliers of injectables, market directly to the public. And the surgeon becomes an intermediary in this, so that the public become the customer of the surgical supplier rather than what in the ordinary course of events would be the correct way, that the doctor is the customer and the controller of the product. (Dr Fred)

The 'correct way' – where doctor is main protagonist – is compromised by the power of the brand. Doctor is recast as middleman. Botox® is only a brand name but has been marketed so strongly that all the recipients I spoke to thought of it as 'the product'. The surgeon continued:

> It's a great name, very hard to break, its like being called Hoover instead of vacuum cleaner or something like that, or Durex instead of sticky tape – its like that, its something that's clear in the public's minds. And they've managed to link their name to the product so accurately that it will be very hard to break. (Dr Fred)

My Labour, and My Leisure Too[9]

The inside of the brochure says 'you stress. You squint into the harsh sun. You concentrate. And over time those expressions leave their mark on your face making you look older, tired or stressed'. This embodies the notion of anti-ageing cosmetic surgery being about trying to look 'better, not younger' (analysed closely in the next chapter). While the older self is almost inevitably more tired, it is no longer acceptable to display this, despite makeover culture valorising work and labour as parts of 'lifestyle'. The blurring between work and leisure (perhaps most clearly articulated in television shows like *Backyard Blitz* where heavy-duty landscaping is confused with a fun weekend) has resulted in a strange dichotomy: work is commendable and desirable but its effects on the body are not (unless they're muscles from gym-work). In turn the eradication of those signs of labour – via cosmetic surgery – becomes an act of labour itself. Work and get wrinkles, work more to pay to have them removed.

In short, Botox® has an agentic presence that appears in the cosmetic surgery world somewhat independently of patients, clinics or doctors. It is an artefact in itself. Latour talks about the importance of 'things', of how non-human actors are necessary in societies. He critiques non-ANT explanations of social order by explaining that they ignore or take for granted things and objects. Important social and political 'constraints' are found in things. For example, 'doors, and other artefacts, act as constant constraints on our behaviour. Though they are physical mechanisms, their effect is indistinguishable from normative or moral control: a door allows us to walk through only at a certain speed and only in a certain place in the wall...' (Collins and Yearley, 1992: 317).

Botox® is one of those things, like a door, that creates a 'constant constraint' – simply because it stills the muscles of the face. But as well as being a physical mechanism it is a thing that has a 'normative or moral control'. In fact it is not about giving the illusion of having led a leisurely life. Rather, it is part of the new presentation of labour within makeover culture, where leisure becomes a form of work, and working – no matter how hard – must never leave us looking exhausted because 'tired is ugly'. Having Botox® and other cosmetic surgery is no longer about denying the marks of labour but is now part of the presentation of a *successful* hard-working self: a person who can afford the treatments, a person who 'looks after herself'. So Botox® is a moral actor in the deployment of cosmetic surgery. It locates itself as a middle-class and desirable accoutrement, a sign of deserved, worked-for wealth and comfort: your botoxed face says that you are part of a deserving group that can afford to choose to look 'better'. 'Botox®. A simple, non-surgical procedure that can dramatically reduce even your toughest wrinkle within days. **So it's really up to you. You can choose to live with wrinkles or you can choose to live without them**' (inVIVOcommunications, Botox® brochure, bold in original).

Agency is superficially located in the hands of the consumer, who has the 'choice' to live either with or without wrinkles in the same way that she has the choice to live with or without a cracked vase. This brochure text acknowledges the hard-earned status of the middle-aged woman who leads a busy life. Serenity is not an option or a desire for her, but its illusion is. Her feelings might include stress or anger but her face must present a smooth consistency. Like the four-wheel drive that she might buy for herself, or a skiing holiday, Botox® is presented as a reward for hard work, as a treat, but also as part of the correct management of public image, part of the staging of enterprise and success. I saw this brochure in the waiting rooms of cosmetic surgeons and also in beauty salons and in general practitioners' rooms. People who may never have contemplated cosmetic surgery for themselves, or only read about it in relation to celebrities, would have picked it up. Botox® – a relatively cheap[10] and effective (although temporary) wrinkle-killer positions itself as a necessity for the contemporary world.

Narrative as Therapy

The rise of makeover culture has by no means obliterated uneven doctor–patient re-lationships. Just as makeover culture has enveloped before/after it has also embraced relations between patient and doctors that are patriarchal and uneven. For Virginia Blum there is still little negotiation in the patient–surgeon interaction. She tells of a surgeon she was interviewing 'turning on' her, demanding to know about her nose job, reassigning her from interviewer to 'defective female plastic flesh' (2003: 21–2).

> There is no choice involved in this relationship. If his effect happens only through my response, I can at the same time argue that my response wells up uncontrollably to the positional power he commands over my body... This institutional power is inextricably tethered to the degree to which women are the perfect subjects of and for cosmetic surgery. (2003: 22)

Cosmetic surgery clearly happens in a misogynist and patriarchal framework. However, patriarchy alone cannot fully explain relations of power in the worlds of cosmetic surgery and makeover. One of the dangers of this mode of analysis is that it can presuppose that gender relations are set and unwavering. Feminist actor-network theorist Susan Ormrod suggests that a more useful set of tools with which to examine gender and technology issues combines ANT and a discursive analysis where 'the social is constructed in and through discourse' (1995: 31). This approach recognises that subjectivity is constructed through text, representation and interpretation. Thus discourse is in constant productive relation with material and semiotic worlds. Latour puts it rather poetically:

> Discourse is not a world unto itself but a population of actants that mix with things as well as with societies... Interest in texts does not distance us from reality, for things too have to be elevated to the dignity of narrative. As for texts, why deny them the grandeur of forming the social bond that holds us together? (Latour, 1993: 90)

Ormrod draws on these ideas to suggest that rather than being oppressed by forces from outside, women are always somewhat implicated in their own oppression (or otherwise) and are 'active in positioning themselves within discourses and in investing a commitment to subject position' (1995: 31). In other words, gender is neither fully pre-existing nor taken for granted but is always made and re-made. Gendered subject positions are utterly tied up with the discursive social-material world, and are thus subject to change and negotiation.

Some of the women I interviewed described being somewhat intimidated in their consultations. However, the general reaction to this wasn't the 'internalisation of disease' and sense of dejection that Spitzack describes, but rather a dismissal of that particular doctor:

> When I went to talk to the surgeon about general appearance I asked him what he would do if he were me and he said apart from taking the fat pads out or having this procedure [blepharoplasty] he would ... inject fat [into my face] – you know how you can take fat cultures from your thighs and put them into your face? – because he looked at my face and thought it was thin. And he thought I would look better with that procedure. And I thought about that and I thought mmmm, no (Simone).

This interviewee attended a consultation wanting to fix her puffy eyelids and also actively sought the doctor's opinion about the rest of her face. When he told her that he thought she should have fat injected into her face she rejected his suggestion quite determinedly. Interestingly, she told me that it was partly because she had dieted for years to be thin and the last thing she wanted now was a fatter face, even if it did make her look younger. She then saw some photos of women who had had the fat-injecting procedure, and thought they looked like chipmunks.

Most of the women I interviewed had shopped around for surgeons and procedures. Some had taken intense dislikes to certain surgeons. One who was seriously considering a facelift told me:

> I already went and spoke to one surgeon ... who was recommended by my GP ... it was a woman ... I didn't like her, I really didn't like her. I didn't like the consultation, I found it, although it was highly informative, and fact-giving, it was ... I found her a bit Margaret Thatcher – 'you will do this and you will do that' – she was a bit kind of authoritative ... I came away shaking ... I put it on the back burner after that consultation so maybe it was quite good, because it made me really think about it. I just didn't like her. (Donna)

Another said 'I went along and he just made me feel really at ease' (Judith). Both connected with their doctors on a level more to do with trust (or lack of it) and understanding than medical expertise. Liking the doctor was important and had a direct impact on the decision to have surgery or not. Another interviewee had thought about breast enlargement for a long time but didn't proceed until she met a surgeon socially. He was the father of her young daughter's schoolfriend and she had many informal chats with him before making her first appointment.

Anthropologist Rebecca Huss-Ashmore has found that for most patients cosmetic surgery is a positive experience described in terms of 'transformation' or 'healing' (2000: 29). Interestingly though, her thesis is that this transformative and healing process does not come about because of the surgery. Instead she suggests it is formed through language, via narratives that are played out by patients and medical practitioners before and after the actual operations. She finds that the process of cosmetic surgery is described by recipients as having had a restorative effect between self and psyche, and body and image: 'I think that it occurs through the creation and acting out of a therapeutic narrative, a lived story in which the "me I want to be" or the "me I really am" is brought into being through the linguistic, emotional, and physical experience of surgery and recovery' (2000: 32).

Spitzack describes this relation in a much more dystopic way: 'the highly *material* "illness" of physical/aesthetic imperfection is "cured" through complex and over-lapping mechanisms of confession and surveillance' (1988: 38). Both viewpoints show the importance of narrative in cosmetic surgery practice and strangely belie the power of the surgery itself.

Opening Black Boxes

ANT says that power is acquired within networks and via convergences and con-nections: 'entities (whether human or non-human) within ... networks acquire power through the number, extensiveness and stability of the connections routed through them, and through nothing else' (Couldry, 2003: 1). These connections are contingent on a series of historical and cultural factors. They are far from 'natural' and yet are often seen as unquestionable – they are what ANT describes as 'black-boxed'.[11]

The power that doctors yield is based in the networks in which they are embedded – in this way they don't exactly 'hold' power, rather, it holds them: its networks converge to exalt them. Traditionally these networks have been made up of elite schooling, professional organisations, universities, hospitals, medical journals and those less visible networks that include supportive wives, hard-working nurses, cleaners and receptionists. In makeover culture the network becomes even more complex as it is heavily mediatised as well as institutional, professional, political and social. Thus part of a surgeon's power comes from his ability to decipher media trends, involve himself in them but not become 'too implicated' in them (like the surgeon denied admittance to the ASPS because of his 'inappropriate' media profile). Foucault reminds us that the birth of modern medicine was tied up with new networked and institutionalised formations of power that allowed doctors to 'see' and to be powerful. He tells how in the eighteenth and nineteenth centuries: 'the medical gaze [began to be] organised in a new way. First, it was no longer the gaze of any observer, but that of a doctor supported and justified by an institution, that of a doctor endowed with the power of decision and intervention' (Foucault, 1973: 89).

I suggest that in makeover culture the medical gaze is undergoing another pro-found reorganisation. Mediatised visualising technologies – all manner of scans and rays – now see into the internal body while television cameras and screens see the external body. The gaze, compacted and focused in the figure of the surgeon through the gathering and centralising forces that Foucault excavated, is now being fragmented in makeover culture. The doctor's status as owner of the diagnostic gaze is still vital but has become segmented: he must share it with all sorts of media and – crucially – with the patients themselves. The surgeon Spitzack visited had customised videos playing in his waiting rooms: strikingly, they featured sets of identical twins. One has surgery and then the other is convinced to do so after seeing her more beautiful 'self'. In makeover culture similar diabolical selling tools saturate the mediasphere. While this means that we are all bombarded with the kinds of images and messages that Spitzack found undermined her body image so thoroughly, it also means that surgeons cease to be sole holders of this kind of information. While Foucault's institutions were hospitals and medical boards, perhaps the most influential institution now supporting and justifying cosmetic surgeons is the mediascape, which influences purchase of equipment, doctor–patient relations and even diagnoses. The doctor's eye, once the primary diagnostic tool in medicine – 'the history of modern medicine is utterly tied up with the development of the gaze as a diagnostic tool' (Foucault, 1973: 89) – is now augmented by a vast media eye, by the patient's increasingly critical eye and by computer images of madeover faces.

The women I interviewed were operating in a slightly different set of power relations to those Spitzack experienced. Makeover culture means that cosmetic surgery has become a kind of shopping: shopping for a surgeon, for a procedure, for a product and for a place to recover. In makeover culture cosmetic surgery is one of many consumable items designed for 'improvement' of the self. Surgeons are still powerful but their status as sole determiners of procedures, aims, needs and beauty has been compromised and is always up for renegotiation.

Importantly, makeover culture positions cosmetic surgery as part of a range of optional aesthetic modifications rather than as a treatment for an illness. Surgeons express both pleasure and dissatisfaction about this: while they mourn their decline in autonomy and status, they acknowledge that stronger patient knowledge and better dissemination of information about cosmetic surgery equals more business. This change perhaps also means that responsibility for shady practitioners is now more broadly spread – the onus is very much on the consumer to research the expertise of her practitioner – as the title of an Australian documentary about cosmetic surgery says, *Buyer of Beauty, Beware* (2006).

The Internet creates a new landscape in the cosmetic surgery world, and the vast amount of free information it provides means that the distribution of agency and the human actors within cosmetic surgery has been altered. Further, the growth of powerful brand names in the arena like Botox® – but also Newfill®, Restylane® and Perlane® – complicates the network of actors negotiating, co-opting and undermining each other. These cultural shifts show that feminist analyses of cosmetic surgery undertaken largely in terms of doctor–patient power relations are not adequate in contemporary makeover culture. The Pygmalions of makeover culture are multiple and intertwined nodes of surgeons, recipients, media products like *Extreme Makeover* that dictate and reflect trends, and strange new entities like Botox®.

Conclusion

The view of doctor/man/creator versus patient/woman/created is one fraught with gender inequalities. Not only does this line of analysis re-create the dichotomy that it describes, it also keeps the action focused on the simple dyad of doctor/patient: there is a closed, two-handed relationship here at best, and at worst the patient is also obscured, leaving only the heroic doctor standing, sweating and labouring for his own glory (Davis, 2003: 41–57). The doctors I interviewed were painfully aware that there were networks larger than themselves at play, that theirs was an industry being re-created by other industries, particularly by the popular media, and that the cosmetic surgery industry was morphing at a rate they found difficult to keep up with. One told me, when I asked him whether he had a computer imaging system so that clients could see digitally created before and after photos of themselves before surgery, '[I don't, but] I'll end up doing it, because that's what the market wants, everyone wants it, and we're unfortunately driven by what the media tell us we've got to tell our patients' (Dr Young).

The making of Galatea occurs in the real world and in the mythical one, out of material stuff and out of magic, and comes about because of Pygmalion's loathing, lust and also his loneliness. Pygmalion and Galatea are actors inside a network of materiality, myth and misogyny. The contemporary cosmetic surgeon operates as a decentralised actor in a network where he is simultaneously lover, father, salesman, aesthete, medical expert, competitor, artist, advertiser and servant. He may morph into a Galatea himself. In makeover culture there are messy assemblages and moments where Galatea may be unfaithful to her origins, may turn on her creator, or may actively employ his expertise to her own ends. She is likely to be a discerning shopper, a canny ingestor of research and a knowing and aware consumer.

Cosmetic surgery is a world where agency is negotiated and movable through doctor–patient relationships and interactions, where human and non-human players such as Botox® have roles of high importance. There are no paramount agents here but rather a series of actors who define each other. Many of these actors 'push' the networks that they exist inside, pointing to possibilities for changes in focus and power: some of these are examined in the following chapters.

–4–

Stretched Middle Age
Mothers, Daughters and Fairy Tales

...the lady one day asked her mirror – 'Mirror, mirror upon the wall, Who is the fairest fair of all' it answered – 'O Lady Queen, though fair ye be, Snow-White is fairer far to see'. The Queen was horrified, and from that moment envy and pride grew in her heart like rank weeds.

Grimm, 'Little Snow White'

If you do suffer from eye bags ... you may be comforted to know that there is nothing you could have done to prevent them as they are genetic and the only solution is surgery. (Hambleton-Jones, 2005: 62)

This chapter is about cosmetic surgery in relation to temporality, ageing and inter-generational relationships. It examines these themes through three strands: the notion of the 'stretched middle age', analyses of interview materials and close media analysis. The first strand argues that cosmetic surgery is part of a suite of anti-ageing technologies wherein individuals enact compulsory, desirable and normative stretched middle age. In the stretched middle age chronology is indeterminate and 'looking good' is subtly differentiated from 'looking young'. Although cosmetic surgery seems to mimic the signs of youth, my interviewees strongly denied chasing youth and instead spoke about 'looking good for one's age' and becoming 'better, not younger'. The second strand interprets responses to do with time and ageing. Interviewees expressed complex and specific reasons for their anti-ageing cosmetic surgery: I argue that they were designing, not denying, their ageing process. The third strand is a close-reading approach to media analysis, showing how one set of texts and images works, prism-like, to direct light on some of the broad cultural logics that surround cosmetic surgery, in particular those to do with intergenerational relationships.

Youth and Old Age

You love your mum. Sure you do. But be honest. Have you ever noticed the Serious Crow's Feet Problem she has? Winced at the way her chin triples itself? Ever thought quietly to yourself, heck, I hope I don't take after her in all departments?

Gloss: The Essential Anti-Ageing Magazine, 1998: 26

The quote above is from the now-defunct Australian publication *Gloss: The Essential Anti-Ageing Magazine*. Although the magazine did not enjoy a long life, it is part of a group of high-production 'glossies' that emerged in the late 1990s in Australia including *Australian Cosmetic Surgery Magazine*, *The Art of Cosmetic Beauty* and *Body, Health and Beauty*, which are all still in circulation. They are merchandised in newsagents' women's magazine sections and are devoted to providing information, advice, opinion and advertising about beauty products, cosmetic surgery, health, ageing and well-being. Anne Ring, an Australian sociologist who specialises in media and health, argues that these magazines were created in line with the progressive deregulation of medical practitioner advertising in Australia. She shows that they contain ethically questionable links between journalism and advertising (1998, 1999, 1999a, 1999b, 2002). Like *Extreme Makeover*, the specialist cosmetic surgery magazines comprise an arena where advertising and editorial are linked and sometimes indistinguishable. Because cosmetic surgery came to prominence as 'infotainment' in the same period as media hybrids like 'advertorials' and 'edutainment' it developed hand in hand with a series of ethically problematic mediascapes built around consumption. To examine the status of intergenerational relationships between women inside just one of these mediascapes is a focused endeavour that ties in with much wider concerns.

Mary Russo, author of the much-loved *The Female Grotesque* (1994), notes that part of the over-developed world's presentation of abundance is via 'arbitrary contrasts and competitions which seem natural or self evident'. One of these arbitrary competitions or 'false choices' is what she calls the 'commodification of generational difference' (1994: 178). She quotes Guy Debord:

> Wherever there is abundant consumption, a major spectacular opposition between youth and adults comes to the fore among the false roles – false because the adult, master of his life, does not exist and because youth, the transformation of what exists, is in no way the property of those who are now young, but of the economic system, of the dynamism of capitalism. *Things* rule and are young. (Debord, *Society of the Spectacle*, quoted in Russo, 1994: 178–9. Debord's italics)

Cosmetic surgery is one of these *things* – a product fundamentally linked to the 'commodification of generational difference'. 'Matis skincare has decided to give you the option of staying young. It boasts twenty-three products that "mimic" the components of a young skin…' (editorial about a face cream in *Gloss*, 1998: 14). In an era that offers improved cancer treatments, effective medications for heart disease and prosthetic devices such as artificial hips and pacemakers we might suppose that the prospect of old age – at least in wealthy parts of the world – would be more palatable than ever. But media and popular culture's representations of old age overburden us with negative stereotypes. While youth is privileged and is associated with sexuality, independence, beauty and productivity, ageing is degraded as frail, useless, unattractive and dependent (Biggs, H. 2002; Biggs, S. 1999; Bytheway, 1995; Friedan, 1994; Gilleard and Higgs, 2000; Macdonald, 2001). 'Youth' is a relatively new category, developed as part of Western capitalist industrialisation after the First World War (Hareven, 1995: 123; Hine, 1999: 237–8). And indeed, the rise of the 'cult of youth' has been proportional to the decline of old age as a respectable, productive and interesting state of life (Fischer, 1978; Gillis, 1975, 1993). Cultural theorists Mike Featherstone and Andrew Wernick put it succinctly: 'consumer culture with its images of youth, fitness and beauty lifestyles ... produced a new set of exclusions of older people' (1995: 7). A *New Yorker* journalist, recalling the Catholic Church's condemnation of Tagliacozzi's operations, comments that 'a culture that insists on the appearance of nubile availability among women old enough to be grandmothers may be as tyrannical as one that requires the syphilitic to wander noseless forever, reviled by all' (Mead, 2006: 90). Miserable representations of the elderly lead to social, political, legal and medical discrimination (Biggs, H. 2002: 175). For women, ageing also means being squeezed into social invisibility (Gibson, P. 2000) and ugliness. This tendency is so acute that 'ageing has been and may yet be experienced as a kind of "trauma"' (Kaplan, 1999: 171; also De Beauvoir, 1970; Gullette, 1997, 2004; Woodward, 1995).

Ageing bodies are never simply organic structures subjected to decline over time; they are continually inscribed with cultural meanings, they reflect societal influences and attitudes. As an added complication, although the process of ageing may traverse countless subtle permutations, the life course is traditionally divided into two extremes: youth and non-youth, with the former almost always being much more desirable. Despite their vastly different representations, youth culture and older age are connected. Kathleen Woodward points out that youth culture currently works hand-in-hand with patriarchy in the denigration of older women: she quotes Australian activist lesbian Barbara MacDonald: 'youth is bonded with patriarchy in the enslavement of the older woman. There would, in fact, be no youth culture without the powerless older woman' (1995: 89). Similarly, there would be no youthful beauty without its opposite, aged ugliness (Bordo, 1990, 1993; Brand, 2000; Davis, 2003; Tseëlon, 1995).

Thomas Walz notes that popular culture's representations of ageing people's sexuality has changed in recent years. He documents a movement in popular media that shows older people as healthy, engaged with the social world and attractive. Importantly though, positive light is only thrown on those older individuals who 'are ageing well (i.e., who look and act young)' (Walz, 2002: 99). Feminist scholar Deborah Covino, in an analysis of the magazine *Modern Maturity*,[1] calls this media phenomenon 'happy ageing' and notes its dedication to the 'productive management of longevity' (2004: 101). In makeover culture individuals who are deemed to be 'ageing well' are working at displaying efforts at stretching middle age. One of the technologies used to do this is cosmetic surgery.

Stretched Middle Age

Discourse around cosmetic surgery is about regaining or maintaining youth and beauty and about the 'management' and 'control' of ageing bodies. In makeover culture, active resistance to ageing is an important consideration for many adults and can even constitute a 'lifestyle'. Chris Gilleard, a psychologist who specialises in old age, and Paul Higgs, a medical sociologist, argue that the quest for good health and the prevention of morbidity are now 'central to the renegotiation of public and private responsibilities in contemporary society' (2000: 128). Care of the body is increasingly interwoven with social responsibility as 'costly old age' is seen to drain government-funded health and welfare systems. In user-pays health systems the imperative to stay fit and healthy is even more poignant. Body disciplines that minimise medical resources and help keep us 'productive' into old age come to be seen as virtues (Chaney, 1995; Gilleard and Higgs, 2000: 128). This postmodern virtuous old age – especially for women – abandons traditional notions of age as a period of stasis and rest, or less positively as a period of slow degeneration. Instead makeover culture obligates its subjects to perform 'lifestyles' until the day they die (Katz, 1995: 69). A magazine editorial says 'in the future, there will be no excuse for looking a day over the age of 35' (Boland, 1998: 28). Middle age then, is not a transit lounge passively inhabited between youth and old age. It is an increasingly significant, actively worked-upon and cherished life-phase with flexible borders.

In the stretched middle age a person's corporeal chronology is rendered less significant than their perceived ability to elasticise their middle age by way of pharm-aceuticals, hormone replacement therapies, cosmetic surgery, dieting, exercise, social activities, financial independence and the compulsory 'youthful outlook'. Cosmetic surgery is an increasingly important element in the toolkit for the stretched middle age. In this context it is less about reclaiming or reinventing youthfulness and more about attempting to create a look of indeterminate age or 'agelessness'.

The notion of a stretched middle age involves multifarious levels and areas of consideration. To describe it as a 'period of life' is inaccurate as its very existence makes borders and categories – that mark subjects as being a certain age – indefinite. Youth is a nebulous category in the stretched middle age where people ideally look 'ageless'.[2] A smoothly stretched appearance wherein age is vaguely indeterminate and one always looks 'good' is the platonic ideal of cosmetic surgery. The reality, however, is that the ideal must be constantly strived for, maintained and updated via continuous renovations and restorations. A 'stretching' of time implies a continuous energy, a temporality that is gradually and evenly expanded. But in order to perform an indefinite, possibly infinite, period of looking 'good for your age' a series of jerky ruptures is necessary, a set of transforming events that create folds at key moments in the lifespan. These are the moments in which the production of 'staying young' or 'looking one's best' is carried out.

In the case of cosmetic surgery these necessary ruptures are created by doctor–patient narratives (as discussed in the last chapter) and by the actual operations, anaesthetics and post-operative recovery periods. They happen in the space between 'before' and 'after' – a space that grows in significance, spatially and temporally, inside the stretched middle age. And as I have explained, 'after' in makeover culture is the new 'before', quickly moving from celebrating its success to denoting the start of a fresh quest for improvement. Another way to view this phenomenon is to see the 'between' bleeding out of its previously set boundaries and becoming paramount. 'Still' moments in time help create the illusion of a stretched middle age, and although they are often hidden from the public eye they mark the places on the body – literally, metaphorically and temporally – where changes have occurred. Featherstone and Wernick have described the ageing body as 'never just a body subjected to the imperatives of cellular and organic decline, for as it moves through life it is continuously being inscribed and reinscribed with cultural meanings' (1995: 2–3). Bodies and subjects are inscribed during these moments of transition. Individuals may have only one cosmetic surgery operation or may thread 'maintenance' procedures throughout their lives. Thus, while the results of the surgeries are important, the operations themselves are also significant and difficult moments in life that belie the smoothness of time that the ideal of a stretched middle age promises. It is during these moments of change, rupture and transition that transformations occur, allowing the continuance of the stretched ideal to flow.

Margaret Morganroth Gullette, a feminist cultural critic who has written much about ageing (1997; 2004) characterises the way in which the ideal of progress intersects with conventional developmental narratives: 'we have all been taught from childhood on through everyday practices and celebratory occasions that we relinquish a past self only to come into a same-but-better one. What a shock then, when our age suddenly means that we encounter the reverse cultural story: middle age as decline' (2004: 50). For Gullette, these counternarratives present a future that can only be 'better' or 'worse' (2004: 197). I suggest that the stretched middle age is one way of trying to reconcile better and worse. For example, often after surgery, dieting or gym-work people in middle age declare their bodies to be 'better' than when they were twenty: such modifications work to upset chronological stages of rise and fall, and of ability and decrepitude.

Temporality and Durée

A well-known dialogue between feminist philosophers Rosi Braidotti and Gail Weiss highlights ways in which feminists have tackled thinking about temporality and new technologies. In her *Nomadic Subjects* (1994) Braidotti presents a pessimistic analysis of new reproductive technologies and condemns their practitioners whom she characterises as male scientists seeking to gain control of women's bodies.

She argues that emerging reproductive technologies metaphorically freeze time (1994: 47) and thus undermine a peculiarly feminine/maternal understanding and experience of duration and becoming. The relationship between mother and foetus is temporally and spatially compromised, if not hijacked altogether, by technologies like *in vitro* fertilisation. In exploring the 'temporality of the techno-body' (1999: 163) Gail Weiss responds strongly to Braidotti's argument. Weiss suggests that while new reproductive technologies should worry feminists they also offer some exciting new ways to view and experience bodies and time. She suggests they might even offer possibilities for 'new ways of linking bodies up to one another, expanding their interconnections, and, in so doing, increasing their intercorporeal potentialities' (1999: 174). Weiss deploys theories of time and temporality from Henri Bergson's *An Introduction to Metaphysics*. For Bergson, time and temporality are different: time is 'objective' – measured, clocked, mappable and separated into discrete chunks. Temporality, or 'durée', is 'subjective' – it is how we experience time, how we perceive ourselves travelling and having travelled through it. Time is outer-awareness while durée is inner-awareness and, while the two are linked, their separateness calls for different philosophical methodologies: these are *analysis* and *intuition* respectively. I will briefly describe these two methodologies.

Analysis moves around an object, weaving strands of seeing. The more strands, the deeper the understanding, and yet this understanding can never be complete. Many points of view are necessary and many strands are used to link the unknown object with those more familiar. Thus understanding of an object builds up and is almost manufactured. *Intuition* on the other hand involves not links, threads and layers but immersion: utter involvement with an object, diving into it so as to experience its 'unique being', which is inexpressible. Intuition is 'intellectual sympathy' where one places oneself within an object in order to *coincide* with what is unique and inexpressible about it. Coinciding means *existing with* and is different from observing, marking, linking and comparing, which are all aspects of *analysis*. Because *analysis* aims to understand an unknown object by linking it to elements already known, it is about translation and representation – it relies on symbols and resemblances. Bergson says that analysis, in its 'eternally unsatisfied desire to embrace the object around which it is compelled to turn' builds up an 'always incomplete representation' and an 'always imperfect translation'. *Intuition* on the other hand, is 'a simple act' (Bergson, 1955: 23–4).

Bergson suggests that durées are never isolated but always interconnected and suggests that through a 'violent effort' we can extend ourselves indefinitely, and possibly even transcend ourselves by intuitively grasping this continuum. Part of seeing and experiencing the interconnections between the durées of techno-bodies and our own durées is 'the recognition that technology is part and parcel of our own durée…' Technology is not something that should be viewed as outside, or 'out there' but rather as 'within our own bodies, facilitating the death of solipsism by affirming the intercorporality of time' (Weiss, 1999: 170). Weiss advises that we should not call certain technologies monstrous 'until we have interrogated [their] intercorporeal implications and effects. And, to the extent that we are embedded and encompassed within the techniques and practices we critique, such an interrogation can never point the finger at a monster without a mirror being present' (1999: 175). New reproductive technologies, then, have the power to disrupt our understanding of durée, 'a durée that extends, transforms, and transcends itself through these very technologies' (1999: 113). Through the rest of this chapter I *analyse* interview and media material to show that cosmetic surgery – which can so easily be theorised as a 'freezing technology' in relation to age and time[3] – can also be understood in terms of durée. I wonder if an understanding of the durée of cosmetic surgery may reveal a potential to disrupt traditional notions of temporality. Following Weiss's suggestions about new reproductive technologies I ask whether cosmetic surgery offers new ways of experiencing connections between bodies. My last section, 'Immanent Change', works less analytically and more *intuitively*, endeavouring to coincide with the 'unique and inexpressible' bond that two women described when they underwent cosmetic surgery together.

Designing – Not Denying – Ageing

One of the issues I covered in the interviews was that of temporality. I wondered how a person who has 'erased' ten or fifteen years from her appearance deals with notions of time – time as experienced both internally (durée) and externally (chronological time) – and whether there is a tension between the two. I wanted to find out how issues of age are negotiated post-operatively: if she now looks and feels younger, how is actual chronological age dealt with? My assumption was that somehow the offending years would be negated or pushed into remission. For example, if someone says she is fifty but is really sixty-five, then in order to maintain believability she must blur or eradicate fifteen years of experience. Frankly, I expected people to tell me that they regularly lied about chronological age after having cosmetic surgery. In fact I found quite a different set of attitudes toward time and ageing. While most interviewees had sought eradication of some ageing signs they all avidly denied lying about their age. Many of them had modest expectations of the physical results of their cosmetic surgery and didn't actually think it would make them look younger. Importantly, there was still a strong desire and hope for *transformations* connected to cosmetic surgery. These transformations were about enhancing the display of health and fitness, eradicating signs of past trauma, signalling a new outlook on or approach to life, or rewarding hard work.

Better, Not Younger

Most interviewees vehemently stated that rather than trying to look *younger* they were trying to look *better*. The rhetoric of 'better not younger' is also found in advertising and promotional rhetoric around some cosmetic surgery. Many cosmetic surgeons now say they don't aim to make people look younger but rather 'more attractive', 'improved', 'good for their age' and 'the best they can be'. Even though most interviewees conceded, when pressed, that the signs of youth are concurrent in our society with the signs of attractiveness (primarily signified by smooth, taut skin) they still maintained that they weren't trying to pretend they were younger per se, but rather trying to 'look good for their age'.

For Virginia Blum, 'better not younger' is part of a horrendous scam: 'A forty-eight-year-old patient ... is so thrilled with her new look that she assures us, "I plan on maintaining my face and body so I can keep getting better and better". But she won't get better and better. She will just keep making interventions in what is getting, from the surgical standpoint, worse' (Blum, 2003: 197). But in makeover culture's logic she is getting 'better and better', although not in the sense of actually looking younger. This patient is embracing the labour of makeover culture and a state of constant becoming. Doing this through cosmetic surgery may, as Blum insists, render her surgically vulnerable and unhealthy but I suggest that that is, tragically, beside the point. The positive rhetoric of 'better and better' denotes movement and growth in abstract ways relating to display: in makeover culture a face altered by cosmetic surgery is proof of a developing and improving self. Blum's stance is outside any position wherein continual surgery could be seen as positive and sensible. An *intuitive* approach allows me to see that the woman who describes herself becoming 'better and better' is a successful citizen of makeover culture.

The youngest of my interviewees stood out in her responses to the temporality-related questions. Simone was a successful professional who had just celebrated her fortieth birthday party in great style with family and friends and was about to undergo a blepharoplasty, her first cosmetic surgery operation (although she had previously had Botox® injected into her forehead and collagen injected into her lips and nasolabial lines). A few days before her scheduled operation she was quite clear about the balance between the hope for transformation and the more 'sensible' approach of looking 'better not younger'. Early in the interview she made it clear that the doctor had told her she would look 'better not younger' and she worked this rhetoric into her answers: 'I don't know whether I'll look younger but I expect to look better. So far as when I look in the mirror I see a person with very puffy eyes and that's the first thing that I see. Having this done will apparently remove the puffiness.' Further into our conversation I asked her whether she expected her life to change after cosmetic surgery and her answer was much more complex, worth quoting at length:

> That's a very confronting question. I think, I could answer it very tritely and say no, I don't think my life will change because I think that really probably it won't, but I have this hope – and I haven't really thought about it until you asked me this question ... I look in the mirror and I think, what I'm hoping is, after the procedure I'll look in the mirror and not immediately see the bags under my eyes, so I won't be so self-critical.

And as a result of not being so self-critical, I might be more positive about myself, and therefore more positive in my life, and therefore my life will be better because I think only I can make my life better. So I'm old enough to realise that I'm not going to look twelve and men aren't going to flock to me as a result, but it's done to make me feel, sort of much more, a happier person. Or to be less negative about myself. So in that sense I hope it effects a change in the way I see myself.

Simone's hope for self-transformation was carefully couched within realisable physical goals (eyes that aren't puffy) and within the rhetoric of happiness being a result of 'being positive'. The prospect of failure was also built into her answer ('really probably my life won't change') but, nevertheless, the expectations weighing on the simple eradication of eye-bags were great. A domino effect was hoped for: non-puffy eyes would lead to feeling less negative about herself which would lead to being happier.

Growing Old Gracefully

The phrase 'growing old gracefully', like the Pygmalion story discussed in the last chapter, is deployed by different and even warring camps around cosmetic surgery: 'On the one hand, it is argued that procedures such as facelifts, chemical peels and liposuction can assist us in growing old gracefully. On the other, growing old gracefully means refusing to tamper surgically with the evidence of ageing.' (Fraser, 2003: 74) Both approaches are linked to underlying values of the 'natural': one believes nature should be left alone, the other thinks it should be 'contained, moulded, and improved upon' (Fraser, 2003: 75). Like the term 'natural', 'growing old gracefully' is mobile, equivocal and often moralistic. The statement 'I'm growing old gracefully' may indicate not having cosmetic surgery but could equally be the opposite. In makeover culture it is increasingly the latter: for example Oprah Winfrey has begun to ask her celebrity guests if they would consider *not* having cosmetic surgery rather than if they would consider having it. A book that accompanies the BBC 4 makeover series *10 Years Younger* begins with the line

You're probably thinking, what's the big deal? Why should I care about the number of wrinkles I have on my face? Why should I try to defy the course of time and turn back the clock? What happened to ageing gracefully? Well, I couldn't agree with you more, as long as you're truly happy with yourself and the way you look. (Hambleton-Jones, 2005: 7)

It is the qualifying 'as long as' that makes any look that doesn't include high maintenance grooming unacceptable. Certain celebrities who have clearly had no cosmetic surgery are labelled 'brave'. When cosmetic surgery becomes the norm, individuals who don't have it must explain themselves, must have an arsenal of 'bravery' and talent to fall back on.

Camille, a 56-year-old housesitter and pet minder who had undergone a lower face ('S') lift, a blepharoplasty and a chemical face peel two and a half years before the interview, said when I asked if she would have anything else done in the future, 'no, no more – that's enough – I had what I wanted done – no, no [laughing] now I can grow old gracefully'. The interviews showed an interesting separation of inner and outer representations of time: along with a strong desire for certain unwanted *signs* of ageing to be minimised or wiped clean, there was a simultaneous acknowledgement and even a celebration of actual chronological age. Camille believed she had partly *chosen* how and when to age. Her cosmetic surgery had given her options about how to present the visible signs of being middle-aged. In saying 'now I can grow old gracefully' she was not *denying* her ageing process via cosmetic surgery but *designing* it – 'grace' for her signified control gained through surgery.

Special Circumstances

I asked interviewees whether they felt there were any special circumstances in their lives that led to cosmetic surgery:

> Oh definitely. This is really, um, to remove, I don't know if it's the last trace, it's the last obvious trace physically, the last physical trace of breaking up with my de facto partner back in '98. And then basically becoming a very serious alcoholic for several years which led to, well I don't know if the alcohol has led to the puffy eyes, but that's what I see now, they are puffy. They might have come along anyway because of my age, but they probably weren't assisted by all this alcohol and this misery. So I'd just sort of like to erase that. (Simone)

Simone felt that a relationship break-up had contributed, by way of alcohol, to the appearance of her eyes. I said 'so you're having cosmetic surgery to eradicate the trauma of this break-up of the long-term relationship four years ago?' and she was quick to correct me:

> I wouldn't say it's to eradicate the trauma. I'd say it's to eradicate the physical appearance, the signs of the trauma... On one level its almost like well, at least to look at my face, we might go back to – I don't expect to look seven years younger – back to just looking, not looking younger, I can't explain it because I don't want to be younger, and the rest of my body would betray my age in any event, but looking like I didn't have a really shitty time getting over somebody in the last four years. [I want to look] as if I broke up with somebody, had a bad few months and then righted myself and went on, like most normal people do. Most people don't sit there and drink a bottle of wine a night and cry and smoke and all that sort of stuff.

Other interviewees answered the 'special circumstances' question with corporeal facts – lopsided breasts because of heart surgery as a child; severely sunburned skin;

losing vast amounts of weight so the stomach skin was like an empty supermarket bag. Only Simone related her unwanted physical feature to an emotional event. While she didn't want to pretend the trauma had never happened, she did want to be rid of the constant physical reminder of it. Just as the former de facto partner was now well and truly out of her life, she also wanted to erase the legacy of the break-up from her face. Cosmetic surgery marked a turning point in her life and was linked with other 'life-improving' practices:

> I do concede that having this done [the cosmetic surgery] has been triggered by turning forty. I've got no doubt about that. This is the year of giving up smoking, not drinking as much, having plastic surgery... So it's trying to sort of regulate my life so that I can go forward... trying to set myself up for the next ten years with a better base than where I was. (Simone)

Simone's answers show how hopes around cosmetic surgery are intertwined with emotional turning points, and can be part of a 'package' of self-improvement. Although aware that turning forty had 'triggered' the cosmetic surgery, she had no desire to actually look younger per se. She was aiming to look like a more 'normal' forty: someone who hadn't drunk a bottle of wine a night for four years. Certainly using this reckoning she was truly aiming to look 'better not younger'.

Balancing the Body

While health and fitness are anti-age technologies used to fashion the self, they do not necessarily fit into the beauty ideal – a fit person may be wrinkled, covered in age spots or grey-haired. But our visually oriented culture increasingly demands that 'looking after one's body' be aesthetically obvious – cosmetic surgery is one way to show this. So along with eating bran, keeping fit and dressing well, some people will have cosmetic surgery operations simply to show they are looking after themselves. Closely linked to this is the practice of rewarding oneself with cosmetic surgery for having successfully maintained a health or fitness regime – the cosmetic surgery procedure is the icing on the cake, the visual indicator that we are transformed in more ways than having simply lost weight. One interviewee, Anne, a 49-year-old with two pre-teen children, had spent three years and about $20,000 (AU) on a personal trainer and gym fees. She had been overweight for more than twenty years and lost about thirty kilos. She said:

> I've spent all this money and time doing this and it's been really successful. But with losing the weight there's no shape to [my face] anymore. I feel like it's all drooped. [The 'S' lift and neck lift] will make my face fit my body more... well it's my face that people see first... I want to be fit because my children are teenagers.

For Anne, being fit and slim did not complete her picture of a rejuvenated self: she also needed to delete wrinkles and 'excess' neck skin. She linked having cosmetic surgery to being fit and losing weight and saw it as a reward for herself: 'I know I'm just as healthy without it, of course! But it's just a small thing to make me feel better … otherwise the weight loss doesn't really help me [in looking younger]'. Again, looking younger and being fit and healthy were utterly intertwined: being slim with a wrinkled neck 'doesn't help' her, because she knows she will be seen as old before being seen as slim. As Woodward points out (1991), age tends to cancel out other defining identity factors, even gender. So it is not surprising that the visual cues associated with 'looking after oneself' may take precedence for some individuals over health practices. A facelifted woman who is unfit or unwell may still be perceived as healthier than her sister who is well and fit but has wrinkled skin. This privileging of the appearance of health is something cosmetic surgeons also pick up on in their advertising:

> You've worked hard to keep your body trim and fit and your positive attitude has helped to keep mind, heart and spirit youthful. Now, cosmetic surgery's latest breakthroughs can do the same for your face so that it's a more accurate reflection of the inner you. Dr. Sachs also discusses cheek implants, chin implants, facial liposuction, lip augmentation, rhinoplasty, facial rejuvenation, laser skin resurfacing, and scar removal. (Michael Evan Sachs MD, http://www.michaelevansachs.com/printdocument.asp)

A more practical reason for cosmetic surgery was explained by Danielle, who at nearly sixty years had lost a massive fifty-five kilos. For her, weight loss and cosmetic surgery were directly linked in the refashioning of a specific body part – her arms:

> If I'd lost the weight earlier [my skin] would've bounced back more. But I had the big flaps and I just couldn't get into some clothes. Stretchy stuff was okay … [but] if a dress had slim arms they wouldn't squeeze into it… If I wore a sleeveless dress I'd be size ten and I loved that, but my arms didn't go [with the rest of my body].

'Bat wings' is a description of the upper arms when the skin hangs or sags below the muscle when the arm is lifted. It is also sometimes called 'bingo arms', associating it with a predominantly working-class activity and intimating its undesirability for class and aesthetic reasons. The solution for Danielle was to have the soft skin on the inside of her upper arms cut away; the scars she bore from elbow to armpit were striking. She took a strange pride in not having had liposuction and justified her arm-lift as a trade off:

> I thought about it [liposuction] but I knew it [the weight] would just come back… I lost weight by changing my diet and exercising every single day, that's the best way to do it 'cause [the weight] won't come back unless you go back to coke and chips … I didn't

have [liposuction] at the beginning because it was better to do it with willpower. But at the end I needed [cosmetic surgery] because there was nothing I could do about the sagging.

For both Anne and Danielle losing weight created a perceived imbalance in their appearances. A slim body is associated with youth and must therefore be topped with a face that doesn't 'sag'. Similarly, a slim body must be seen as slim and taut all over, and having one body part (in this case the arms) that doesn't 'bounce back' after weight loss is seen to spoil the whole effect. Both women justified their cosmetic surgery by proving that they had the willpower to change their bodies. Having done everything they could through dieting and exercise, cosmetic surgery was merely an adjunct to their own achievements. Danielle in particular was scornful of people who choose liposuction over dieting. For her, the hard work of weight loss justified cosmetic surgery but otherwise she considered it only for the weak-willed. Thus successfully doing makeover in one part of your life (dieting) leads into needing to do it in another (having surgery). And simultaneously, the success in the first instance also justifies the second instance: makeover is its own reward.

No Excuse for Looking Old

Danielle's cosmetic surgery was also justified because 'there was nothing I could do about it'. Her sagging arm skin was unalterable except with surgery. So in fact there was something she could do about it, but she needed to be an active consumer and employ an expert. A philosophical or practical acceptance of what is 'unalterable' is not necessarily an admirable quality in makeover culture. To say 'I have wrinkles, I have sagging skin, there's nothing I can do about them' is in many ways now 'incorrect', on moral and technical levels. Increasingly in makeover culture the choice is not to have cosmetic surgery rather than to have it. Just as a contemporary woman attending an important public event will probably feel the need to wear make-up, the middle-aged woman of the mid twenty-first century may well live in an environment where cosmetic surgery is the absolute norm. For middle- and upper-class women the decision not to have cosmetic surgery will be a political (or an aesthetically perverse) one, a resolution that says certain things about the bearer of wrinkles or the carrier of jowls. In other words, a face unmarked by cosmetic surgery – or rather a face that retains the marks of age – will be a face that makes a statement.

Mutton Cut Up as Lamb

In Disney and post-Disney versions of the fairy tale *Snow-White and the Seven Dwarves*, the wicked stepmother is punished at the end by accidental death – she falls down a ravine or chokes. But in pre-Disney versions of the story she must take part in her own sickening murder. She decides to attend the ball being held in celebration of her stepdaughter's wedding, unaware that her enemies – including her stepdaughter – are expecting her and have devised a special welcome:

> The evil queen was so petrified with fright that she could not budge. Iron slippers had already been heated over a fire, and they were brought over to her with tongs. Finally, she had to put on the red-hot slippers and dance until she fell down dead. (Grimm, 1987: 222)

There has been much feminist analysis of the negative influences that fairy tales can have on young girls' self-esteem, given that fairy-tale heroines patiently await princes to set them free, are ideal and uncomplaining domestic workers, and have outward beauty that indicates inner perfection. But what do such tales have to say to older women? Apart from the occasional benevolent fairy godmother, the only ageing women in these narratives are those who are desperately grasping at fading beauty, demented with jealousy of their daughters, and ready to commit murder, infanticide and abuse to maintain or gain power. Often they suffer horrible deaths or punishments. Less gruesomely, the burning red shoes may represent menopause with its hot flushes, just as the Sleeping Beauty's pricked finger represents menarche. But either way ageing is depicted as utterly undesirable and its dwellers contemptible. Many contemporary stories echo ancient narratives. Here I focus on a set of present-day tales about mothers, daughters, youth, age, power – and cosmetic surgery.

As I have already noted, it is impossible to attempt a cultural analysis of cosmetic surgery without paying close attention to the media products that comment upon it. In the case of cosmetic surgery this shows that media do not only represent the practice but also produce it. They express and promote its deployment as desirable or undesirable, necessary or frivolous, normal or abnormal; its results as beautiful or ugly; and its experience as excruciating or just mildly uncomfortable.

Mothers' and Daughters' Age Old Problem

Cosmetic surgery is a perpetual and popular subject in women's magazines. It has also spawned its own magazines: specialist glossies devoted to cosmetic surgery and related topics. Suzanne Fraser has identified several cosmetic surgery genres, including the popular magazine genre (2003: 61–96). Building on her meticulous findings I identify a sub-genre inside the magazine genre – the mother/daughter/ cosmetic surgery story that is found in specialist cosmetic surgery magazines and more general women's magazines. These pieces usually feature celebrity mother/ daughter comparisons but may also include the narratives of 'normal' people. I argue that they strongly express a contradiction that lies at the heart of discourses around contemporary cosmetic surgery, namely, that while cosmetic surgery works to annihilate the markers of ageing, it simultaneously relies on a continued divide between age and youth.

This media analysis focuses on two multiple-page spreads specifically devoted to the issue of mothers, daughters and cosmetic surgery in the magazines *Gloss* and *NW*.[4] *Gloss* was the short-lived publication mentioned earlier and *NW* (formerly *New Woman*) is a weekly magazine available in many outlets in Australia including supermarkets. Predictably, they position cosmetic surgery as an antidote to the visible signs of ageing. Less predictably, they advocate cosmetic surgery as a 'solution' for youthful daughters and for ageing mothers. *Gloss* has a suite of interviews, articles and commentaries collected under the headline 'Like Mother, Like Daughter'. The *NW* piece is called 'Age old problem' (Broadbent 2002: 22–5). It places stars' ages next to their names and gives them an ageing score out of ten on the 'wrinkle rater'. Significantly, the score is not based on the star's looks but on how her mother has aged.

Each star in the *NW* article is paired with her mother, and it is the mothers' faces that come under vicious scrutiny: they are criticised for having 'sagging jowls', 'laughter lines', 'turkey-gobbler necks', 'permanent frowns', 'tired eyes', 'crows feet' and 'thick noses'. These are presented as ominous signs of what lies ahead for their still-beautiful daughters. We're told that in twenty years' time, Gwyneth Paltrow will be 'wrestling with wrinkles', Geri Halliwell will have 'thin lips' and Catherine Zeta-Jones will have 'heavy eyelids'. Poor Nicole Kidman 'is already showing the problem areas that will plague her in old age'. Of the nine celebrity daughters compared to their mothers only one is determined to be *unlikely* to require cosmetic surgery eventually.

The aim of this kind of scrutiny and almost apocalyptic rhetoric is to keep the ageing female body within the borders of acceptable femininity – that is, youthful femininity – by predicting and 'fixing' transgressions even before they occur. Fraser notes that in magazine discourse 'appropriate femininity has two forms; first and ideally – youthful, and second, when youth is no longer possible, committed to the pursuit of a youthful appearance as an endorsement of youth as the ideal manifestation of femininity' (2003: 74, also see Gullette, 2004). So the ideal feminine body must be presented as youthful, or at least as doing work to try to appear youthful. Legitimate femininity is either genuinely youthful or is dedicated to simulating a youthful appearance. As Simone De Beauvoir painfully observes: 'From the day a woman *consents* to growing old, her situation changes. Up to that time she was still a young woman, intent on struggling against a misfortune that was mysteriously disfiguring and disforming her; now she becomes a different being, unsexed but complete: an old woman' (1970: 595, my italics). The *consent* to ageing is crucial because the stretched middle age is dedicated to a continual struggle against the signs of age. Thus, cosmetic surgery is easily presented as something that's utterly correct to desire and indeed crucial in the enactment of ageing: it is presented as an indispensable rather than an optional tool for the stretched middle age.

While the article in *NW* works by emphasising perceived negatives due to ageing in the faces of the mothers, a similar piece in *Gloss* works by complimenting the mothers for the cosmetic surgery they *have* had. Three sets of mother/daughter celebrities are analysed by one of Sydney's most famous cosmetic surgeons, Darryl Hodgkinson. He estimates, from photos, that all three of the mothers have had extensive cosmetic surgery, ranging from three to seven operations each. He describes the mothers in glowing terms: Blythe Danner, Gwyneth Paltrow's mother, is 'quite youthful', Ivana Trump, mother of Ivanka, is 'transformed', and Janet Leigh, mother of Jamie-Lee Curtis, is 'very pretty'. The daughters' faces are analysed against the mothers' to see how they will fare in comparison, and Hodgkinson categorically states: 'for all of these stars to maintain a youthful appearance, cosmetic surgery will be required as each generation ages' (1998: 24).

Intriguingly, both of the articles feature the Hollywood actress Gwyneth Paltrow and her mother Blythe Danner. Two similar photos of the pair are used to illustrate seemingly contradictory arguments: while the *NW* article states that Danner's 'jowls' are a big problem, the *Gloss* article suggests she has probably had a nose job, facelift, browlift and eye surgery, and compliments her on her 'youthful appearance'. *NW* analyses the mother's face unfavourably and presents her as having not had cosmetic surgery: the daughter is duly warned about how not to take after her. *Gloss* examines the mother's face positively, assuming she has had cosmetic surgery, and she is complimented on having corrected her faults: here, the daughter is told she should follow in her mother's footsteps or risk ugliness. So although the articles treat the mother quite differently – in one she is praised, while in the other she is ridiculed – the shared conclusion is that the daughters will definitely need cosmetic surgery.

These articles lock mother and daughter together in endless mirrored pairings where each can only refer to the other. It seems that without cosmetic surgery the mother is forced to look at the youthful beauty that she no longer has, while the daughter can only see the utterly undesirable face that awaits her. Only cosmetic surgery can release them from this depressing bind. The mother/daughter relationship is represented as symbiotic: pictures from both articles show them as intertwined, overlapping and touching. Each couple is carefully framed so they are on their own: mother and daughter have no reference points apart from each other. Different colours separate the different pairs and some images even have their backgrounds removed, so the visual language here implies that this twinning is all there is: mother and daughter are inseparable. In the subtext the mother's wrinkles are presented as active and malevolent, about to invade the daughter and take her over, while the daughter's youthful beauty haunts the ageing mother, constantly reminding her of her own shrinking lack. This was a cultural dominant that most of my interviewees adhered to and spoke about.

Some of the women express profound interest in not looking like their ageing mothers. Simone told me:

I'm about as old now as my mother [was] when I first begin to [see her] as a woman, as opposed to my mother ... I've sort of realised that I'm quite like her now ... I got her body ... I always noticed this thing about my mother's body, which was ... that she had like a fat build up in her thighs ... I can't remember when I first noticed my own thighs, but certainly now, I definitely know that ... the worst part of my body is my thighs, which is why I'm thinking about going and having liposuction.

And in an inversion of sorts, some expressed pleasure at looking more like their daughters: one 38-year-old said after liposuction: 'My butt looks like my 14-year-old daughter's ... I never would have dreamed that was possible' (quoted in Karash and Smith Knight, 2000). A woman who had breastfed four children told me after having breast implants:

Before, I had nothing left at all. All I had was a nipple and it was hanging over itself like a crease... [Now] I'm rapt, totally rapt, going shopping and trying on clothes is just so great, I can do it with [my 16-year-old daughter] and I don't feel bad because, you know, she has the most lovely little round breasts. (Judith)

Jocastan Power

The turning-away from her mother is an extremely important step in the course of a little girl's development. (Sigmund Freud quoted in Hirsch, 1989: 91)

mothers and daughters need alternative models for relating to one another outside the 'family plot' ... (Ray, 2003: 113)

The cover of this *NW* shows Lisa Marie, Elvis Presley's daughter, and her mother Priscilla (Figure 8). These two women have done precisely what the *NW* and *Gloss* articles seem to recommend: they have taken full advantage of aesthetic technologies of the self, particularly cosmetic surgery, and each is carefully performing the stretched middle age. In the article inside they are ridiculed for their efforts while simultaneously being held up as beautiful individuals to be emulated: 'there's something a bit weird about a mother and daughter who look the same age. Both Priscilla and Lisa Marie Presley are said to be fans of plastic surgery and, as time passes, whatever work they're having done seems to be turning them into twins' (*NW*, 30 September 2002: 22–3). This is an example of contradictory ideological complexes weaving together to sustain a dominant cultural logic. Contemporary popular texts like those analysed here emphasise both the yearning for a closure of the generation gap and a horror of losing traditional markers of, and margins between, age groups.

This juxtaposition of fear and desire highlights an inconsistency that lies at the heart of anti-ageing cosmetic surgery discourse because, while it deconstructs

Figure 8 Cover of Australian *NW*, 30 September 2002

or even annihilates the markers of ageing, cosmetic surgery nevertheless relies on a continued divide between age and youth. Hence, in order to promote anti-ageing cosmetic surgery as a tool with which to enact middle age 'properly' many texts around it reinforce repressive generational stereotypes while simultaneously promising escape from them. By privileging the fraught paradigm of the two-handed mother/daughter struggle women are locked into the unbeatable slow machine of clocked and chronological time. The grimmest extension of this viewpoint is that we view the future with a sense of dread and loss, looking either at our daughters, who flaunt the youth that we have lost, or at our mothers, who inhabit the undistinguished, unrespected position that awaits us as we inevitably age and decline. It is this sad paradigm that texts such as the *NW* and *Gloss* articles analysed above present: in the guise of offering transformation and escape they shut down the possibilities of alternative temporalities and in fact lock us into a constant battle against time.

The stretched middle age means that old and clear boundaries between generations are blurred. As technologies of the madeover self proliferate – from hair dye to cosmetic surgery to bio-reproductive developments – they bring anxieties and even feelings of panic to the surface. Mother/daughter/cosmetic surgery texts express that alarm neatly because they recognise the possibilities of technologies that render age less important, therefore offering all sorts of potential new freedoms and novel experiences of temporality and spatiality. But they are also caught up in a deep-rooted mythic horror of compounded generations: the classic Oedipal state where two adjacent generations struggle and even war with each other.

Freud's Oedipal complex – wherein the young boy wishes to become his father, naïvely at first by desiring to marry his mother and kill his father – is part of the boy's development as a human, moving him from the presocial to the social and allowing him to achieve maturation as an individual both within the family and the wider society (Gatens, 1996: 52–3; Hirsch, 1989: 28–9). For women the Oedipal complex describes conditions where we compete with, undermine or hurt each other in order to be more successful within a patriarchal system. Hence 'the bond between mother and daughter, daughter and mother, must be broken so that the daughter can become woman' (Irigaray, *Ethique*, 1984: 106, translated by and quoted in Hirsch, 1989: 43).

In the ancient Greek drama that provided Freud's template, King Oedipus commits material crimes of incest and patricide. But these crimes flag a far greater offence to do with his correct position in time: he oscillates between generations, ignorant of his proper place, travelling 'backwards' to marry his mother and 'forwards' to become his daughters' brother. Keeping this in mind and turning the prism slightly to focus on the mother he marries, Jocasta, I suggest a 'Jocastan Complex' where the mother becomes or remains powerful and desirable by challenging her assigned place in chronological time. She marries her son, thus becoming 'younger', and experiences dual or triple relationship roles (as mother, grandmother and sister) with her daughters. She is the pivot in a series of events that twist the normal flow of time: she refuses the negative role assigned to her because of her age. Partaking of cosmetic surgery might then be described as a Jocastan action: it is one way for women to maintain or regain central positions in the active adult world, avoiding the marginalisation that comes with age.

In Oedipal situations tensions and confusions – and of course tragedies – occur because of generational enmities. Oedipal nightmares result from families being too intimate (in Sophocles' *Oedipus* of course it is actual reproductive incest) so the urge to flee such closeness is strong. One way of viewing anti-ageing cosmetic surgery and the stretched middle age positively is as a way to alleviate Oedipal tensions by simply allowing mother and daughter to occupy the same temporal space, and to effectively banish the generation gap, at least aesthetically. While the daughter may use cosmetic surgery to escape the tyranny of her mother's genes and to distance herself from her aesthetic fate, the mother concurrently uses cosmetic surgery to come closer to how the daughter looks. But this coming together is highly problematic, because cosmetic surgery, while seeming to offer an alternative to Oedipal tensions by minimising the generation gap, also does exactly the opposite.

Marianne Hirsch (1989), Kathleen Woodward (1995) and Ruth Ray (2003) all offer feminist readings of the Oedipus myth and alternate paradigms. For Hirsch, woman-centred myths such as the story of Persephone and Demeter are more useful than *Oedipus*. She says that they have 'hegemonic power ... delimiting force, and ... explanatory potential' (1989: 29) but also insists that new theoretical paradigms – that focus on maternal perspectives and don't rely on a divide between mothers and daughters – are vital. Woodward suggests inserting the oft-forgotten grandmother into the mother/daughter equation in order to surpass the Oedipal binary. Her revision of the mother/daughter plot encourages us to be flexible about notions of chronology and temporality, seeing ourselves *always* in the bodies of our mothers and grandmothers, rather than in a dreadful future: 'the figure of the older woman ... was in fact present in my past all along, and [she will be] present in my future, time willing' (1995: 92). Feminist gerontologist Ruth Ray argues that while tensions between mothers and daughters can be used to initiate personal growth we also need other stories through which to relate to each other. She acknowledges that 'in the practice of daily life, it is difficult to resist the pull of the old Freudian psychodrama of mother/daughter conflict. Yet, we must try' (2003: 120).

And what we may get when we try is what Mary Russo describes as 'provisional, uncomfortable, even conflictual, coalitions of bodies which both respect the concept of "situated knowledges" and refuse to keep every body in its place' (1994: 179). As Weiss suggests, through 'violent efforts' of understanding and intuition we may alter our understanding and experience of durée. We may even use technologies like cosmetic surgery – that in many ways try to 'freeze' us inside set generational camps – to extend and transform our relationships, to disrupt conventional notions of temporality, and experience different connections between bodies. Intergenerational relationships in this schema may be highly fraught with never-ending dialogues, conflicts, negotiations and alliances, but they are not impassable: their boundaries are penetrable.

Instances of dialogic connections between bodies are more plentiful in fiction than real life. In *The Female Grotesque* (1994) Russo shows how Fevvers, the winged woman in Angela Carter's *Nights at the Circus*, and her mother Lizzie, 'a gnarled old leftist', work together to create an intertwining of old and new and a productive merge of two generations. She argues that 'the spectacle of the new is produced and can therefore be counterproduced' (1994: 179). The characters of Fevvers and Lizzie represent an 'intergenerational grotesque' (1994: 178) similar to the one Mikhail Bakhtin analyses in his evocative description of ancient terracotta figures of senile, laughing, pregnant 'hags'. Fevvers's wings signify youth and newness to most characters in the novel but Lizzie sees in them the 'Annunciation of my own Menopause'. The wings on the younger woman's body balance the onset of menopause in the older woman's. They represent new growth and are a metaphorical pregnancy: one body becomes reproductive as the other farewells that possibility. The key is that the existence of the wings allows Lizzie to see her menopause as transmogrative 'annunciation' rather than loss. Russo notes, 'the figurative biological clock is communal' (1994: 178). So here intergenerational bodies present themselves and interpret each other as joined and separate. In this view old and new are interlocked – showing that the new need not be unequivocally tied to youth.

Immanent Change

Feminists should not only analyse the destructive Oedipal ways that cosmetic surgery's discourses pitch women against each other, engendering anxiety and dread – as I have done in the media analysis above – but to try to identify or suggest alternative paradigms. One such alternative reading of the mother/daughter/cosmetic surgery relation comes from deep inside the practice itself. There is a 'trend' in mothers and daughters presenting to plastic surgeons together. Forty-four per cent of member-surgeons of the American Academy of Facial Plastic and Reconstructive Surgery reported that mother/daughter pairs had consulted them in 2003. While there are no previous statistics for comparison, the fact that the question was included in the 2003 survey suggests that the phenomenon had increased (AAFPRS 2003 Survey, 2004: 6). Although problematic in all sorts of ways that beg further feminist research, for my purposes the presentation of mothers and daughters to cosmetic surgeons *together* is significant. It points to a phenomenon that may run parallel or even in opposition to an Oedipal situation where women are in competition with each other. I suggest, *intuitively*, rather than through a systematic *analysis*, that cosmetic surgery – and other less violent deployments of the stretched middle age – could be used in new ways for women to enjoy relationships that do not rely on competitiveness and opposition. Future research into the attitudes, feelings and relationships of mother/daughter pairs who have undergone cosmetic surgery might surprise us. Unlike the editorial about the Presley women, an article in London's *Daily Mail* allows a mother and daughter pair to tell their own story and keeps editorial comment in the affirmative: 'heads turn when mother and daughter Carol, 48, and Sarah Hamilton, 24, walk down the High Street, their admirers oblivious to the generation gap between these two petite blondes...' (Levy, 2000). Sarah had breast augmentation while her mother Carol had an eyelift and lip implants; they shared a hospital room. Post-surgery Carol said, 'for the first time in ages, I played the protective role of a mother ... I washed and brushed Sarah's hair, opened doors for her and fed her. It was like having a baby again. The whole experience made us feel incredibly close'. Sarah said, 'I feel proud to walk down the street with such a stunning, young-looking mother' (Levy, 2000). For this pair cosmetic surgery seems to have re-emphasised traditional mother/daughter roles while simultaneously redesigning them as equals. These two 'petite blondes' are of course deeply implicated in all of the normalising and repressive aspects of cosmetic surgery, but they are also enacting a Jocastan wish-fulfilment of becoming 'sisters'. The ways in which they interact with cosmetic surgery and define it in terms of their relationships with each other may provide feminists with alternative means of thinking about the 'warring generations' aspects of cosmetic surgery.

Conclusion

The stretched middle age is not a gradual progression between youth and old age but rather an indefinitely stretched period of makeover. Although its aim is not to *re-create* youth it uses the markers of youth to stave off or balance the markers of old age. 'Staying young', which in the schema of makeover culture means successfully negotiating the various practices and performances of anti-ageing, is argued by Gilleard and Higgs to be a tri-faceted process made up of exercising consumer choice, being financially independent so as to resist the stigma and marginalisation of being an 'old-age pensioner', and having the cultural know-how to be accepted as not too distanced from youth culture (2000: 128). There is a fourth facet that the first three are dependent upon: being able to 'read the signs' of an ever-morphing set of judgements about what an acceptable display of age is. In other words, being able to place oneself securely inside the stretched middle age, and thus perform as a good citizen of makeover culture.

While cosmetic surgery grows as part of a suite of body technologies and lifestyle practices that are working to create and maintain the stretched middle age, its positive possibilities are largely ignored by popular media that prefer to encase it within ancient discourses that privilege conservative panic. Specifically, fear and terror of ageing is still embraced. Rhetoric around anti-ageing cosmetic surgery continually re-emphasises the contained dichotomy of two standardised states of being, especially for women – young and old – by adopting the signs of one in order to stave off the signs of the other.

Repositioning our attitudes towards technologies like cosmetic surgery may offer entirely new ways of seeing and experiencing temporality, and could lead to the superfluity of terms such as 'generation gap'. Sadly, while cosmetic surgery grows as part of a suite of body technologies and lifestyle practices that are working to create a swelled period of middle age into which almost every adult will potentially fit, the discourses around it use outdated and repressive paradigms that undermine the potentially innovative possibilities that it offers.

As part of a set of technologies and life practices that are creating a stretched middle age, cosmetic surgery offers multiple and varied new ways for intergenerational relationships to be enacted. The physical markers that differentiate people at thirty, forty, fifty and sixty may be replaced by an extended middle age, which could allow infinite opportunities for ageism to diminish and for more lateral relationships to develop.

In this schema the ageing queen might not bleed and burn to death in red-hot iron shoes in order for the princess to rise to power. Instead, mother and daughter might dance with each other at the ball, lovingly and generously twirling their pasts and futures together.

–5–

Makeover Misdemeanours

Magazines and Monstrous Celebrities

> it will never be known what the next monster will look like; nor will it be possible to guess where it will come from.
>
> Rosi Braidotti, 'Signs of Wonder and Traces of Doubt'

Monsters have a special place in the cosmetic surgery world. The celebrities I analyse in this chapter have been identified in popular magazines as grotesque or monstrous. They are famous women who have 'gone too far', are seen as ageing *disgracefully* or using cosmetic surgery improperly. They occupy complex roles within makeover culture. They are the special agents of an abject, hybrid otherness that cosmetic surgery – as an emerging technology – requires to make itself legitimate. They are necessary for the practice's integration and normalisation; they are the 'unnatural' measuring sticks against which the 'new natural' can be measured, accepted and condoned. Through them I examine the regulation, definition and policing of the normal and the monstrous within makeover culture. I suggest that makeover culture holds special regard for abjection and hybridity, two important characteristics of monstrosity. I show how 'normal' individuals must be both abject and hybrid in order to perform cosmetic surgery correctly. Makeover culture stringently regulates these acceptable modes of abjection and hybridity; I call them 'proper' abjection and 'proper' hybridity. I offer brief explanations of monstrosity, abjection and hybridity, and then explain 'proper' or 'discrete' abjection and hybridity. I then examine three 'indiscretions' performed by celebrities – indiscretions that violate the rules of proper abjection and hybridity – in order to explain why those individuals are deemed monstrous and how their monstrosity works to support makeover culture.

Monstrosity, Abjection and Hybridity

The definition of monstrous at any moment is determined by countless social and historical factors: 'monstrous' is not an immutable category but rather subject to constant reinterpretation. Many theorists working with the term start with the unknowability of the monster. Philosopher Rosi Braidotti describes it as 'the most irrational non-object ... slippery enough to make the Encyclopaedists nervous...'

(1996: 150) while cultural theorist Margrit Shildrick explodes its meaning to include 'any being who traverses the liminal spaces that evade classification' (2002: 5). Actor-network theorist Steven D. Brown argues that monsters are 'category errors' (1999: 147) because they fail to fit properly into safely anchored domains. Mary Russo suggests that listing stereotypes is a useful, if flawed, way to convey meaning. Her taxonomy gives an indication of what is meant by monstrous without trying to narrow it down: listing is a way of naming the monstrous while leaving room for additions. 'Naming represents a particularly vivid way of recalling the persistence of those constrained codings of the body in Western culture which are associated with the grotesque: the Medusa, the Bearded Woman, the Fat Lady, the Tattooed Woman, the Unruly Woman, the Hottentot Venus, the Starving Woman, the Dwarf.' (Russo, 1994: 14)

While accepting that the monstrous is by definition mutable and unknowable, it does have two enduring broad characteristics: abjection and hybridity. Abjection in relation to bodies happens when boundaries are opened or violated. Mary Douglas argues in her foundational symbolic anthropological work *Purity and Danger* (1979) that: '*Any structure of ideas is vulnerable at its margins. We should expect the orifices of the body to symbolise its specially vulnerable points... Spittle, blood, milk, urine, faeces or tears by simply issuing forth have traversed the boundary of the body. So also have bodily parings, skin, nail and hair clippings, and sweat.*' (1979: 121) And philosopher Elizabeth Grosz summarises that 'the abject is what of the body falls away from it while remaining irreducible to the subject-object and inside/outside oppositions' (1994: 192). The abject may vary according to place and time but it always reminds us of our penetrable or leaky borders, of our uncontainability and our susceptibility to infiltration. Hybridity is closely related to abjection, also dealing with borders, margins, contaminations and (mis)categorisations. While many hybrids are completely acceptable, *monstrous* hybridity refers to objects or subjects that contain juxtapositions or interweavings that are mismatched or incongruous. The hybrids that form between technologies and the human body are often seen as monstrous, especially when the technologies are new. For example, *in vitro* fertilisation, machinic transplants and the *Visible Human Project* have all been characterised as somewhat monstrous (Waldby, 2000; Zylinska, 2002). Cosmetic surgery, also seen as a new technology, is grappling with its status in relation to hybridity – many discourses around cosmetic surgery work with notions of foreign objects in bodies, of 'unnatural' pieces of plastic or silicone merging with 'natural' flesh.

'Proper' Abjection and Hybridity

The monstrous is outside and therefore 'other'. In a discussion of makeover culture it is important to note that it can also be *between*. Russo writes, 'the grotesque body is the open, protruding, extended, secreting body, the body of becoming, process, and change' (1994: 62–3). So as well as defining the 'normal' by being what it is not, the monstrous-grotesque is where 'becoming, process, and change' actually occur. Makeover culture is at its heart about processes of transformation and therefore has an intense relation with monstrosity.

All bodies that undergo cosmetic surgery are abject at some stage, especially during operations and recovery periods. Any body in a process of transformation is abject – sweat, blood and tears are seen by makeover culture as steps on the path towards bodily improvement. In this way, abjection is an important part of the makeover process. But abjection is dangerous. Kristeva describes it as frightening and abhorrent: 'The in-between, the ambiguous, the composite. The traitor, the liar, the criminal with good conscience, the shameless rapist, the killer who claims he is a saviour... Abjection is ... a terror that dissembles, a hatred that smiles ... a friend who stabs you. (Kristeva, 1982 [1974]: 4)

How then, can makeover culture both embrace abjection as a key step on the pathway to self-improvement and restrain its menacing aspects – aspects of mess and uncontainment – that threaten an established order? The problem of abjection is dealt with in makeover culture in two ways: firstly, specific spatial and temporal frames are designated in which the abject is acceptable: the operating room, the period of quiet recovery, 'during' photos as shown on certain cosmetic surgeons' websites and certain mediascapes like *Extreme Makeover*. Importantly, all of these sites privilege before and after, so the 'during' in which the abject occurs is tightly bracketed by images or descriptions of comfortable stasis.

Secondly, makeover culture *projects* monstrous abjection on to certain bodies so that its own version of 'proper' abjection can be normalised. Georges Canguilhem explains in his foundational medical-philosophical work, *On the Normal and the Pathological* (1966, reprinted 1978), that ideas of normality are formed in relation to the establishment and then rejection or attempted elimination of abnormality. He also argues that normality is entirely dependent on its environment and varies in relation to time and space. In a simple but effective example he says: 'with a disability like astigmatism or myopia, one would be normal in an agricultural or a pastoral society but abnormal for sailing or flying' (1978: 118). Similarly, Marilyn Monroe was the goddess of her time yet her body would be unacceptable on today's red carpets – she might even be listed in the 'They Need Lipo' section of *Awful Plastic Surgery*. 'Normality' is contingent on place and time. We are currently witnessing a violent process of negotiation about what is normal in the makeover environment, played out in popular magazine texts. These magazines are arenas where cosmetic surgery, in trying to establish itself as normal, reacts aggressively towards what it wants to eject: what it endeavours to make monstrous. The negotiation of the normal in these contexts relies on a tug between different ideological systems; as I have shown in previous chapters, it is by being inclusive of inherent contradictions that a paradigm like makeover culture draws its strength. The celebrities discussed in this chapter play a vital part in makeover culture's containment of abjection: they are its 'over-participants', spectacular cosmetic surgery monsters who are ridiculed, set apart and determined as 'not us'. They represent abject monstrosity because their intense relationships with cosmetic surgery, viciously scrutinised by the media, have rendered their bodies metaphorically always-open and uncontainable.

All bodies in makeover occupy categories of hybridity. Indeed, with its ceaseless renovation and supplementation of the self, makeover culture is largely about performing 'proper hybridity'. 'Expressing oneself' through clothing or home decorating, as we are exhorted to do by television makeover programmes, is a form of hybridity – an augmentation of the self with objects. Less metaphorically, cosmetic surgery creates hybridity by inserting substances like plastic, silicone and saline into the body. This hybridity is considered 'proper' so long as it adheres to certain rules of discretion. *Awful Plastic Surgery* is a good example of when and how cosmetic surgery hybridity is praised and when it is vilified. As I explained in Chapter 1, the site delineates strongly between appropriate and inappropriate cosmetic surgery, with sections like 'Ooops, I Messed Up My Face' and 'Scary Celebrities', which feature 'awful' cosmetic surgery where hybrid monstrosity is spectacularised. However, the site's 'Good Plastic Surgery' section congratulates celebrities for getting their hybridity right, for example: 'Natalie Imbruglia went from no boobs to cute saline ones. They look mighty nice!' and 'Madonna is the queen of good plastic surgery. She had her nose slimmed in the early 90s.' The site's definition of 'good' cosmetic surgery is summed up in relation to singer Jennifer Lopez's supposed nose job and lip reduction, neither of which I can even discern: 'she's an example of good plastic surgery, because the changes are not extremely noticeable and [they] enhance her looks'.

Cosmetic surgery's hybrid monstrosity designates those who fuse together and display odd or unacceptable combinations. For example, the sculpture/human juxtaposition that is Jocelyn Wildenstein's face is an obvious mix of organic and manufactured elements, most notably a large chin implant. Similarly, the old/young and sexy/abhorrent confusions that happen around ageing celebrities like Farrah Fawcett and Cher are partly due to displays of 'unseemly' hybridity. In makeover culture celebrities who deliberately exhibit or even flaunt their hybridity are as monstrous as Kristeva's 'killer who claims he is a saviour'. Prosthesis is an important part of hybridity because it can emphasise abjection or lack, calling into question the integrity of the body. Cultural theorist Joanna Zylinska writes, 'A prosthetic extension reveals a lack in the corpus to which it is attached, the very need for, or even a possibility of, such as attachment of extension indicating an original incompleteness, or perhaps unboundedness, of the self' (2002: 215). Cosmetic surgery procedures that involve augmentations or implants make this clear:

> Courtney Love is back on the rampage. Before she was arrested this week, she went to Wendy's where she flashed patrons … her implants have become so hard that they have made ripples in her skin. All together now, let's yell 'Ew, yuck, Courtney'. Hopefully,

the courts will unfreeze her bank account so that she can get new implants. Her Franken-tits are scary. (*Awful Plastic Surgery*)

The monstrosity identified in this text is not to do with having implants but rather with the fact that Love (rock-star, actor and Kurt Cobain's widow) has drawn attention to them: the ripples in her skin emphasise that prosthetics are present and belie an illusion of 'naturalness'. Smooth, demure implants are 'mighty nice' but those that call attention to themselves become 'Franken-tits'. Cosmetic surgery's continued growth relies on hybridity being normalised – on the cultural and bodily 'acceptance' of foreign objects – but makeover culture demands that those foreign objects be incorporated as parts of the self and 'blend in'. Bodies like Love's, which either actively or inadvertently display their prosthetics, extend the moment of aug-mentation beyond its temporal and spatial boundaries. By showing scars or lumps the illusion of seamlessness is destroyed and the strict temporal and spatial bound-aries designated for monstrosity inside makeover culture are violated.

Celebrities and Two-Faced Texts

When connected to celebrities, cosmetic surgery is glamorised, normalised and demonised. It is alternately presented as the weird obsession of another breed, extraordinary and not an option for the average person, or as a glamorous commodity to be aimed for, something desirable. David Marshall's cultural study of what he calls the contemporary celebrity system suggests that celebrities are 'marketable commodities' (1997: x). He shows how contradictions work together inside this system:

> In one sense, the celebrity represents success and achievement in the social world... In another sense, the celebrity is viewed in the most antipathetic manner. The sign of the celebrity is ridiculed and derided because it represents the centre of false value... The celebrity sign effectively contains this tension between authentic and false cultural value (1997: x–xi).

Here is another example of ideological complexity – contradictions working in the service of a cultural dominant – in this instance ridicule/admiration and mundanity/otherworldliness highlight and create the status of the celebrity. These ambiguities and tensions are particularly played out via the powerful scrutiny to which bodies of female celebrities are subjected. Marshall writes that 'the intense focus on the body and its reformulation is central to the construction of the female star. The body itself becomes the expression of and the control of the public personality' (1997: 266–7). Virginia Blum argues that there is a deep relation between celebrity culture and cosmetic surgery and that the star system has in fact created a beauty norm that in turn gives rise to widespread adoption of cosmetic surgery:

Of course, stardom can happen only in the context of a large audience that converges in the celebration of the iconic actor. Consider how necessary this institutionalisation of star culture has been to the creation of a culture of cosmetic surgery. In order for cosmetic surgery to be appealing, not to mention a viable professional solution, enough of us have to agree on standards of beauty ... the star is both the standard and an instrument of standardisation. (Blum, 2003: 55)

This is unsubtly manifest in *I Want a Famous Face*, a US reality TV show styled similarly to *Extreme Makeover* but featuring individuals who want to look more like certain celebrities, usually for the sake of furthering their careers. This programme is the example par excellence of the intertwining of the film and television industries with the 'morphing industries' of cosmetic surgery. Twin teenagers want to look like Brad Pitt to become models and then actors (they begin acting lessons after the cosmetic surgery); a *Playboy* model wants to look like Pamela Anderson and a plus-size model wants to look more like British actor Kate Winslet. The programme demonstrates that stars create universal standards of beauty that are held up as ideals: if your beauty doesn't mimic or at least refer to the two-dimensional image of a star in print or on screen, then it isn't proper beauty. The flip side to this is that, while ordinary people may have cosmetic surgery to look like celebrities, celebrities must have cosmetic surgery in order to keep looking like their on-screen selves. Comedienne Joan Rivers, who said 'I wish I had a twin, so I could know what I'd look like without plastic surgery' uses her cosmetic surgery experiences as material for her routines (http://www.brainyquote.com/quotes/authors/j/joan_rivers.html). Others share the pressure they feel to have cosmetic surgery: 'I work in an industry where if you don't get a little nip and tuck, a lady of my age is going to end up playing Katie Holmes's great-grandmother in the Dawson's Creek reunion. I'm never going to be Halle Berry, but I want to look as good as I can.' (Kathy Griffin aged 42, 14 July 2003, *People Magazine*)

Some stars 'fail' in their cosmetic surgery attempts. No longer able to live up to the 'star standard' they smash down to earth. Farrah Fawcett, former 'golden girl' of the 1970s' television programme *Charlie's Angels*, was referred to on the cover of the Australian *New Idea* magazine (28 February 2004) as a 'Fallen Angel' because of her cosmetic surgery (see Figure 9). What is the point of such vilification, and why is some cosmetic surgery described as 'awful' while some is praised?

Relations between monstrousness and normal are emphasised by Susan Bordo, who points out that in a society preoccupied with body size bulimics and anorexics are likely to be displayed in lurid and grotesque detail: 'such presentations encourage a "side show" experience of the relationship between the ("normal") audience and those sick individuals on view ("the freaks")' (1990: 85). As I stated above, weight-loss dieting is only 'normal' when held up against a monstrous 'other' like anorexia. I suggest that a parallel normal/pathological dichotomy is set up in the world of cosmetic surgery: as it becomes mainstream and, as one magazine writer puts it

Figure 9 Cover of Australian *New Idea*, 28 February 2004

'more and more of us are making a decision once reserved for the rich and famous' (Tulloch, 2004: 137), those who 'overdo' cosmetic surgery in the same way that anorexics and bulimics 'overdo' dieting are displayed as freaks. And like the ideal glamorous body size, which exists in a tiny margin close to severely underweight in medical terms, the ideal surgicalised aesthetic occupies a precise point on a vast spectrum of possible cosmetic surgery looks. A certain exact range of results is carved out and negotiated as 'normal'.

> Preparation for the Oscars begins at Christmas, with enough stars begging for appointments with their plastic surgeons for it to be referred to as the plastic surgery season ... I ... removes brow wrinkles, collagen ... plumps up lips, and new this year are FotoFacials – intense pulsed light therapy used to tighten the skin. (Broadbent, 2002: 27)

> On the set of *Monster-In-Law*, Jane wowed all with her new, stretched head. Looking more like a woman in her 30s, Jane's face was a far cry from what she sported at the Golden Globes in January. 'Jane looks amazing', says a cast member. (Lang, 2004: 16)

Stars are often characterised as deranged and hyper-vain, 'begging' their surgeons for treatment. Cosmetic surgery results are criticised but also implicitly praised in this sort of journalism: Broadbent, quoted above, suggests that cosmetic surgery is a desperate measure but chooses to describe Botox® as able to remove wrinkles rather than as, say, 'freezing the face', which is another popular way to describe its effects. And she writes that collagen only 'plumps up lips' without mentioning syringes, allergic reactions or numbness. Lang, writing for the Australian *Woman's Day*, makes Jane Fonda monstrous by saying she has a 'stretched head' but simultaneously describes her look as 'amazing', usually a compliment. Suzanne Fraser neatly characterises the tone of such articles as one of 'mild titillation, where the reader is invited to wonder at the strange, sometimes sad and often extravagant cosmetic surgery experiences of famous people. Such pieces can express a range of emotions from curiosity to horror, pity or admiration at once.' (2003: 62)

Her reading accepts a distance between subjects and readers of such writing where one world voyeuristically reads about the inhabitants of another. But I suggest that there is something deeper going on here. The double-edged approach of much writing about cosmetic surgery indicates cosmetic surgery's cultural situation in the early twenty-first century, which is between normal and monstrous practice; between beautiful and grotesque results. The ideological complexity of these internally contradictory texts creates a dynamic interplay that continually recasts and redefines monstrosity and normality in relation to each other. Canguilhem reflects that 'the normal is not a static or peaceful, but a dynamic concept' (1978: 146), and that the normal is established 'by devaluing everything that the reference to it prohibits from being considered normal...' (1978: 147). So the abnormal does not come about separately from the normal but rather it is that which has been ejected and excluded from the normal: 'that which diverges from the preferable in a given area of evaluation is not the indifferent but the repulsive or more exactly, the repulsed, the detestable' (Canguilhem, 1978: 147). Monstrosity – 'the repulsed, the detestable' – becomes a preoccupation during periods of intense cultural change precisely because the normal is negotiated through it.

The cultural and social dangers in having cosmetic surgery, in terms of being abject- or hybrid-monstrous are especially prevalent for women in the public sphere. Mary Russo recalls gleaning as a child that 'making a spectacle out of oneself seemed a specifically feminine danger' (1994: 53). Her broad analysis of the dangers of being caught in the public eye resonate and parallel the dangers that I identify for women, celebrities in particular, when doing cosmetic surgery: 'these women had done something wrong, had stepped, as it were, into the limelight out of turn – too young or too old, too early or too late – and yet anyone, any woman, could make a spectacle out of herself if she was not careful.' (Russo, 1994: 53)

The unbounded arena of cosmetic surgery has variable borders of acceptability: being able to gauge when to start and when to stop the procedures or 'maintenance' is a vital part of the success of the project. Individuals who are deemed to have had 'too much too often' or 'too much for too long' are likely to be ridiculed by the media, their cosmetic surgery procedures outweighing any other news about them. Celebrities and indeed all women, as I showed in Chapter 4, tread a fine line between losing their status because they are 'old' and losing their status because they are 'old trying to be young'. Conversely, some women become celebrities merely by virtue of their cosmetic surgery; who would know of Jocelyn Wildenstein or Jordan if not for their spectacular cosmetic surgery as reported in popular magazines and tabloids?

Cosmetic Surgery Disasters

Articles found in popular women's magazines about monstrous cosmetic surgery come under headlines like 'Celebrity Plastic Surgery Disasters' and expose stars who have 'gone too far' – 'when some stars go too far in their quest to look prettier and younger, the results are shocking' (Renshaw, 2002: 17). The 'disasters' generally constitute overstepping boundaries in three broad areas:

- age-appropriateness;
- presentations of correct femininity and gender; and
- what might be called the blind embrace of a perverse aesthetic.

These three categories of indiscretion are extensive and overlapping but for my purposes here it is useful to delineate them. In the following three sections I address the ways in which cosmetic surgery is represented as being done wrong, and consequently how its recipients are shown as monstrous. In the 'age-appropriateness section' I draw on Mary Russo's theorisations of the grotesque, particularly her engagements with Mikhail Bakhtin's 'senile, laughing hags' in order to discuss representations of the ageing celebrities Cher and Farrah Fawcett. In the 'femininity-done-wrong' section I deploy Joan Riviere's psychoanalytic articulations about a mask of femininity in order to engage with representations of celebrities – in this case Meg Ryan and Pamela Anderson – who respectively perform their femininity 'right' and 'wrong'. 'Perverse aesthetics' are examined, again mobilising Russo's notions of the grotesque, via Jocelyn Wildenstein.

Indiscretion One: Ageing Disgracefully

The cover of the January 2002 Australian magazine *NW* featured a striking extreme close-up photo of Cher. Inside were ten pages devoted to cosmetic surgery. The cover photo closely frames Cher's heavily powdered face: it looks stretched out but heavily wrinkled around the eyes; her hooded eyelids are bulbous and glittering with purple eye shadow (Figure 10). Headlines around the picture yell 'Plastic Surgery Disasters' and promise 'Shocking New Pics'. A quote placed below Cher's chin between postage-stamp sized photos of Anna Nicole Smith, the *Playboy* model who married a geriatric billionaire and was known for her extensive cosmetic surgery before her death in 2007, and Jocelyn Wildenstein, a New York socialite famous for her feline-styled cosmetic surgery states 'They're all freaks'.

Cher and Farrah Fawcett are regulars in this style of reporting. While Cher still elicits praise for her music and tours and is occasionally touted as being in excellent shape for her age, Fawcett is primarily a figure of ridicule. The tone is often malicious. Cher is compared to cheap cuts of meat: 'the list of body parts she has tinkered with reads like an economy sausage – they include her nose, teeth, cheeks, stomach, buttocks and navel' (Renshaw, 2002: 16). The list of negative descriptors is almost endless, including adjectives like excessive, distorted, unnatural and weird. But her main crime seems to be that despite all her cosmetic surgery, she is now looking 'old'. An 'eyewitness' to the filming of one of her video clips told *NW* that 'when you got up close, you could see the ravages of time under the special lavender-coloured foundation she had on'. The *NW* article reveals that Cher has been 'forced to turn to lighting trickery and heavy makeup to conceal her true appearance' (Renshaw, 2002: 16). She is shown as dishonest and desperate – just like the evil fairy in *The Sleeping Beauty* and the wicked stepmother in *Snow-White* she must resort to 'trickery' to appear young enough to be in her own video.

Fawcett is another regular in articles about monstrous cosmetic surgery:

> she turned up looking totally unlike her former self, having had her nose shockingly re-sculpted to reveal huge nostrils. Her previously modest pout had been transformed into

Figure 10 Cover of Australian *NW*, 21 January 2002

a gloss red 'trout pout', and her eyelids appeared to have been pinned back to such a degree that she almost looked like an alien. (Bromley and Vokes-Dudgeon, 2004: 4)

To theorise these representations of aged monstrosity I am deploying Mary Russo's reading of the work of Mikhail Bakhtin, particularly her writing around his analyses of the 'senile, pregnant hag' (Russo, 1994: 1). Bakhtin describes some ancient terracotta figurines found in Kerch, in The Ukraine. They are statuettes of women who are aged but pregnant, dying but laughing: 'There is nothing completed, nothing calm and stable in the bodies of these old hags. They combine a senile, decaying and deformed flesh with the flesh of new life, conceived but as yet unformed... Moreover, the old hags are laughing.' (Bakhtin quoted in Russo, 1994: 63) Russo insists that the figurines are more than embodiments of the grotesque, and much more than examples of the inverse of the 'monumental, static, closed and sleek' ideal Classical body. They are 'loaded with all of the connotations of fear and loathing around the biological processes of reproduction and of aging' (1994: 63). She adopts the figurines to write about how maternal bodies overlap boundaries and generally disrupt 'the political economy of the sign as it is produced in dominant discourse' (1994: 67). I draw upon them here in a similar way, to look at how 'overdone' cosmetic surgery bodies also disturb order, straddle borders and create disquiet.

The confronting and contradictory Kerch figurines compare well with common representations of the bodies of Cher and Fawcett. Cher and Fawcett have youthful visages but are chronologically beyond middle age – the parallels between them and the Kerch figurines lie in the juxtapositions inherent in their embodiments, in the ways they intertwine traditional opposites: age and beauty, fertility and decrepitude.

The Kerch statuettes embody oppositions: they are rotting and disfigured on the outside but produce and hold life within. The surgically modified woman is an aesthetic inversion of the laughing and senile pregnant hag: Cher and Fawcett are shown to be smooth and 'preserved' on the surface but are old – chronologically postmenopausal – and barren on the inside. In both ancient and contemporary texts there is a fascination with juxtapositions: decay versus creation, surface versus interiority. Cher and Fawcett are Kerch figurines turned inside out, the idea of an inappropriately-grasped youth playing on their skins instead of in their wombs. They are makeover culture's 'laughing, senile hags' who exemplify disharmony and incongruity and embody 'inappropriate' extremes. They threaten order with their obvious hybridity.

Joanna Freuh describes the ageing female body as 'uncharted territory, outside cultural maps of conventional femininity...' (1996: 82). As I showed in Chapter 4, this is a body that has an extremely small and prohibitive space in contemporary Western culture. One way to deal with being relegated to this 'uncharted territory' is to have cosmetic surgery: this is something that many celebrity women do. But those who get it 'wrong', like Cher and Fawcett, enter a different kind of uncharted territory. Just as the unaltered ageing feminine body is often displayed as monstrous, so is the body that has been altered 'too much'. Fawcett's lopsided nostrils and peaked eyes may be aesthetically confronting but part of the fear we feel when looking at her it is because she has taken action, however misguided, against being relegated to the outskirts. Articles such as 'Celebrity Plastic Surgery Disasters' demonise this active, unconventional femininity. 'Insiders believe Farrah, 54, has recently acquired a new Michael-Jackson style nose, which – as our picture shows – has tipped her over the edge from well-preserved to plain weird. Farrah has always refused to grow old gracefully. In 1995 she posed for *Playboy* and smeared herself in mud for a nude video.' (Renshaw, 2002: 18) By comparing Fawcett to Michael Jackson via her rhinoplasty, Renshaw is making more than an aesthetic observation, since to my eyes Fawcett's nose doesn't even look like Jackson's. Jackson is often depicted as being of dubious morals, gender and sexuality. Thus to be metaphorically burdened with his nose Fawcett is being marked as strange and somewhat abhorrent. Further, she is shown through this one damning comment to be of dubious gender: she has embraced the mask of femininity so entirely that her 'real' gender is called into doubt.

Noeleen O'Beirne says wryly, in an article that discusses her own personal and theoretical dealings with ageing, 'it would appear that a feminine continuum does not exist for women who survive into old age' (1999: 111). While nude videos and *Playboy* shoots are nothing unusual for Hollywood starlets, for Fawcett to partake of such overtly sexual and feminine acts at fifty is unacceptable to many popular magazine journalists and their readers. Her age overrides her femininity and her sexuality: a seriously overt performance of either of them leads to ridicule, and she is subjected to it here by being accused of the worst cosmetic surgery crime imaginable: having Michael Jackson's nose.

For Margrit Shildrick, ambiguity is what defines the monstrous body as fascinating and disturbing: 'it is not that the monster represents the threat *of* difference, but that it threatens to interrupt difference – at least in its binary form – so that the comfortable otherness that secures the selfsame is lost' (2002: 303). Fawcett's cosmetic surgery interrupts the difference between those 'successfully' growing old in makeover culture with the help of body-disciplining procedures like cosmetic surgery, and those who are failing at the performance of acceptable ageing by simply 'letting themselves go'. She has seemingly followed all the correct paths but has ended up looking 'wrong'. Her results now blur boundaries and interrupt difference and she becomes monstrous, embodying both horror and fascination. 'Her stunning looks as one of the Charlie's Angels captivated a generation of men... But Farrah Fawcett is looking far from angelic these days. Instead, one trip to the plastic surgeon too many has left the '70s sex bomb looking decidedly odd.' (Renshaw, 2002: 16) It only took Fawcett 'one trip too many' to overstep the boundary between beauty and horror: this exemplifies the arbitrariness of these boundaries and also the harsh punishments awaiting those who overstep them.

Indiscretion Two: the Lopsided Mask

While figures like Cher and Fawcett are vilified for their cosmetic surgery, there are others whose cosmetic surgeries evoke ambiguous reactions: they are alternately represented as beautiful and monstrous. With them it is as if popular magazine discourse can't make up its mind: are they monstrous or not? Have they had inappropriate cosmetic surgery or not? Are they beautiful? At the time of writing Dannii Minogue is being equally and alternately depicted as having successful and unsuccessful cosmetic surgery, as are Roseanne Barr, Meg Ryan, Sharon Osbourne and Pamela Anderson. I suggest that the level of vitriol against these uncertain stars is inversely proportional to the status of their careers, so a well-received movie might provide a respite from being judged surgically monstrous. The oscillation in discourse surrounding them shows that they inhabit a highly contested zone where the risk of being monstrous is everywhere.

In its tenth anniversary issue (March 2002) the magazine *Who Weekly* featured a mock board game based on the past ten years of Pamela Anderson's life. The game is headed 'If it's not her breasts, it's her boyfriends. Pamela Anderson's now you see 'em, now you don't decade left us stuck between Kid Rock and a hard place' (*Who Weekly*, 2002: 110). The game, in snakes and ladders style, traces Anderson's rise from *Playboy* centrefold in 1992 through to her engagement to rock musician Kid Rock in 2002 via one marriage, two children, a divorce, a few boyfriends, a successful television career and one movie flop. While the love life is not strikingly different from many women's, what makes Anderson eminently burlesque and easy to parody is her breasts. She had her famous implants removed in 2000 because of worries about silicone leakage, but then decided on bigger saline augmentations in 2001. 'Now you see 'em, now you don't' suggests that vacillating between implants is unacceptable. The in–out–in breast augmentations are characterised as monstrous because the hybridity here is unstable. Their removability highlights the body as abject: open and penetrable. It is shown as a container lacking stern definition, as quintessentially monstrous. These breasts are also threatening because they highlight the presence of, and the ability to remove, the mask of femininity.

Joan Riviere wrote in her foundational article 'Womanliness as Masquerade' (1986, first published 1929) that 'women who wish for masculinity may put on a mask of womanliness to avert anxiety and the retribution feared by men' (1986: 35). 'Masculinity' refers to the privileges and stimulations that came with being male and were unavailable to most women in the early twentieth century. Riviere focuses on 'a particular type of intellectual woman' – the equivalent of our contemporary mythological 'superwoman' – who has a successful career wherein she competes with or outshines men, is a superb housewife and mother whilst also being 'properly feminine' in her appearance and demeanour. This notion of being 'properly feminine' is of interest here.

Riviere's analysis has been highly influential for many feminist scholars (Doane, 1982; Irigaray, 1985) and has had varied interpretations. My reading of it is that it is mainly about self-protection: women who desire powers associated with masculinity and who work towards having them, but who believe (usually accurately) that they will be punished for taking what is not 'rightfully' theirs, assume the mask (shown via 'excessive' signs of femininity) as a measure against retribution. Riviere theorises that womanly masquerades are what make the achievements of women palatable to men: without them most women would not only fail to qualify for the recognition they deserve but would also be punished for their 'masculine' achievements. Certainly, women who have achieved high status in contemporary society have not done so without huge effort, compromises and a series of never-ending skilled enactments of various gender roles. Judith Butler (1990) has shown that these are not usually calculated performances but rather culturally taught and conditioned, and largely unconscious. The correct performance of femininity is vital for most women, and I think more so for those in the public eye, something Julia Baird has recently demonstrated in relation to Australian women politicians (2004). It is also amply shown in the figure of Margaret Thatcher with her trademark handbag, a quintessential feminine marker.

The mask of femininity calls into question ideas of essential or 'natural' femininity. It suggests that if it is possible to stage femininity, then it is also possible to un-stage it. Russo says, 'to put on femininity with a vengeance suggests the power of taking it off' (1994: 70). Here then is the reason that Anderson's small–big–small–bigger breasts are unacceptable: they demonstrate that femininity is unstable. Riviere's work complicates this, suggesting that the masquerade is not an act per se because it cannot be distinguished from a women's 'true self': 'The reader may now ask how I define womanliness or where I draw the line between genuine womanliness and the "masquerade". My suggestion is not, however, that there is any such difference; whether radical or superficial, they are the same thing.' (1986: 38)

This is one of the central concerns of Steven Heath's article 'Joan Riviere and the Masquerade', written fifty-seven years later. With great sensitivity Heath guesses that Riviere herself was one of those remarkably uncategorisable and problematic intellectual women whom she studied. He implies that her article was autobiographical, or that it at least works through the topography of Riviere's own position in relation to her male psychoanalyst colleagues (one was Sigmund Freud). For Heath, the crux is the apparent travesty of a mask that is all there is, a masquerade that hides nothing: 'the masquerade says that the woman exists at the same time that, as masquerade, it says she does not' (1986: 49). He explains this in terms of femininity being seen as *not masculinity*, and therefore being fundamentally about dissimulation: 'In the masquerade the woman mimics an authentic – genuine – womanliness but then authentic womanliness is such a mimicry, is the masquerade ("they are the same thing"); to be a woman is to dissimulate a fundamental masculinity, femininity is that dissimulation.' (1986: 49) Russo puts this idea succinctly: 'femininity is a mask which masks nonidentity' (Russo, 1994: 69). If womanliness *itself* is a masquerade, if there is nothing else, then mimicry such as cosmetic surgery could be seen to be of little consequence. Lifetimes of efforts, suppressions and performances – all the continuous rituals observed in the enactments of femininity – might easily make a 'little nip'n'tuck' seem an insignificant step in an ongoing process of self-protection tied in with self-definition. But for Heath these tensions create 'a tourniquet of reassurance and disturbance' (1986: 54). The masquerade provides reassurance as it preserves life and protects from danger, like a tourniquet, but causes harm if it is applied with less than exact pressure. Ideally, the mask facilitates equilibrium, a balancing act between risk and security that can so easily be performed wrongly. In order to serve its purpose the mask must be strong and stable but not obvious as performance. The Thatcher handbag is again a perfect example – she got it 'right'. If the mask brings attention to itself it will suddenly be hybrid-monstrous, and/or abject-monstrous, prosthetic, revealing a lack in its host. Grotesque 'outings' of celebrities like Cher and Farrah Fawcett show that they perform femininity obviously. Their masks, via cosmetic surgery, have tilted and become visible – they don't quite fit any more. Their cosmetic surgeries don't encourage a suspension of disbelief but rather bring attention to the masquerade. Anderson is ridiculed in the same way for bringing attention to her mask: for wearing it with a vengeance but more importantly for showing that it is removable.

For all the violent 'outing' around falling stars like Fawcett, whose every procedure is viciously scrutinised, there is a corresponding eerie silence around the cosmetic surgery of celebrities who still enjoy A-list status. Often it seems that journalists and audiences are willing to collaborate in the fantasy of wrinkles just disappearing overnight with the help of a healthy diet or a new-found interest in yoga or Pilates. An interview with Meg Ryan in the same edition of a *Marie Claire* edition that featured a highly critical report on Chinese women having their legs surgically lengthened[1] politely neglected to mention her cosmetic surgery. 'Though she turned 40 last November, the former high-school homecoming queen appears 10 years younger in person. Up close, there's not a discernible blemish or crease on her face...' (Gold, 2002: 84). The interview shows complicity between interviewer and interviewee in what is *not* said:

> You look incredible – even better in person. But when you stare at yourself in the mirror, is there anything you'd change?
>> *I wish my legs were longer. I wish my feet were smaller. I wish my hair was longer.*
> Do you worry about getting wrinkles?
>> *What are my choices? Not to get older? I'm all right with it. I'm really all right with the whole shebang. I like seeing the life on people's faces and in their eyes.* (Gold, 2002: 86)

For the moments when stars can do no wrong, media participate in the collective endeavour of maintaining the mask of femininity. In 2002 Ryan's mask was still utterly tied up with her acceptable femininity and her status as star. Accordingly, her cosmetic surgery went unmentioned. Such support is utterly conditional and only extends – usually for a short period – to those who manage to juggle appropriate femininity, ageing and having cosmetic surgery. So the mask of femininity is related to monstrosity and cosmetic surgery in various ways. It will be 'exposed' as hybrid-monstrous and phoney if deemed age-inappropriate, as in the case of Fawcett and Cher; it may be silently supported if connected to a powerful woman or looks like 'good work', and it will be abject-monstrous if it calls attention to itself by being unstable, as in the case of Anderson's breasts.

Indiscretion Three: Beautiful Aliens

Russo explains how the concept of the grotesque can embody the 'grotto-esque' style of art that emerged 'only in relation to the norms which it exceeded' (1994: 3). The Classical style that preceded it was linked to what was seen as the natural order, exemplifying harmony and 'true' representation. Grotesque art was the nemesis of the Classical, overrunning margins and creating hybrids: 'combining vegetation and animal and human body parts in intricate, intermingled, and fantastical designs' (Russo, 1994: 3). The new style created fury in Classical champions: 'if we can draw the human head perfectly, and are masters of its expression and its beauty, we have no business to cut it off, and hang it up by the hair at the end of a garland' (Ruskin quoted in Russo, 1994: 5).

Jocelyn Wildenstein was a low-profile New York socialite before she became internationally infamous during an acrimonious divorce in 1999 from her billionaire art dealer husband. He said she had a 'bizarre proclivity to have continuing plastic surgery, hair transplants and tattooing, which has submitted us to public ridicule' (Alec Wildenstein quoted in Delves Broughton, 1999). In the style of a true makeover culture citizen she simply retorted that cosmetic surgery was part of her 'health regime'.

Wildenstein's face, featured here on a magazine cover (Figure 11), appears too 'moulded' for reality. None of her features are overly strange in themselves: an aquiline nose, almond-shaped eyes, high cheekbones, defined, thick lips and a strong chin. But together they form an aesthetic that is distanced from the mainstream. Wildenstein looks like a 'beautiful' alien, and apparently she is 'ecstatic with her work. She feels beautiful. She looks in the mirror and she loves what she sees. She got exactly what she wanted' (Renshaw, 2002: 17). And this is what really disturbs and enrages some people: that she is happy in her monstrosity (some find her attractive: she has no shortage of lovers). Wildenstein is demonised largely because she is *pleased* with results that are considered ugly by the mainstream: it is one crime to have too much and 'wrong' cosmetic surgery, but a worse one to be happy about it.

Figure 11 Cover of Australian *NW*, 7 November 2005

The painter Zeuxis took on the task of painting Helen of Troy, but could find no model beautiful enough. The solution was to use many different women as models, choosing the most beautiful features of each to create an idealised whole. Thus the mythical beauty of Helen was preserved – no single living woman could do her justice. Paradoxically, while Helen's beauty was reinforced as utterly otherworldly it was also shown to be easily re-composed or mimicked from an assortment of disparate pieces. So idealised beauty is both unattainable and eminently constructible. The undertones of monstrosity are strong here: monsters are often made from a collection of fragments. Our most famous and loved monster, Frankenstein's experiment, the flip side to the lovely Helen, is constructed from the body parts of corpses which were nevertheless selected for their beauty: 'His limbs were in proportion, and I had selected his features as beautiful. Beautiful! Great God! ... now that I had finished, the beauty of the dream vanished, and breathless horror and disgust filled my heart' (Shelley, 1985, first published 1818: 101). The monster, created by a scientist from corpse parts and electricity, is entirely hybrid: he remains in parts and is never 'whole' and hence is never human, never accepted. The cosmetic surgery recipient can suffer a similar fate via media representation: Frankensteinian analogies imply that she is less than human, wholly created by science, a messed-up mix of elements and technologies.

Fragmentation works both for and against ideas of beauty. The cosmetic surgery 'experts' routinely consulted by journalists (they may be beauticians, 'Hollywood insiders' or surgeons) will uniformly praise one celebrity's nose, arms, lips or skin, separating that part from the rest of the body. Such body parts almost have their own lives – cosmetic surgery recipients tell surgeons 'I want Halle Berry's lips' – but like good children they return home often enough to reconnect and enhance the body from which they sprouted. A good example is Nicole Kidman's feted translucent skin, probably the result of intensive peels to remove freckles, and her tiny sculpted nose, both of which are regularly isolated and described as excellent. They add to her stature. However, when too many body parts become independent they are deemed too disparate: wayward children who no longer lend harmony or respect to their host body. Jocelyn Wildenstein's features do this: her cheeks, her eyes, her forehead and her lips are all striking enough to be deemed untoward. When combined they form a grotesquery that means their host can only be deemed, at best, perversely beautiful.

The cosmetic surgery recipient, made up of organic and non-organic elements, is a collaged hybrid. She must massage a place for herself within the realm of the beautiful and avoid the grotesque/monstrous. Her hybridity is acceptable if she adheres to strict rules to do with femininity and age. But only a couple of misplaced steps – a lopsided nose job, features that don't 'match', a movie flop, even wrong make-up – and she will become grotesque, quickly aligned with Frankenstein's monster rather than Zeuxis' Helen.

Spectacle and Carnival

Bakhtin and Russo argue that the grotesque body is 'first and foremost ... a social body'. In contrast, the freak body or the body-on-show is outside of the social. These two kinds of body can also be characterised by the cultures they thrive within: for Bakhtin the freak body is part of a culture of spectacle, linked to the Enlightenment and Modernity. The grotesque body is part of a culture of carnival, cognisant with the Middle Ages and early modern Europe (Russo, 1994: 61). In medieval times the grotesque was eminently accessible and was not distanced through the tropes of theatre but was performed off stage and in the streets by the general populace. In contrast, Russo identifies freaks such as people in circus sideshows as part of a new bodily canon of the late nineteenth century that both superseded and incorporated the grotesque: the freak may 'appear, reproduce, or simulate the earlier carnivalesque body described and idealized by Bakhtin' but it does so in an entirely different context. Spectacle maintains distance between audience and exhibit while carnival encourages reciprocity: 'audiences and performers were the interchangeable parts of an incomplete but imaginable wholeness' (Russo, 1994: 78).

Bakhtin's descriptions of grotesque bodies in carnival show that they were neither distanced from nor objectified by their observers but were rather participatory figures, blurring boundaries between genders, species and social classes. The idealised carnivalesque body was democratic, exuberant and, importantly, indistinguishable from the social body: 'the grotesque body is ... the body of becoming, process, and change ... the grotesque body is connected to the rest of the world' (Russo, 1994: 62–3). In contrast the freak body is cognisant with spectacle and is definitively *different* from its audience, housed in an abnormal body that is outside of the social. It is part of a set of visuals based on objectification and a demarcation between audience and exhibit. The former carnivalesque symbiosis between performers and participants is cleaved apart, creating an interruption and a gap that allows some people to be voyeurs while others must become spectacles. Russo argues, via Bakhtin, that 'spectacle was the antithesis of the carnivalesque' (Russo, 1994: 38).

I suggest that in makeover culture the distinctions between spectacle and carnival, between grotesque and freaky bodies, are problematic. Spectacle is about making clear delineations between the normal and the monstrous, while carnival deliberately muddies separations. While there are strong elements of spectacle and audience/exhibit segregations in the display of cosmetic surgery monsters, there is also something carnivalesque about the ambivalence that the texts examined in this chapter have towards their subjects. The implicit glorification of cosmetic surgery – the means by which these monsters have fallen from grace – encourages audience members to join in. In this schema, people on *I Want a Famous Face* don't seem so deranged: they are merely participating in a carnivalesque makeover culture where lines between spectacle and audience, celebrity and ordinary person, are all cross-able. Texts like the ones analysed above, where cosmetic surgery is simultaneously normalised and monstrified, co-join audience and exhibit. Flawed stars, despite often being characterised as despicable, suggest a carnivalesque combination of audience and exhibit, a connection that the rules of spectacle prohibit. The representation of certain cosmetic surgery recipients as monstrous contrasts with the positive rhetoric that surrounds the practice in many of its medical and social guises. These oppositions mean that the person who undertakes a surgical re-creation or reclamation of self is brave indeed, for eventually she will probably be damned if she does and damned if she doesn't.

Conclusion

The ideal self in makeover culture is unstable compared to the contained self of modernity, which is 'supposedly fully present to himself, self-sufficient and rational' (Shildrick, 2002: 5). The makeover culture self, although not fickle, is flexible and always-in-progress. This means that in makeover culture the differences between bounded selves and uncontained others are often unclear and therefore highly contested. Monstrosity shares unstable and morphing characteristics with makeover culture's 'always-becoming'. Monstrous figures analysed in this chapter show how close mainstream and liminal cultures are in makeover culture. Makeover's monsters are not non-humans outside of culture but beings who are deeply, inextricably embedded in the heart of the dominant discourse. They are practitioners who do their culture 'too much', people who dwell not on the outskirts but at the core. This chapter has shown how they are constructed as monstrous for specific reasons to do with normalisation. In the cosmetic surgery world an enforced and media-generated monstrosity counterbalances the increase in and acceptance of cosmetic surgery procedures that might otherwise be deemed generally offensive. The subjects who bear this burden are the abject- and hybrid-monstrous others against whom a morphing notion of normality is measured. Chapters 6 and 7 explore a different kind of monstrosity: one that has been designed and sought out by its subjects via cosmetic surgery and one that baffles people even more than that of Jocelyn Wildenstein.

−6−

Sleeping Beauties
Lolo Ferrari and Anaesthesia

Because I could not stop for Death—
He kindly stopped for me—
The Carriage held but just Ourselves—
And Immortality

Emily Dickinson, 'Because I could not stop for Death'

Lolo Ferrari was in Cyprus before we got her ... she'd had so many hands on her that there was a hole between her breasts – so we had to fix her.

A curator describing the Lolo Ferrari waxwork on display at the
Checkpoint Charlie Museum in Berlin, Reuters, 2005

Lolo Ferrari was a French pornographic star. Born Eve Valois, she changed her name to Lolo, which is French slang for breasts and mother's milk (Greer, 2000). In the late 1990s she became known for her appearances on the BBC late night show *Eurotrash* where she was a sometime presenter. She could be relied upon to deliver pithy and risqué soundbites in a sexy French accent along with the spectacle of her massively augmented breasts. Ferrari's chosen bodily configurations were of extreme proportions: after between eighteen and twenty-five cosmetic surgery operations (reports vary), most of them to enlarge her breasts, she became literally mythic, resembling an ancient fertility goddess or the graffiti project of a horny adolescent. Her breast implants were supposedly the biggest in the world, winning her a place in the 1999 *Guinness Book of World Records*. She died early in 2000 at the age of either thirty or thirty eight (again, reports vary) of what was first thought to be an overdose of prescription anti-depressants. Later her husband and manager, Eric Vigne, was arrested and charged with her murder by suffocation (Henley, 2002, 2002a).[1] Whether suicided or murdered, Ferrari is a full-blown tragic figure: the Marilyn Monroe or Kurt Cobain of a world at the nexus of celebrity, cosmetic surgery and pornography. The last series of photos taken of her show that each breast ended up about the size and shape of a basketball: the great silicone sacs had distorted the skin on her petite frame so that it became dark and inflamed, riddled with stretch marks. Her aureoles were the size of her palms. One of the myths around

129

Ferrari is that like 'Elephant Man' John Merrick she had trouble sleeping because of her unusual body. Whether true or not, she was probably in serious muscular and dermatological pain.

There is a compelling kitsch poetry about Ferrari's life. She was utterly self-aware and simultaneously self-destructive, humorous and melodramatic. Like some of the other celebrities of the cosmetic surgery world such as Cindy Jackson, the self-styled Barbie doll and member of Mensa (cindyjackson.com), and the musical genius Michael Jackson (who I discuss in Chapter 7), Ferrari occasionally displayed comic, biting insight into her own created self. She declared: 'I'm like a transvestite... I've created a femininity that's completely artificial', and 'I hate reality – I want to be wholly artificial' (http://www.goodbyemag). Her ability to poetically self-analyse and her philosophical depth make cultural analyses of her life even more compelling. She embodied many contradictions: she was simultaneously victim and successful businesswoman, little girl lost, exploiter and manufacturer of her own assets. Ferrari carried her staged femininity like a shield but also like a weapon of self-annihilation, eventually making it, literally, so heavy that it became unbearable.

Most writing about Ferrari – apart from that found in pornographic magazines – is quick to define her as severely disturbed, even as suffering from body dysmorphia. She is held up as an example of what not to do in articles that purport to give a balanced view of cosmetic surgery. Here I attempt to avoid judging or 'diagnosing' Ferrari and focus instead on two intertwined aspects of her cosmetic surgery. The first is the most obvious: her breasts. I examine them in relation to gigantism, normalised notions of femininity, and as symbols of the transition from girl to woman. The second takes one of her most striking statements – that she loved being under anaesthetic – and analyses it in order to look at how immobility, stasis and death are crucial parts of makeover culture.

Lolo's Enchanted Slumbers

> After surgery, you lie in bed waiting for your day. Instead of obscuring your face, the bandages seem more like a blank field of possibility – of the beauty promised, of the happy ending to the surgical story. (Blum, 2003: 11)

The notion of magical transformation during cosmetic surgery is common: some of my interviewees expressed wonder when describing their awakenings. One said:

> Oh definitely, I was so excited, at the prospect of being a new person, and I know when I woke up and you know I looked down and could see these breasts looking up at me and you know they were strapped and I also had a maternity bra on and I thought it was hilarious to be quite honest that I had these breasts that you could actually see, sitting up in front of you. But from the very first day I was just so thrilled with them, really. (Patricia)

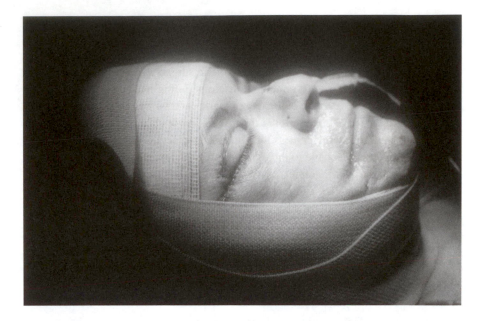

Figure 12 Michelle Del Guercio, 'Bleph Stitches: woman with fresh stitches and bandages after extensive elective surgery' *Plastic Surgery* series (http://www.mdmedicalphotography.com/), photo courtesy the artist

Ferrari took this further, declaring: 'I adore being operated on ... I love the feeling of a general anaesthetic – falling into a black hole and knowing I'm being altered as I sleep' (http://www.goodbyemag). Purporting to love the *actual anaesthetic* is something I did not find expressed elsewhere in the cosmetic surgery world. However, the idea of unconsciousness leading to transformation is not new. It has strong roots in myth, particularly in fairy tales like *The Sleeping Beauty* and *Snow White and the Seven Dwarves* and is nicely illustrated in one of its contemporary forms via Michelle Del Guercio's photograph 'Bleph Stitches: woman with fresh stitches and bandages after extensive elective surgery' (see Figure 12). These tales can be used as portals into an understanding of Ferrari's actions within makeover culture and into some of the mythical promises of cosmetic surgery.

Ferrari's complete openness about her cosmetic surgery, not to mention her striking appearance, made her subversive. She never indulged in the discourse that upholds 'natural looking femininity', an entirely problematic concept itself as I explained in Chapter 1. In this way she is like Orlan – discussed in the next chapter – a French performance artist who has strived valiantly to highlight the *processes* of cosmetic surgery in addition to the results it creates (Ince, 2000; O'Bryan, 2005). Via a series of semi-public operations, Orlan shows the *becoming* of cosmetic surgery: the gory, messy and bruised stages of transformation between before/after. Although

Ferrari's operations were behind closed doors she also embraced this state of constant becoming. There was never a finished result for her; she underwent constant metamorphosis and interminable stasis, having the same operation repeatedly. Orlan and Ferrari, two extreme practitioners of cosmetic surgery, are opposites in relation to agency. Orlan remains determinedly conscious during her operations, directing the proceedings, talking to the audience. In stark contrast Ferrari completely gives herself over to the surgeon, describing the loss of power via general anaesthetic as a joy that she 'adores'. Her happiness with unconsciousness (almost for its own sake) is unseemly and unacceptable to the mainstream, which puts it on a par, in terms of good taste, with her pornographic movie roles. Like the stereotypical promiscuous woman who seeks out sex and enjoys it too much, Ferrari is too vocal about her taste for oblivion. In a culture where self-control is paramount the notion of loving anaesthetic is abhorrent but also seductive. In this way Ferrari's cosmetic surgery project is as subversive as Orlan's.

Enchanted Castles

Fairy tales are seductive fantasies in which glorious transformation happens in sleep. In *The Sleeping Beauty*, newborn princess Briar-rose is cursed by a vengeful old fairy (wicked mother figures in fairy tales are almost always old, and therefore depraved – as I showed in Chapter 4, age alone can be enough to signify evil). The curse placed on Briar-rose by the crone-fairy means she will die on her fifteenth birthday, but her fate is lessened by a good (and young and beautiful) fairy. So at age fifteen Briar-rose pricks her finger on a poisoned spinning wheel needle (a loaded phallic symbol) and sleeps for a hundred years along with everyone in her castle. The century passes, a prince wakes her with a kiss, and they live happily ever after. But for my analytical purposes here it is the 'between-time', the hundred years of sleep, that is paramount.

The hundred-year entombment mimics death in its immobility but preserves the princess's beauty without decay. The entire castle and its contents are unaffected by the century gone: after the enchantment is lifted 'the cream was not sour for all that a hundred years had passed, nor was the butter rank' (Rackham, 1920: 106). As the century ticks away Briar-rose occupies a place between life and death. Arthur Rackham, author of the best-known version of the tale, uses signifiers of both death and life to describe her:

> She was lying upon a couch with her lovely hair spread out like a stream of gold; and, oh! No words can tell how beautiful she was. Softly the Prince came near and bent over her. He touched her hand; it was warm as in life, but she did not stir. No sound of breathing came from her parted lips, fresh and sweet as the petals of a rose; her eyes were closed. (Rackham, 1920: 94)

Although she has no breath her lips are 'fresh' and although inert she is warm. The mixed life/death description shows that her state is different from either sleep or death: it is something more like purgatory or limbo, a state of between/becoming, a state common in fairy tales. Novelist and mythographer Marina Warner notes that these moments of limbo are commonly interpreted in academic literature as a 'slow incubation of selfhood ... [and] eventual sexual fulfillment' (1994: 219–29). But Warner herself prefers to see them as symbols of the 'dark times' that can follow the first encounter between an older woman and her new daughter-in-law. A combination of these two readings leads me to suggest that such sleeps are a fantastical way to bypass uncomfortable, messy, transformative teenage and early-adult years. We simply fall asleep as pre-teens and wake up as fully-fledged adults with heroic, adoring husbands and our difficult mothers and mothers-in-law out of the way.

In the stories the supreme beauty of the sleeping, or dead, princess is dwelt upon – her immobility is part of her desirability. Thus the chief fascination in the fairy tales is not the curses or in the happy endings but the poison-induced living embalmment of their heroines.

In Rackham's version of *The Sleeping Beauty* the process of the castle entering hibernation is told in rich detail over eight paragraphs (compared to only two paragraphs about the kiss and the happy ending). The hundred-year entombment is richly elaborated, with a thick hedge providing an insulatory protection for the sleepers:

> And all round the castle there grew up a hedge of thorn, tangled with ivy, woodbine and creeping plants, so dense that from a distance it seemed like a little wood. Higher and higher it grew, closing round the castle like a wall until all that could be seen was the top of the highest tower, and the flagstaff from which the royal standard hung limp and motionless. (Rackham, 1920: 74)

The cursed castle is unaffected even by the wind and the flaccid flag indicates a lull in sexual activity – only to be reactivated by the virile prince once he penetrates the pubic hedge a hundred years later.

Briar-rose is beauty personified in this frozen temporality that denies a century of ageing. The fascination in the story of *The Sleeping Beauty* lies not in the curse or in the happy ending but in the living embalmment of its heroine: in the preservation of her youth over an entire century, in her 'escape' from the power of an evil mother figure, and in her symbolic transformation from child to woman.

Snow White's Glass Coffin

Like Briar-rose, Snow White is also immobilised by a wicked mother figure. Her stepmother, demented by Snow White's beauty, instructs a hunter to take her into the woods and kill her. Taking pity on the child he sets her free and she ends up living with seven dwarf miners. But the stepmother finds out she is alive and pays a visit in disguise, giving the girl a poisoned apple. Snow White then 'dies'. The dwarves 'were going to bury her, but she still looked as fresh as though she were alive, and still had her beautiful red cheeks'. So they make her a glass coffin 'into which one could see from every side', where she lay 'for a long, long time, and her body didn't decay. She looked as if she were sleeping, for she was still as white as snow, as red as blood, and her hair was as black as ebony' (Grimm, 1973: 269–70). Like Briar-rose she is neither dead nor alive, not breathing yet 'fresh'. Her coffin and Briar-rose's castle are quarantine stations where the girls stay out their transitions into adulthood. These structures hide transitions, making the move from helpless child to powerful woman (both girls become Queens) appear effortless.

Snow White and the Seven Dwarves is more overtly sexual than *The Sleeping Beauty*. When the seven dwarves come home to find Snow White seemingly dead their treatment of her body is sensual:

> No breath came from her mouth, and she was dead. They lifted her up, looked to see if they could find anything poisonous, unlaced her, combed her hair, washed her with water and wine, but nothing helped; the dear child was dead and stayed dead. They laid her on a bier, and all seven of them sat down and wept for her, and wept for three whole days. (Grimm, 1973: 269)

While unconscious Snow White undergoes foreplay – preceding her marriage to the Prince. This is not initiated by the heroine so the taboos about the expression of female sexuality are bypassed. Partly because her lovers are dwarves (and therefore not 'whole' men) but more importantly because she is unconscious, Snow White can be safely lifted, unlaced, combed, washed and wept over (by seven strong labourers no less) without having to face the punishments that might normally await sexually active girls. Her temporary death is licence to experience the forbidden while also providing her with a seamless transition into sexual adulthood.

Lolo Ferrari's Anaesthetics

The state induced by anaesthetic – fatal if not administered properly – complements the poison-produced deathlike sleeps that Snow White and Briar-rose experience. Lolo Ferrari endeavoured to make other aspects of her own life magical, and lived as if enchanted. Her house in the south of France had a white picket fence, a pink interior and she favoured princessy outfits complete with tiaras. Others have picked up on the fairy story aspects of her life, including *Marie Claire* journalist Elisabeth Alexandre: 'She was really very touching. You wanted to imagine her in a dream world with a big, airy house and white bunny rabbits and pink butterflies and friends who would like her truly for what she was, not for the money they could make out of her. The reality was very different.' (quoted in Henley, 2000)

Ferrari's narrative also features an evil mother, whom she told reporters was hateful, overbearing and castigating:

My mother told me I was ugly and stupid... She said I was only good for emptying chamber pots. I wanted to be an anaesthetist, but you can't learn with a mother like that. Actually, I'm like my mother. She thinks she's ugly too. When I was born, it was herself that she saw and she stuck all sorts of negative stuff on me. She did all she could to stop me living. My mother was always very unhappy with my father. My father was this macho guy who was never there and deceived her openly. So she revenged herself on me. She told me I was revolting too, that no one would ever want me. She hit me sometimes with a riding crop. I was frightened and I was ashamed; I wanted to change my face, my body, to transform myself. I wanted to die, really. (quoted in Henley, 2000)

She describes a horribly tragic real-life fairy-tale scenario, right down to the Cinderella chamber pots. Cosmetic surgery operated as Ferrari's 'curse', the poisoned instrument by which she would 'die' and yet awaken magically transformed, having escaped her evil mother and become beautiful. Instead of eating poisoned fruit or pricking her finger or becoming an anaesthetist herself Ferrari had anaesthetics. Her deep embrace of them is not a strange sickness confined to a single individual but a slight twist on the everyday cultural logics of makeover culture and stretched middle age, which valorise endless transformation into something better but also endless stasis or agelessness. *Extreme Makeover* promises a 'truly Cinderella-type experience'. Anaesthesia provides both stasis and the promise of transformation. I have argued that in makeover culture the *process of becoming* is more desirable than awakening, more important than reaching a point of finality. Is it any wonder then that Ferrari chose to enter anaesthesia over and over? She spent her whole adult life having operations or working towards them, effectively cancelling out an ordinary transition into womanhood, and when she wasn't actually in the 'black hole' of anaesthetics that she loved so much she created a perpetual twilight for herself with prescription sedatives (Henley, 2000).

Warner says that 'the idea of awakening, sometimes erotic but not exclusively, goes to the heart of fairy tale's function' (1994: 417). Certainly when Snow White and Briar-rose wake up their worlds have changed – they are fully-fledged sexual adults and their enemies have disappeared or been reduced to a non-threatening state. But stasis is also vital to these narratives. Stasis, created by anaesthesia in cosmetic surgery, is a between-state that both mimics and denies death. Paradoxically, animation is neutralised so that transformation can occur. The princesses bypass the often painful and fraught temporal processes that would have seen them confront their powerful mother figures and develop from girl to woman. Instead, they enter periods of hibernation from which they wake transmogrified, desirable and strong. Similarly, cosmetic surgery recipients' transformations are linked practically and mythologically with the 'little deaths' that anaesthesia creates. Dan, a recipient on *Extreme Makeover*, mumbled happily as he slipped into pre-operative unconsciousness, 'I'm going to Disneyland', and indeed he was: the finale for the episode was his 'Reveal' and wedding combined, in Disneyland. Dan instinctively and literally linked anaesthesia, transformation and his final, fantasy destination: his anaesthetic promised him a pathway to a land of magic and a happy ending.

What a Lovely Corpse

For literature scholar Elisabeth Bronfen, Snow White's transparent coffin 'elicits an aesthetic viewing' (1992: 102). In it she becomes an art object – the dwarves even write her name in golden letters on its side – subjected to the gaze and set apart. Importantly, the prince does not love her before she 'dies': Bronfen asserts that it is only once the fluid feminine body is cleansed, purified, immobile and available for the uninterrupted gaze – in other words only because she has become an art work – that he desires her so strongly. It is significant that he demands possession of the entire coffin – the display, not just the body – from the dwarves. Importantly, his erotic desire is only at the level of viewing: seeing the princess's still, undemanding body is connected with pleasure and with possession in much the same way as gaining pleasure from looking at pornography is usually connected to purchase or ownership of the erotic image. Bronfen continues: '...Snow White performs the apotheosis of one of the central positions ascribed to Woman in western culture; namely that the "surveyed" feminine body is meant to confirm the power of the masculine gaze' (1992: 102). She says that the figure of the immobilised 'dead' woman on display depicts both female sexuality and death, which are 'the two enigmas of western culture' (1992: 99).[2] When women's bodies like Snow White's are inert and exhibited, both death and female sexuality are contained and controlled so that the threat that each presents to the living, masculine subject is diminished. Such representations render the 'mutable, dangerously fluid, destabilised feminine body ... cleansed, purified, immobile' (Bronfen, 1992: 99).

Ferrari's body takes on the form of an artwork via the same mechanisms. She is rendered inert by her anaesthetics and becomes an aesthetic object[3] – whose primary function is to be looked at sexually – because of her breasts. Her implants, the *products* of her moments of immobilisation, are also a permanent disavowal of the 'mutable, dangerously fluid' woman's body that Bronfen describes. Semiotician Gillian Fuller notes that 'In a seeming mock commentary on Irigaray's fluid metaphysics of female desire, Lolo has had 23 litres of silicone pumped into her breasts, yet this bountiful fluid does not result in process only more product. Something that was once subject to the instabilities of gravity and chance are now stable, hard and above all big.' (1997)

Ferrari's breast implants are uncontained by the usual temporal and spatial boundaries to which mammaries are subject. As a pornography star she is available, indefinitely and forever, to a sustained gaze that parallels the unreturned gaze that Snow White undergoes while she is incapacitated.[4] I suggest that her own statements about loving anaesthetics are implicit recognition of this linkage but also a way of claiming and subverting the masculine gaze. She actively becomes passive (a contradiction in terms similar to 'passive aggression') and thus gives voice to the ideal, immobilised figure of perfect femininity.

Passivity need not be all negative, certainly submission and surrender can be active and chosen, especially in sado-masochistic sexual scenarios. Susan Bordo points out in her discussion about the trend towards 'soft' portrayal of male bodies in advertising campaigns that the act of offering oneself is in fact far from passive: '"passive" hardly describes what's going on when one person offers himself or herself to another. Inviting, receiving, responding – these are active behaviours... It's a macho bias to view the only real activity as that which takes, invades, aggresses' (Bordo, 2000: 133).

Using this logic, undergoing cosmetic surgery may be a forceful rather than a passive act. This is part of Kathy Davis's line: whether cosmetic surgery comes from feelings of inadequacy or not, to actively work against an unacceptable appearance, to say 'I am not this face or body' and then to *do* something about it is a form of defiance (1995). Texts like *Extreme Makeover* also present cosmetic surgery as something that courageous individuals undertake in the name of self-determination. But Ferrari is very different from the women Davis interviewed and especially different from recipients of extreme makeovers. The cultural contradiction where women are negatively construed as 'passive' by the many perpetrators of cosmetic surgery within makeover culture if they don't have cosmetic surgery, but also 'passive' by many feminists if they do have cosmetic surgery, is one that Ferrari seems to inhabit. Rather than using cosmetic surgery to fix a 'deformity', as did Davis's interviewees, or to 'amend the abject body' so it might join part of a clean and smooth community of similar individuals (Covino, 2004), as recipients of *Extreme Makeover* are doing, Ferrari forcefully and continually redesigned herself as a singular caricature for the male gaze. She did this in such a confronting way that it cannot be seen as merely bending to fit a stereotype.

Bronfen uses Freud's theory of scopophilia, where he asserts that there are two linked categories of desire – visual and tactile – to theorise the attraction of the 'dead' beauty.

The 'embalmed corpse' satisfies as an object of sight and alleviates the viewer of any need to progress to the 'normal sexual aim'. Death sanctions what would otherwise, for Freud, be a perversion – the exclusive privilege of the gaze as it becomes, supplants, and excludes the sexual activity connected with touching the other. (Bronfen, 1992: 102)

Freud asserts that – normally and healthily – visual desire leads to tactile desire. In other words, enjoyment in seeing progresses to a desire to touch what we see. Bronfen theorises that in the figure of the permanently sleeping beautiful woman or the embalmed corpse these two categories of desire are collapsed: there is visual desire, but the desire to touch is either not acceptable or not possible. Further, when death is connected in this way to the inaccessible – to that which is untouchable – death itself also becomes remote and therefore unthreatening, completely other; it cannot touch the viewer: 'any image of death contains as one of its signifiers the observer's survival' (Bronfen, 1992: 102). The anaesthetised, augmented, pornographic Lolo Ferrari is similarly completely visually available but untouchable. Pornography, but especially I would argue pornography that represents hyper-feminine pneumatic bodies like Ferrari's, obfuscates the possibility of touching. The link is strong between Lolo Ferrari and the immobilised feminine bodies that Bronfen asserts conflate desire and tactility. Ferrari's love of anaesthetics was the literal manifestation of this parallel: her work as a pornography star and her specific body modifications are the metaphoric manifestations of it.

Our Breasts, Lolo's Breasts (*)(*)[5]

It is significant that the operation Ferrari chose to undergo repeatedly is the one that most differentiates a woman from a child: breast augmentation. Most cosmetic surgery operations work at making the appearance increasingly youthful: dermabrasions ideally create a baby-like skin, blepharoplasties widen the eyes, lip enhancements give the mouth a perpetual baby pout. But breast augmentations work at the other end of the mother/infant dyad. A full bosom signifies fertile, sexualised adulthood and represents the opposite of childhood asexuality and innocence. Ferrari's breasts are an extreme example of the symbolic move from girl to woman. What Ferrari most resembled was a skinny little girl playing dress-ups with breasts made out of balloons. So here the transition from girl to woman turns around on itself, circling back to its opposite: the breasts might appear to represent fertile womanliness but in fact represent only themselves, as they are clearly a costume. This is something recognised in popular culture too: a mocking headline on *Awful Plastic Surgery* about then-teenaged Hollywood actress Lindsay Lohan said 'I'm Not A Little Girl, See I Have Fake Tits' (awfulplasticsurgery.com). The dress-up aspect of Ferrari's breast-performances highlights her ironic embrace of this notion. On her body it is played out to its physical extremes: identity becomes utterly bound up with the ultimate feminine signifier, and that signifier itself is 'false'. Ferrari herself said 'I've created a femininity that's completely artificial' (http://www. goodbyemag). Perhaps she was aware of Riviere's 'mask of femininity' or maybe she just intuitively understood it. Either way, she was an articulate analyst of her own condition.

Perhaps the purpose of breast implants in makeover culture is, more than anything else, the implants themselves. Marianne Guarena, author and star of the website 'YES THEY'RE FAKE!' did not want 'natural' looking breasts. For her, the fakery was part of the appeal: 'I am thrilled to finally be getting my new boobs!! I am so excited I feel as though I am on a high. I have always wanted fake-looking, round boobies and here I am about to get me some, not to mention get my fat sucked out and put in my face! lol!' (http://www.breastimplants4you.com/journals/marianne_highprofiles.htm)

I suggest that a new aesthetic is evident as part of makeover culture where artificiality works as an end in itself, where the clearly manufactured is prized over an organic or 'natural' look. One interviewee had to describe her new breast implants to me because we were talking on the telephone: 'Oh, I wouldn't say they look a hundred percent natural ... they're quite spaced, separated. And now, I mean, it's like coz I've lost that four kilos I'm too skinny to have such big breasts. And they're up high and real perky, there's no sag. They look more sexy than natural ones! [laughing]' (Judith)

Deborah Covino writes that in contemporary Western culture 'the ideal body is an aesthetic image, conceived and presented as or in a medium other than flesh' (2004: 4). Using this logic the less 'fleshy' implants appear to be the more desirable they are. But there are two other reasons for the desirability of noticeably 'unnatural' breast implants. Firstly, many celebrities and 'beautiful people' have large and obvious augmentations. While in surgical-aesthetic terms these might be seen as 'failures', in terms of cultural capital they are (literally) connected to hugely successful, rich and famous people. In this way it is by association that some of the aesthetics of cosmetic surgery that aren't quite 'right', that look a little strange, for example bee-stung lips, over-high breasts and tightly pulled faces, become desirable-in-themselves – 'I have always wanted fake-looking, round boobies'. Secondly, makeover culture valorises works-in-progress. The breast that is 'finished' and 'natural looking' blends in and looks like it has always been there. While this is the ideal outcome for some, others prefer to extend its obvious artificiality into infinity. With a large, high, 'unnatural' breast the operations may be temporally ended but makeover remains 'present' into the future. What is the point of having implants, of making yourself over, if nobody knows?

Feminists and other scholars have shown that in the late twentieth century the privileging of the image of the pubescent girl made the ideal female image progressively younger, slimmer, taller and more androgynous (Bordo, 1990; Stratton, 1996). Despite the desirability of the androgynous body, small breasts (commonly attached to thin bodies) were pathologised, labelled as 'micromastic' or 'hypomastic'. Sander Gilman notes that 'small breasts come to be seen as infantilizing, and the sagging breast as a sign of the ravages of age' (1999: 249). Breast implants fix these problems. They are placed high on the chest to minimise 'fall', their shape remains round forever (not, of course, if they burst or encapsulate), and of course they abolish smallness. Breasts have been subject to various expectations at different times in history, depending on what sorts of bodies are 'ideal'.[6] Jon Stratton offers a useful historical analysis of the changing (historical) 'ideal' woman's body, especially the radical shift to a body with minimal fat in the second half of the twentieth century: 'it became slimmer, while breasts and buttocks became problematic' (1996: 151). Naomi Wolf has noted that until the mid twentieth century various distributions of sexual fat were considered attractive (1991). We only have to consider whether liposuction would have been favoured in the Victorian era, or breast implants favoured by 1920s' bound-chested flappers, to see that cosmetic surgery practices are determined by whichever ideal body type dominates at a given time. This is not to say that cosmetic surgery simply reflects fashion. In fact, as cosmetic surgery becomes more accessible and 'normalised' it can be seen itself as a contributing force in the dictates of fashion: which came first, the breast implant or the Wonderbra?

Put simply, breast implants promise a way to regain 'femininity' (curves) without getting fat. This is not to say that the only women who have augmentation surgery are those who are thin and muscular, but rather that the ideal feminine body is based around firm flatness that can be further 'improved' with select augmentations. The most pervasive, powerful and normalising set of disciplines upon which contemporary heterosexual women's bodies are shaped is that of the tyranny of slenderness (Bordo, 1993; Chernin, 1994; Hesse-Biber; 1996). Surgeries that make bodies bigger via augmentation and implantation, or smaller via liposuction and flesh and skin reduction, cannot be viewed without considering this paradigm. Thus cosmetic surgery's privileging of gigantism (as in breast augmentation) for some body parts can only be understood when it is paradoxically situated within a framework of smallness. Bodies subjected to cosmetic surgery are usually bodies firstly structured and processed by a disciplinary surveillance structured around slender tautness.[7] Breast and lip augmentation surgeries, particularly as they relate to notions of gender, must be discussed in conjunction with the slenderness normalisation process. The tightly contained feminine ideal will often lack the curves that are considered erotic, and here is where cosmetic surgery comes in. Buttock implants are still rare but lip implants and breast augmentations are common ways to make the body bigger and more 'womanly'. So contradictory elements work in tandem to create a cultural dominant: two seemingly opposite logics of body modification – one that reduces and values the small, one that augments and values the full and generous – conjoin to create the culturally functional and acceptable contemporary 'feminine body'.

Dieting and gym-work create ideal feminine bodies that are thin, upright and hard – in other words phallic. In turn, breasts become a most problematic region of the female anatomy because they define the body as that of a woman while simultaneously detracting from its phallic quality. Jon Stratton suggests that while large breasts don't strictly fit into a phallic ideal they are aesthetically and culturally necessary because they reassure the man that the 'male' (phallicised) body he sees before him is in fact female:

as a consequence of cultural fetishism, men want women both to have breasts and to have no breasts, which is further compounded because the process of reducing body size to fit phallic ideals reduces breast size. One reason for the attraction of breast augmentation surgery is that with it a woman can have a phallic body with clearly emphasised breasts. (Stratton, 1996: 161)

Just as periods of magical slumber transform persecuted girls into desirable women, 'domesticating' them, implants also 'tame' the phallic female body, bringing it back into line as primarily gendered feminine.

There is another layer of anxiety around breasts because they simultaneously represent maternity and eroticism, aspects of womanhood that are almost obsessively disjoined at most cultural sites. Phenomenologist Iris Marion Young identifies the patriarchal dependence on a division between motherhood and sexuality as 'one of the most overdetermined dichotomies in our culture' (1990: 198). She finds that the conflicting discourses of mothering and sexuality constitute the main expectations of women in relation to their breasts, making both arenas fraught. But Young also implies that 'breasts are a scandal' because they resist limiting themselves to these conflicting discourses, and shatter the border which creates this division (1990: 199). Fuller says that breasts are contradictory because they symbolise both motherhood and sexuality: 'breasts rupture the stability of the categories they are meant to delimit: in one imagining the breast is cloaked, covered by the head of a suckling child, in another it is revealed and fully fetishised in magazines like *Hooters* and *Big Ones*.' (1997) Fuller is reviewing a 1997 exhibition by Sydney artist Suzanne Boccalatte called *Generation Airbag* (Figure 13). Structured as an altar to Ferrari – presciently a few years before she died – pairs of bronze mirror-finished breasts were placed on the floor making a runway-like row of 'lights' leading up to a huge photo of Ferrari, topless. Fuller suggests Boccalatte is contextualising Ferrari's breasts as 'an almost perfect disavowal of the threatening mother – they are complete pornographic objects inasmuch as these tits are all sex and no reproduction' (1997). The artwork exemplifies not only the many contradictions around Ferrari herself but also contradictions that are inherent in all breasts. For Fuller, 'each [brass] tit can be read as a clone dropping off the mother tit or as a discarded body bit that doesn't make the grade (indeed casting 'imperfections' have been left intact)' (1997). The disciplinary discourse of heterosexual femininity requires that women straddle the border between sexiness and 'good mother', but breasts somehow defy these oppositions, never being solely sexy or maternal. This is one of the reasons that breasts are so problematic: they are, in some important sense, unable to be categorised, straddling two axes of femininity, the reproductive/maternal and the sexy.

Young states that in our patriarchal culture, 'focused to the extreme on breasts', women *feel* that they are judged – and often *are* judged – according to the size and shape of their breasts. A woman's experience may be as varied as the size and shape

Figure 13 Suzanne Boccalatte, *Generation Airbag* (1997). Installation at the Performance Space Gallery, Sydney, featuring life-size photo of Lolo Ferrari and brass balls, photo courtesy the artist

of breasts themselves, but her 'life experience' and her 'breasted experience' will be linked, for breasts are '*in question* in this society, up for judgement ... and [woman] has not escaped the condition of being problematic' (1990: 198).

Susan Bordo asserts that a constricted, smooth profile without bulges or protuberances is now the ideal rather than thinness per se. Anxieties about bulges and lumps can be seen as a metaphor for fear and loathing of 'internal processes out of control – uncontained desire, unrestrained hunger, uncontrolled impulse' (Bordo, 1993: 89). The alien in the body is the horrifying bulge, flab or sag, and displaying control over it allows people to define themselves as good makeover citizens: 'the well-muscled body has become a cultural icon ... the firm, developed body has become a symbol of correct attitude; it means that one "cares" about oneself and how one appears to others, suggesting willpower, energy, control over infantile impulse, the ability to "make something" of oneself.' (Bordo, 1993: 94–5) While we may dutifully labour inside makeover culture's gyms and diets to 'make something' of ourselves, our breasts remain recalcitrant as one of the few body parts which cannot be made firm or 'improved' through exercise or dieting. In order to make something of one's breasts they must be implanted.[8]

The Gigantic

Breast implants do not unproblematically bestow acceptable femininity. Like the celebrity cosmetic surgery that I discussed in Chapter 5, if not 'done right' implants create dissonances and engender hatreds by being wrongly shaped, too scarred or – more commonly – too big. The 'too big' implant indiscretion is the most visible one and therefore the most demonised by popular media. Ferrari shares this category with women like Jordan, a page-three model and star of *British Celebrity Survivor*, and Anna Nicole Smith, whose death in 2007 bears many similarities to Ferrari's. These B-grade celebrities fit a 'giant feminine' category: they overcompensate for being phallic. While I think that Smith and Jordan unwittingly overstepped the very margins they sought to reconstitute, Ferrari was quite aware of the borders she was transgressing. In this way her breasts are feminist: they break down barriers, they consciously push the feminine body beyond its patriarchal casings. Fuller describes Ferrari as a 'feminist bad girl' whose high, tightly encased, upright breasts are the embodiment of a 'hyper femininity' that both subverts and critiques 'the braless, freeswinging and ultimately maternal breast of the 70s feminist good girl' (1997). Perhaps upholding Ferrari as an embodiment of third wave feminism is stretching my point. Nevertheless she certainly enacts a form of femininity that is overtly subversive and complicit, and that makes a running and ironic commentary on itself.

Susan Stewart says in her poetic book about narratives of the miniature and the gigantic, *On Longing* (1993), that fantastic gigantic body parts become symbolic environments in themselves, engulfing their surroundings and their bearers: 'what often happens in the depiction of the gigantic is a severing of the synecdoche from its referent, or whole' (1993: 89). For example, she shows how the enormous and consuming breasts depicted in *Gulliver's Travels* become environments in themselves, swallowing up their world, including the narrator. She explains that the sense of being engulfed comes about via the position of the observer: '[with gigantism] the partial vision of the observer prohibits closure of the object. Our impulse is to create an environment for the miniature, but such an environment is impossible for the gigantic: instead the gigantic becomes our environment, swallowing us as nature or history swallows us.' (1993: 89)

Most pornographic images centralise the vulva or anus, emphasising woman's receptivity. But images of Ferrari, no matter what angle they're taken from, are dominated by her breasts. Outrageously out of scale with her tiny frame they threaten to engulf the viewer and have indeed already engulfed Ferrari, who is supposedly their environment – they are huge blots on the landscape of her body. She initially 'ingested' them by buying them and taking them in, but they then metaphorically swallowed her such that they *are* her. The gigantic is without containment: combined with the synecdochical over-signification of the part, it is this that makes Ferrari's breasts overwhelming, anti-receptive, a visual 'opposite' to the standard spreadeagled pornography bodies.

The breasts themselves became fetishist symbols of the all-powerful, threatening mother figure who dominates her daughter's life as described in many fairy stories: Ferrari's augmentations simply replaced the power that her mother wielded over her as a child. She remains simultaneously separate and connected to them, and gains freedom from the tyranny of the mother only by replacing it with the might of her ever-expanding mammaries. In a traditional fairy tale the transformations that Ferrari underwent while under anaesthetic would have freed her from the wicked and controlling mother or stepmother. But in this fairy tale for makeover culture her breast implants created a new 'bad' mother, one that through gigantism became environmentally and historically overwhelming. Ultimately – and predictably – Ferrari's transformations had the opposite effect in her life to those of Snow White and Briar-rose, serving only to replicate the condition she had tried to escape, and setting up an alternative oppression. This is her tragedy and the reason her story had to end in suicide or murder rather than with a kiss from a prince.

Tumescent Citizenship and Surplus Embodiment

> That shit isn't natural either. They could've recycled all the plastic in this bitches chest and made a few bumpers for a couple SUV's ... Lolo Ferrari, who was billed as 'the woman with the biggest breasts in the world' and had a reputed 71-inch (177.5 cm) silicone-enhanced bust and was as **ugly** as her tits were big. As soon as they rule out that one of those tits of hers didn't get a mind of its own and roll up on her face in her sleep, I think they might have a case against the husband. (Shabazz Steward)

The above quote, taken from Nkrumah Shabazz Steward's popular web log, is a florid yet typical example of common attitudes towards Ferrari. Vilification is standard in writing about her while mockery and misogyny abound. Most myths connect her breasts to her death:

- she died in surgery;
- one of the implants burst and her breast became gangrenous;

- both implants burst on an aeroplane because of cabin pressure;
- the weight of them suffocated her by pressing on her lungs; or
- (Shabazz Steward's novel variant quoted above) they rolled up and smothered her.

In an Actor-network theory analysis the breasts would in fact *be* semi-autonomous actors, in which case stories about them taking on mythic proportions and 'turning against' their creator might be even more resonant. The rhetoric in the myths around Ferrari's death suggests that having transgressed so many boundaries she *deserved* death-by-breast – for many, and the breasts coming 'alive' and killing her is an apt ending to her story.

Cultural logics around deeply transgressive individuals position them as lesser citizens, as unworthy, and as ultimately expendable. English scholar David Russell notes that many critics working around citizenship locate the nexus of 'moral worth' in the body (2004: Bit 3). The ideal citizen is corporeally invisible, with a 'neutral' body that doesn't stand out: 'the ability to make the body abstract, invisible, and non-identifiable has been the most desirable quality for a citizen to possess' (2004: Bit 4). He suggests that good citizenship is embodied by white middle-aged and middle-class men (something confirmed with a quick glance at the Australian or British Parliaments or the US Congress) while women, the disabled, the poor, blacks and foreigners – people who are visible because of their embodiment – are often considered to be lesser citizens. These 'problem citizens' suffer because of 'surplus embodiment' (Russell, 2004: Bit 6) and may seek to diminish or minimise their corporeality in order to gain legitimacy. As I showed in Chapter 2, cosmetic surgery is often used to exactly these ends – 'ethnic' cosmetic surgery diminishes signs of racial difference, while extreme makeovers minimise signs of poverty and disability. Cosmetic surgery is in many ways an attempt to 'blend in' and a way to invisibilise the self's corporeality: it is a kind of uniform. The ways in which Kathy Davis's interviewees talked about their surgeries fitted this model. They didn't want to be more beautiful and noticeable but more 'normal' and less noticeable. This is where Ferrari differs strongly from the average cosmetic surgery recipient. Rather than deploying cosmetic surgery to rectify some form of surplus embodiment and therefore join the ranks of the normal she used it to create surplus embodiment.

Russell argues that '"surplus embodiment" and "citizenship" remain inextricably tangled and mutually exclusive' (2004: Bit 18). He shows how white male pornography stars are successful because of their excessive embodiments: large penises or other remarkable features are what their careers are built upon. He focuses on Ron Jeremy, a performer in 1980s' sex films known as 'The Hedgehog' because of his round shape and hairiness. In the same industry and in a similar way Ferrari gained fame and success because of her surplus embodiment. However, Russell shows that when these individuals attempt to integrate into the mainstream their tumescence marks them as unworthy of normal citizenship. As I showed in the last chapter, successful cosmetic surgery in makeover culture is predicated upon embracing a uniform aesthetic and being able to demonstrate understanding of just how much surgery is enough. Ferrari's tumescent citizenship, gained via cosmetic surgery, makes her a spectacular and in some ways successful failure. She is an important part of the ideological complexity of makeover culture; her exclusion from respectable citizenship because of cosmetic surgery makes her the exception that proves the rule.

Closure, or Second Burial

Elisabeth Bronfen uses the work of religious anthropologist Robert Hertz to describe how bodies like Snow White's – immobile 'art' works – cannot be sustained. Eventually, they must either *properly* die or be reanimated. Hertz examined societies that practised primary and secondary burial rites, and asserted that in these rituals death was not a singular event but rather a progression: a transit that ends in total separation from the world of the living after going through a series of 'between' stages. He described the double death rites of the Olo Ngaju people of Borneo where two burials – one 'temporary' and one 'final' – occur before death is fully accepted (MacDonald, 1999). During the first burial period the dead person is understood to be neither in this world nor in another but rather in-between, occupying a role of doubleness. The doubleness, necessary but problematic, is later ended with the enactment of a second burial, after which the spirit of the deceased is unified and definitively sent to the other world.

Bronfen suggests that during the first burial's transition stage the corpse represents a temporary triumph over death and a kind of immortality – it is dead and alive. But she asserts that eventually and inevitably 'this dangerous though fascinating interzone must cease' (1992: 104). Put simply, the living cannot sustainably co-habit with the dead. The corpse-object of the first burial works as a link between worlds that cannot and should not remain open permanently. She asserts that the first burial corpse is a fetish that makes desire merely optical, rendering death visible but untouchable. However, the reassurance that this provides is dangerous in the long term. This is because ultimately the corpse represents nothingness: it no longer has a living referent. Second burial then puts it finally to rest, severing its connection to the living world and replacing it with monuments that may resemble the deceased but are definitively representational. This is why life is described in such richness around the 'first burials' of the 'dead' princesses: the descriptions emphasise that 'first burials' create environments in which the dead share space with the living.

Contained and everlasting bodies like Snow White's in her coffin or Ferrari's in its pornographic frames deny the mutability of the feminine body and also death itself. They stave off temporality and work to reassure the viewer that he is both masculine and alive. It is not only the object of the gaze but also the gazer who is outside of temporality, and this must also come to an end: staving off time is eventually an act that cannot be sustained. Bronfen notes that representations of, and narratives about, dead feminine bodies eventually require reanimation or decomposition.

Second burial need not be literal. In a culture like ours, where the dead disappear rapidly and the 'transit passage' is hidden or denied, this is particularly the case. We rarely have the opportunity to view or deal with real dead bodies: many people's first and last contact with the deceased is via a closed coffin. Our 'first burials' then must come in the form of *representations* of death. Baudrillard says that many of our cultural forms are deathlike and notes, in a theory about Californian houses which could equally be attributed to cosmetically altered bodies that:

> All dwellings have something of the grave about them, but here the fake serenity is complete. The unspeakable house plants, lurking everywhere like the obsessive fear of death, the picture windows looking like Snow White's glass coffin, the clumps of pale, dwarf flowers stretched out in patches like sclerosis, the proliferation of technical gadgetry inside the house, beneath it, around it, like drips in an intensive care ward, the TV, stereo, the video which provide communication with the beyond... (1998: 30)

The surgically enhanced body also has a 'fake serenity', for all the signs of age, wear and tear and grief have been stretched out. It too is filled with technical gadgetry, which keeps it 'alive'; it too strives to be whole unto itself, communicating with 'the beyond', the outside world, without being affected by it. While cosmetic surgery can be read as fear of mortality and disgust with corporeality, it is also precisely the opposite. It involves the killing of a living human part (skin, muscle), and the replacement of the live with the dead (an implant). Similarly Efrat Tseëlon notes the similarities between the processes of preparing a body for mummification and cosmetic surgery. They both paradoxically cut into and thus damage the skin of the body in order to preserve that very surface: 'the aesthetisation of death and the beautification of the living are defensive strategies. They are designed to protect the person from realisation of some lack by creating an illusion of wholeness and immortality' (Tseëlon, 1995: 117).

Makeover culture's 'finished products' are the unlived-in spaces shown in ironically named 'lifestyle' magazines – the perfectly tszujed[9] interiorscapes with every throw cushion placed just so. These 'still lives' are also 'living deaths', as are still pornography images, especially those that feature unreal and plasticated 'living dolls' like Ferrari. The messy stages of makeover culture then, the stages of renovation and surgery where bodies are gaping and open and nothing is contained, lead up to ideal deathlike images, where everything is finalised and static.

Snow White in her coffin is a symbolic first burial and so are many parts of Lolo Ferrari's life. Ferrari enacted her own first burials – an utterly subversive act on a par with suicide – in the form of multiple, much-loved anaesthetics. She was always flirting with the idea of being a fetish, an embalmed, non-fluid, immobile and hyper-feminine representation of death to be gazed upon. But stuck in the groove of a continual stream of first burials, and given that first burial is ultimately incomplete and untenable, Ferrari had to die. Her 'second burial' was her actual death. In fairy stories, the second burial is usually performed as a kind of rebirth, but Bronfen suggests that Snow White's reanimation can be seen as a kind of sacrifice – 'a sacrifice of the haunting fetish, the double' – that which is dead and not-dead. Similarly, makeover culture creates and re-creates bodies that are dead and not-dead, that are, like Ferrari's, hard and implanted, metaphorically dead and alive at the same time. So makeover culture too must have its sacrifices, its martyrs for the cause. The 'sacrifice' of makeover failures like Lolo is necessary for the continuing health of the culture. Like the preserved corpse, Ferrari was a double that had to cease, that was not sustainable. Snow White and Ferrari both finally return to a state that relies on temporality, a state of mutability. In this way Ferrari is makeover culture's biggest fan but also its most infamous martyr.

Conclusion

Lolo Ferrari enacted an extreme and perverse version of makeover culture. She worked and played with cosmetic surgery on literal and mythological levels. Her deliberate agency in inflating the mask of femininity was simultaneously embrace and rejection of it. Her embodiments of makeover culture were as much about *highlighting* the death that it aims to circumvent as avoiding it. She showed that makeover culture is about designing death as much as it is about designing life.

The suspensions experienced by Snow White, Briar-rose and Lolo Ferrari via poison and/or anaesthesia are extended moments where transformation can happen without pain. When used as portals into an analysis of cosmetic surgery, they point to the beginnings of a new understanding of this technology in relation to temporality, namely its complex relation with death and immortality. They also echo makeover culture, which when 'correctly' performed embodies rhetorics of elasticity, adaptability and mobility, in both physical and mental/emotional terms, and is above all a state of constant becoming. Makeover culture, for all its endless construction of newly finished surfaces, also always creates sites that are in disarray, like the dusty 'ruins' of renovations-in-progress, the chaos of redecorating and the mess of the body in and just after surgery. These are all 'little deaths', foreshadowing and 'doubling' for death even as they facilitate makeover culture. The look of a bombed house is akin to the plaster- and debris-strewn renovation-in-progress; the anaesthetic and bruised downtimes of cosmetic surgery make people look like car crash victims. These are reminders that cosmetic surgery and makeover culture are still subject to death and finality and that in fact it is these inevitabilities that they work in tandem with.

By acknowledging that cosmetic surgery within makeover culture involves embracing deathly moments, and that these suspensions-in-time are part of the life of makeover culture at work, feminists are better placed to understand how makeover culture works at deep mythical and symbolic levels. Cosmetic surgery seen through this lens is a new manifestation of an ancient set of symbols about femininity, suffering, transformation and death. This seems to have been something that Ferrari had an intuitive understanding of.

Her eventual real death was no surprise. She said in a late interview, 'All this stuff has been because I can't stand life' (http://www.goodbyemag). Like a dead infant, she was buried with her favourite teddy bear in a white casket that she had chosen herself a few weeks before dying. Perhaps finally in death she managed to prolong forever the delicious 'black hole' she had sought via anaesthetic so many times.

–7–

Makeover Artists
Orlan and Michael Jackson

...that which can only be surprising, that for which we are not prepared, you see, is heralded by species of monsters. A future that would not be monstrous would not be a future; it would already be a predictable, calculable, and programmable tomorrow.

Jacques Derrida, quoted in Zylinska, 'Prosthetics as Ethics'

Orlan and Michael Jackson may be the monstrous mother and child of cosmetic surgery. Monsters threaten and problematise accepted structures and are often seen as harbingers, foretelling disturbances in the established order, heralding or symbolising unwelcome but important change. For Jacques Derrida, the very possibility of a future relies on a 'species of monsters' that exist in the present. A monster need not be horrifying, it is something that 'shows itself [*elle se montre*] – that is what the word monster means – it shows itself in something that is not yet shown and that therefore looks like a hallucination, ... it frightens precisely because no anticipation had prepared one to identify this figure' (Derrida, quoted in Zylinska, 2002: 233). In other words, some monsters not only signify what we are *not* (that which must be ejected or quarantined) but also what we are *becoming*: that which may eventually be embraced. Cultural, feminist and ethical theorist Joanna Zylinska argues that constructive engagements with an unknown future require an ethics of welcome, a modus operandi that is open and hospitable. She suggests that Orlan and the Australian performance artist Stelarc reside within a 'prosthetic ethics of welcome'. They demonstrate the ways that body technologies and body modifications may be used to perform hospitality, openness and invitation to an unknown – monstrous – future. Because Orlan and Stelarc publicly and literally open their bodies to future corporeal, mediated and technical possibilities, they make themselves always already prosthetic. Prosthesis is usually seen as a way to fix lack, a way to create wholeness and autonomy and therefore bounded subjects. But Zylinska suggests that it may also be positioned as 'an articulation of connections and slippages *between* the self and its others' (2002: 216). Unbounded, networked and changeable subjects are created when we look at prosthetics in this way.

Prosthetic couplings, like those that happen in everyday cosmetic surgery, demonstrate that the relationships between what we might label 'nature', 'technology' and 'culture' are interdependent. People who have cosmetic surgery potentially allow for wide conceptual adjustments about identity: their 'technobodies' encourage us to question what it is to be human and how the self is comprised in relation to others. Zylinska suggests that they can be all about positive connections: 'a prosthetic ethics of welcome ... can be interpreted as an ethical figure of hospitality, of welcoming an absolute and incalculable alterity that challenges and threatens the concept of the bounded self' (2002: 217). A similar point is made by phenomenologist Francisco Varela. Writing about his own liver transplant, he suggested that the operation had made him into a 'guest' in his own existence, in his own body:

> Transplantation ... is my horizon, an existential space where I adapt slowly, this time as the guest of that which I did not arrange, like a guest of nobody's creation. This time, the foreign has made me the guest, the alteration has given me back a belonging I did not remember. The transplant ex-poses me, exports me in a new totality. (Varela, 2001, quoted in Depraz, 2002: 93)

Rather than having made him 'whole' and contained again, the imported liver gives him a 'new totality' that is about exposing and opening the self. The liver, supplier of life for Varela, makes him the guest, baffling boundaries between self, other, foreign and indigenous.

In Chapter 5 I explained how cosmetic surgery's 'monstrous others' like Farrah Fawcett become demonised but also domesticated. The proliferation of Fawcett's image across many everyday objects and the constant reduction of her aims and desires to frivolity and failure render her, finally, monstrous but non-threatening. Orlan and Jackson are of a different order. Their body projects are too complex and confronting to be simply discounted as monstrously 'wrong' or 'failed'. While we can reasonably guess at Fawcett's intentions, Jackson's desires are mysterious and Orlan's projects remain bewildering. By making their bodies defiantly open, becoming, prosthetic and digital these two artists resist domestication, instead placing themselves outside of the ordinary and thus embodying – not just heralding – future body possibilities.

Chapter 5 also showed how the self is created in conjunction with the other by way of positioning and using monstrous others to delineate individual boundaries. Monstrous hybridity is about prosthetics that are 'wrong' and 'overdone' and thus obscene: hybrid bodies are acceptable only so long as they stick to certain rules about containment, presentation and decorum. Here I wish to skew this slightly to suggest that the self may also be constructed through the other not by way of rejection but through ingestion. When hybridity becomes an integral part of the performance of self, when bodies are permanently 'othered', they become examples of what not to do, as in the case of Fawcett. But what if those bodies are in some way heralding or embodying a future? What if they are examples of *what to do*, and *how to become*?

The Saint and the King

Orlan is a French artist who became known in the 1960s, 1970s and 1980s for art installations and performances. Many early performances involved the sheets of her trousseau, sometimes stained with blood or semen, while some included striptease in elaborate commentaries on feminism and marriage. In 1971 she adopted the persona 'Saint Orlan' and her work began to revolve around hagiography. All of her art has included strong observations on representations of the female body in traditional art and the status of the woman artist. She uses multimedia, photography, live performance, sound, sculpture and video, and always includes her own body in one form or another.

Since 1990, the year she turned forty, Orlan's work has developed in deeply complex ways that I can only précis here (for further reading I recommend C. Jill O'Bryan's book *Carnal Art: Orlan's Resurfacing*, 2005). Her longest and most famous project consists of multiple cosmetic surgery procedures. She began by making a computer-generated face from an amalgamation of features from icons of Western art: the chin of Botticelli's *Venus*, the forehead of Leonardo da Vinci's *Mona Lisa*, the lips of Boucher's *Europa*, the nose of the School of Fontainebleau sculpture of Diana, and the eyes of Gérard's *Psyche*. Then she set about having her own face surgically altered so it would resemble the amalgamated image (Orlan does not seek to look like Venus or the Mona Lisa, as is often wrongly reported).[1] She called the project *The Reincarnation of St Orlan* (*Reincarnation*). The operations are performed before an audience in what Kate Ince calls 'a weirdly hybrid cultural space' (2000: 21). Hospital theatres are augmented with dancing boys, electronic music, designer gowns, mime artists and giant bowls of tropical fruit (see Figure 14). Orlan creates 'relics' out of her own liposuctioned fat and bloodied gauze and exhibits them in small rounds of Perspex (Moos, 1996). She remains conscious throughout the surgeries, having only epidurals or local anaesthetics, directing the action and reading philosophy aloud.

While my discussion here will mainly focus on the *Reincarnation* work, there are some other Orlan projects important to my argument. One is titled *Self-Hybridations* and is also a form of self-portraiture. It uses digital morphing techniques rather than surgery: a template of Orlan's face is morphed and transfigured so it resembles various hybrid images inspired by ancient Olmec and Mayan standards of beauty. The other projects that fascinate me are quite ungraspable. In fact, I have come to call them the 'fantasy' projects because they are secretive, rumoured and speculative. For example, Orlan has spoken about a project that has a working title of 'an operation of opening and closing of the body'. Her armpit will be sliced open, as deeply as possible – 'to the very viscera'[2] (Brand, 2000a: 312). The gap will be held open while she smiles, laughs and reads, and then it will be sutured closed. She has mysteriously mentioned another operation, shrouded in secrecy: 'the operation will take place in

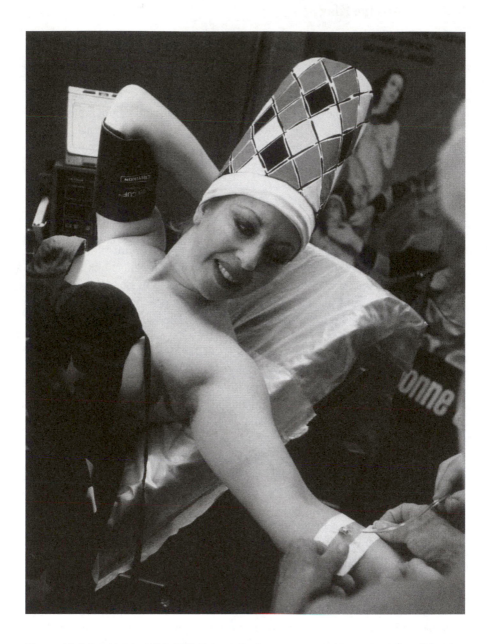

Figure 14 Orlan (6 July 1991) Fifth Surgery-Performance, or, the Opera Operation. Operation conducted by Dr Chérif Kamel Zaar in Paris. Set and props by Orlan, costumes by Franck Sorbier. © ADAGP, Paris and DACS, London 2007

public in a gallery of contemporary art. This operation won't be a cosmetic one, but one which will considerably alter my appearance, and whose aim will be to enhance my physical faculties' (quoted in Ince, 2000: 110).

And she has announced that she will appear in a film called *Painkillers* by David Cronenberg, director of *Crash*, *The Fly* and *Videodrome*. The film will show a fake operation that will open her from 'top to bottom':

> The story is about a future civilization in which pain no longer exists. [Cronenberg] asked Orlan to play her own part in this film, and she offered to perform her ultimate plastic surgery performance. She would then be shot and photographed while reading – laughing and performing – with her body surgically exposed from top to bottom. (http://www.jahsonic.com/DavidCronenberg.html)

Singer-songwriter Michael Jackson worked as a child-performer with his family and then went on to become one of the most famous and successful pop stars of the twentieth century. He was the creator of *Thriller* (1982), still the biggest selling album of all time. His career and his cosmetic surgery are intricately intertwined, with the press nowadays usually more interested in his latest surgical change than his music. Kathy Davis writes: 'Jackson's importance for the music world is undisputed, but it is his bizarre behaviour that receives the most attention in the media. This includes ... undergoing multiple cosmetic surgeries' (Davis, 2003: 81). Lately he has prohibited questions about cosmetic surgery in interviews. But his appearance speaks for itself: over the past two decades he has without doubt received multiple rhinoplasties, at least one chin augmentation and is likely to have had many other procedures. His cosmetic surgery is usually described as very odd, with references to him working at deleting or minimising his blackness, wanting to look like a woman (specifically Diana Ross) and obliterating his nose. 'Wacko Jacko's' appearance is often linked in the media to reports of abhorrent or weird actions that include dangling his baby son from a balcony in Berlin in 2002, sexually molesting children, sleeping in an oxygenated chamber, buying the Elephant Man's skeleton at auction and worshipping at a shrine dedicated to Elizabeth Taylor.

In 1995 Jackson and his first wife, Lisa Marie Presley, were interviewed by Diane Sawyer for *Primetime*:

Michael: I'm a performer.

Lisa: And he is constantly re-modifying something, or changing it, or reconstructing it or, you know, working on some imperfection he thinks needs to be worked on. If he sees something he doesn't like he changes it. Period. He re-sculptured himself. He's an artist.

Michael: I might wanna put a red dot right there one day ... (*points to his forehead*)

Lisa: (*laughs*)

Diane: But ... but ...

Michael: An' two eyes right here. (*touches his cheeks*) (Television interview with Diane Sawyer, 1995, with Lisa-Marie Presley, www.allmichaeljackson.com/interviews/simulchat)

In a rare moment of playful candour, Jackson indicates some aspects of cosmetic surgery that I wish to focus on. This is cosmetic surgery that creates bodies that are unique and unconventional, and that are self-consciously, unapologetically manufactured. The Sawyer interview was a rarity: Jackson usually denies, to varying degrees, that he has undergone multiple cosmetic surgery procedures. A typical statement goes like this:

> I'd like to set the record straight right now. I have never had my cheeks altered or my eyes altered. I have not had my lips thinned, nor have I had dermabrasion or a skin peel. All of these charges are ridiculous. I have had my nose altered twice and I recently added a cleft to my chin, but that is it. Period. I don't care what anyone else says – it's my face and I know. (Jackson, 1988: 229)

'Project' is an easier concept to relate to Orlan than to Jackson: Orlan's cosmetic surgery is clearly project-based and carefully planned, while Jackson's cosmetic surgery is usually denied. His transformations seem haphazardly planned, if at all, and are apparently more subconscious than Orlan's. The trajectory, patterning and impacts of Jackson's cosmetic surgery seem almost accidental, while in contrast Orlan displays careful if not complete control over all performative and aesthetic elements of hers. Regardless of his intentions, Jackson's cosmetic surgery effects are frequently interpreted as deliberate and calculated. Conversely, Orlan's carefully orchestrated project has 'gone wrong' on several occasions – she may never complete *Reincarnation* because of difficulties in finding a surgeon to perform the final operation, which is the construction of a huge nose – and her work is often interpreted in ways she declares are just wrong.

Orlan's Body of Work

As shown elsewhere in this book, cosmetic surgery is part of a set of disciplines that governs appearance, mainly for women, in contemporary Western society. Orlan's *Reincarnation* is a critique of these beauty ideals and practices, specifically those manifested in the arena of cosmetic surgery (Brand, 2000a; Hirschhorn, 1996; Ince, 2000; O'Bryan, 2005). Her critique in *Reincarnation* has been largely of the first aim of cosmetic surgery – dictated by the imperative to beauty – but the fact that she worked at this project between the ages of forty and fifty hints that the project also points to the imperative to remain looking youthful. In an interview with Peggy Zeglin Brand she spoke heavily against Western versions of beauty being (literally) inscribed on the female body. Interestingly, she was less predictable on ageing:

In the past, women, and men too, had a much shorter life expectancy; women often died in childbirth. And very often, people, once they've reached seventy, wind up with a face they don't recognise as theirs any longer. There is a loss of identity because they no longer recognise themselves. They are alien to themselves. And I think that, in this case, when it is too difficult to feel 'other', there is cosmetic surgery (Brand, 2000a: 297).

This rhetoric fits neatly into the notion of external appearance not fitting with an inner sense of self, common in popular discourse around cosmetic surgery, typified by statements like 'the gap between body and state of mind is bridged by plastic surgery... Patients' spirits are uplifted along with their bodies' (plastic surgeon Alan Engler quoted in Covino, 2001: 93). Orlan also mobilises the rhetoric of suffering here where life becomes 'too difficult' because of body image and cosmetic surgery is a justifiable last resort (Davis, 1995). Clearly, her extraordinary relationship with cosmetic surgery doesn't stop her from having some opinions that are compatible with mainstream discourse. In fact she has maintained all along that she isn't against cosmetic surgery itself but hates the way it is used to enforce an unobtainable standard of female beauty. Her distaste for cosmetic surgery regimes doesn't stem from ideals of a 'natural' body that should be left alone: on the contrary, she declares that the body is a mere envelope, and that people should have the chance to remould it as they desire.

The Reincarnation of Saint Orlan

Reincarnation works on three main levels. Firstly, it inverts the traditional doctor–patient dyad. Orlan casts herself as creator and the doctors as expert helpers; she performs 'foreplay' before the surgery by kissing the doctor ('ostentatiously' says one commentator) on the lips, highlighting the doctor/lover parallel that I outlined in Chapter 3. Her wakefulness during her operations is a radical variant on the usual scene of passive patient, active doctor, while her philosophical readings throughout the surgery are a constant reminder that this malleable flesh is also part of a sentient being. She acknowledges the quasi-sexual relationship between patient and surgeon but then takes control of it, de-mystifying the closed doctor–patient relationship by inviting audiences in and broadcasting the operations. Art curator Michelle Hirschhorn writes: 'by directing the reconstruction of her own body, she problematises the traditional gendered relationship between the active male subject position as artist/creator and the passive female object position as matter awaiting transformation' (1996: 111). Nobody has problematised the Pygmalion/Galatea relationship more than Orlan. She has said 'one thing is sure: it is through cosmetic surgery that men can exert their power over women the most' (Brand, 2000a: 296). The inversion of power in her performances has been much lauded: indeed it is often held up as 'proof' that her cosmetic surgery is intellectual and feminist and is done for 'higher reasons'. The active consciousness she performs during operations, where she reads and talks, is said to display 'agency, which has to be demonstrated if Orlan's work is to be acknowledged as feminist' (Ince, 2000: 114). However, I believe it is unproductive to position Orlan as the feminist 'opposite' of women who elect to undergo cosmetic surgery for more common reasons, and simplistic to assume that the demonstration of agency is necessary for a feminist stance. Further, agency in cosmetic surgery does not have to be predicated on simply being awake. As I have showed in previous chapters there are feminist ways to interpret 'garden variety' cosmetic surgery, where women may actively design their ageing. Even someone like Lolo Ferrari, who was extreme in her passivity, in her willingness to surrender to unconsciousness, and in her giving away of agency, may be deploying cosmetic surgery in new, potentially subversive ways. Orlan's project is more extreme and more imaginative than most deployments of the technology, but creating a dichotomy between it and more everyday cosmetic surgery is less fruitful than looking for complementarities between them.

Secondly, *Reincarnation* shows alternative purposes for and products of cosmetic surgery, opening the technology to a myriad of possible uses. Orlan is infuriated when accused of trying to look beautiful:

> the most difficult thing about my work is to make myself understood... [I said to a press conference] 'Look at my head! Will you stop saying I want to look like Venus, which is the image I fight against the most? For me, this is what I want to debunk. And stop saying I want to look like the Mona Lisa. You can see it's not true.' (Brand, 2000a: 304)

The difficulties she faces are because it is almost impossible for people to see that cosmetic surgery need not be about creating beauty or youth: 'my work goes against our customs, our habits, to such an extent that people cannot see it; all they hear is "cosmetic surgery"' (Brand, 2000a: 304). Misreadings of her work happen in the art world and in everyday media: Michelle Hirschhorn had a lot of difficulty finding quality critical work about Orlan, despite the artist having been represented in at least three international biennales, and concluded that 'not only had she been constructed as an aberration in the popular press, and therefore denied credibility as an artist, but seemingly she had been substantially excised from the corpus of contemporary art history as well' (1996: 110).

A decade later there are now substantial writings about Orlan including two dedicated monographs (Ince, 2000; O'Bryan, 2005), two edited volumes (Blistene, 2004; Zylinska, 2002) and a documentary feature film (*Orlan, Carnal Art*, directed by Stephan Oriach). Despite this there are still major, sometimes wilful, misunderstandings of her intent in the popular press: I even saw her absurdly described as a 'biopunk' (*San Francisco Bay Guardian*, 2001).

Although she has borrowed features from iconic beauties, the construction of an attractive face was never Orlan's aim. For example, in appropriating the Mona Lisa's rather bulbous forehead, a forehead that Camille Paglia has described as 'egglike',[3] she now has lumps the size of kidneys just above her eyebrows. She often puts glitter on them so they're highlighted and honoured as things of beauty. Orlan's 'anti-beauty' project can be aligned with the suggestions made by Kathryn Pauly Morgan (1991: 45–7) discussed in Chapter 1. Not surprisingly though, like Morgan's proposal that a feminist cosmetic surgery could include scored on wrinkles, dyeing our hair grey and creating droopy breasts with lead weights, Orlan's ideas about cosmetic surgery being useful for aesthetic purposes other than the creation of 'normal' beauty have not yet been adopted.

Zylinska suggests that the lumps or 'horns' are an example of Orlan embracing 'the possibility of the unpredictable transformation that inevitably "explodes" the humanist discourse of identity' (2002: 226). The work then becomes an ethical project, one that extends beyond Orlan's body and confronts us all. The lumps and her other 'anti-beauty' endeavours not only demonstrate a purposeful move away from mainstream notions of beauty but also highlight the body's leaky penetrability and, more importantly, Orlan's willingness to allow it to be infiltrated. Zylinska suggests that 'through the extension of her body towards absolute alterity, Orlan challenges the confinement of moral agency to an autonomous and bounded self' (2002: 227).

Thirdly, *Reincarnation* prises open the usually closed space in the before/after schematic: remember that this project began a good twelve years before programmes like *Extreme Makeover* began to display operations in progress. Carey Lovelace, a playwright and arts writer, watched a live satellite broadcast of one of Orlan's operations in a New York gallery:

> Soon, the surgeon is sawing away, methodically scraping out flesh from below the hairline. The gallery empties of a third of its audience. After forty-five minutes, the monitor is finally turned off – that's all for now, announces gallery owner Gering, smiling, to the few hardy souls who remain. (Lovelace, 1995: 13)

The period taken to complete the operation is clocked, measurable time that the audience must endure; the forty-five minutes are gruelling, each one counted off by the stoic watchers who are only able to remain because they are 'hardy'.[4] The surgical revelations of *Extreme Makeover* are weak in comparison: the space they open between before and after is sanitised and compressed, bracketed by familiar narratives and promises of transformation, cut down to only a few minutes per episode. By showing *in real time* and *live* performance the acts that must occur for before/after to exist, Orlan creates a powerful temporality where every minute is experienced in excruciating second-by-second totality by the audience. The repulsion that Lovelace describes is because of squeamishness – the revulsion of the abject – but there is also a difficulty in watching labour articulated.

It is the *becoming* that is impossible for some to witness. Victoria Duckett suggests that Orlan's theatricality works against a fetishistic acceptance of before/after images, 'forcing a return to temporal reference and an acknowledgment of the marks of labour' (2000: 221). It is impossible to say whether Orlan's art influenced the mainstream opening of the space of the slash that we see in texts like *Extreme Makeover*. But certainly in makeover culture there is less revulsion around the abject open body and more interest in seeing bodies in process and bodies becoming. However much Orlan herself may hate the idea of being 'adopted' by the mainstream,[5] copycat lumps made with theatrical make-up featured on Parisian catwalks and some of the preoccupations of *Reincarnation* have been co-opted by it. Everyday cosmetic surgery culture now includes twilight sedations (where the patient remains conscious) for 'S' lifts and blepharoplasties; there is much more openness about the details of operations; and patients are increasingly seen as 'clients' with power and control.

Psychoanalyst Parveen Adams has described the spaces that are created when Orlan's face is cut into – for example the gap made when her cheek is lifted away from the bone – as the horrifying unknown: the space between inside and outside. For Adams there is a revelation in Orlan's work because of the emptiness revealed: 'in the space which is opened up... Something flies off; this something is the security of the relation between the inside and the outside. It ceases to exist... There is an emptying out of the object' (1996: 153–4). Following Zylinska's proposed 'prosthetic ethics of welcome' the emptiness need not be vacuous: it may also make space. It is not repulsive but invitational, expressing the ultimate hospitable body, one open to absolute alterity.

Theorising Michael Jackson

Orlan's work is multidimensional and difficult to grasp. But the 'project' of Michael Jackson's cosmetic surgery is even more elusive. Ironically, Orlan writes and speaks abundantly about her work but is often ignored. In contrast Jackson is secretive about his cosmetic surgery but speculation about it is overwhelming. His own output – his body and his texts – contradict each other. His operations exist as much in the titillating discourse around him as they exist on his body. In the next few sections I cover some of the ways that his 'body art' has been theorised. Broadly, he has been described as 'a paragon of sexual and racial ambiguity' (Mercer, 1986: 27) and is portrayed as a shoplifter of images and identities that don't rightfully belong to him: whiteness, femininity, beauty and childishness. This possibly makes him the exemplary monster of our time. Judith Halberstam claims that 'the monster functions as monster ... when it is able to condense as many fear-producing traits as possible into one body' (1995: 21). Jackson's body produces fear about race, gender and the child/adult divide.

It Don't Matter If You're Black Or White

Jackson is African American but no longer black. He is whiter than white, albino white, some say greyish-white beneath the make-up. He insists the change is a result of vitiligo, a condition where skin loses its ability to produce pigment and becomes patchy. The important issue is not whether he suffers from this condition but that he chooses to make his brown patches white rather than his white patches brown. African American literary scholar Michael Awkward insists that Jackson's 'assumption of nonblackness must be seen as neither inevitable nor as ideologically innocent...' (1995: 179). Jackson creates more complexity by proclaiming pride in being black: 'I'm a black American... I'm proud to be a black American. I'm proud of my race' (Oprah Winfrey interview, 1993, quoted in Awkward, 1995: 179).

His 2003 police card shows his pale face but designates him as black (RAC: B). There was concern at his 2005 trial for child molestation that the jury was all white. Clearly Jackson himself, the law, the American public and the countless critics who proclaim him as having 'abandoned' his blackness see Michael Jackson as being black. Indeed, as Awkward points out, his identification as black is quite correctly nothing to do with skin tone: the 'one drop'[6] rule ensures that 'blackness is not necessarily determined by how one looks ... by its very (American) definition, blackness can be masked effectively behind an apparently white physicality' (Awkward, 1995: 180).

Skin bleaching has a long history and is a multi-million dollar industry in the USA, Ghana, Jamaica, the Philippines and India (Charles, 2003; Laforteza, 2007; Robinson, 2004), indicating by numbers alone that Jackson's 'whitening' is probably an extreme example of a common practice. Many critics condemn his bleaching, describing him as 'a poster figure for black hatred' (Toure, quoted in Shaviro, 2003). Kathy Davis suggests that Jackson is an acute example of someone passing: '...Jackson's face evokes discomfort. It is a painful reminder of the legacy of slavery and the ubiquitous racism in the US that has made and will always make cross-racial "passing" a less-than-playful practice' (2003: 85). She suggests that passing is a practice that 'may not be so much about rejecting blackness (or any other marked identity) as about rejecting an identification with blackness that brings too much pain to be tolerated' (Davis, 2003: 87). This argument fits in with her overall analysis of cosmetic surgery as a technology used, largely by white women, to negate features that otherwise make life almost unbearable. So if skin bleaching is common, and if everyone knows Jackson is black anyway, then what is he doing that causes such ire?

The Mask of Whiteness

I suggest that the issue here is the *mask of whiteness*: a mask that works with race as the mask of femininity works for gender. The mask of whiteness, like the mask of femininity, provides only conditional protection. Jackson *overplays* his mask, makes it obvious and therefore confronting, in the same way that Farrah Fawcett overplays her adoption of youthful femininity. Sociocultural masks are usually desirable. For example, the *Extreme Makeover* website demonstrates how black people *should* adopt the mask of whiteness: 'Angela from Milwaukee, Wisconsin, is a clinic clerk who wants her lips and nose reduced, but fears that her African-American identity may be altered'. Angela receives 'a chin augmentation with implant, rhinoplasty, lower eyelid lift, upper and lower lip reduction, tummy tuck, breast augmentation, lipo of hips and waist, laser hair removal, skin Medical peel, at home programme for acne and hyperpigmentation, 6 upper da Vinci porcelain veneers and Zoom whitening' (Season 2, episode 12).

Angela was worked on by '...Dr. Anthony Griffin... A crusader in promoting the new safe ethnic surgical techniques to other plastic surgeons and teaching that plastic surgery does not erase ethnic identity' (*Extreme Makeover* website). Needless to say, there is never any mention of the risk of cosmetic surgery erasing the ethnic identities of white recipients. What Angela ends up with here is a 'whitening' of her distinctive 'black' features: most strikingly her nose is narrowed and her lips are thinned. Importantly, her skin colour is maintained and significantly she appeared slightly *darker* after the makeover. The message is that aesthetically, blackness is acceptable and indeed desirable so long as it is *only colour*: features should be altered to be more like those on white bodies. This 'whiteness' may be metaphoric but is as much about passing as bleaching one's skin is. Sander Gilman points out that the drive to 'pass' is not 'only the desire to "pass" as white, but to "pass" as black' (1999: 116). In other words, there is an acceptable 'black look': 'one can be "black". But "black" turns out ... to be in the eye of the beholder and the hand of the surgeon' (Gilman, 1999: 117). Dr Griffin's and *Extreme Makeover*'s brand of cosmetic surgery justifies itself as 'not erasing ethnic identity' by simply maintaining and darkening brown skin tones even as it does away with other indicators of African heritage. Jackson is doing exactly the same thing but he is far more honest about it. He has minimised, perhaps eradicated, his African American features including his colour. His blanched face brings attention to the mask of whiteness that people like Angela wear. The discomfort he evokes then is not just historical, as Davis suggests, but is also connected to contemporary ways of achieving mainstream black beauty.

In a British documentary called *Michael Jackson's Face* (Humphreys, 2002) music producer Quincy Jones tells how members of the Jackson family, especially the father, Joe, would tease Jackson about his 'Big head. Big nose. Big lips'. This is not cross-racial but intra-racial vilification. And criticism from one's family makes a deep impact. Virginia Blum tells how when she was a teenager her mother arranged for her to have rhinoplasty: 'having a parent criticize a physical feature is a complicated emotional experience that induces both anger and guilt. You feel as though you have let the parent down. Why didn't you come out right?' (2003: 1) Blum's mother took it on herself to fix the perceived aesthetic glitch. Jackson absorbed the paternal criticism and 'fixed' it himself, once he had the means, with a vengeance.

In *Michael Jackson's Face* many photos of Jackson are examined by cosmetic surgeon Jan Stanek. The trajectory of Stanek's analysis shows just how acceptable – commendable even – Jackson's 'whitening' was up to the point where the mask became too obvious.

Stanek looks at a photo of fourteen-year-old Jackson and says, '[here we see] typical features of a person of African origin. His nose is very wide, and very flat. He doesn't have much definition to his tip of his nose. Apart from that he is overall an attractive fourteen year old boy.' He is really saying that Jackson's nose is too African looking: at this stage this is a nose ripe for 'whitening'. He moves on to later photos wherein he identifies various surgeries that have taken place. He consistently describes them as having improved Jackson's face, particularly his nose: 'eight years later... He has had surgery to his nose, it is the overall width of his nose that has changed, including his tip. But his face remains attractive and he has suffered no ill effects from this surgery'. Others were equally impressed with Jackson's transformations. Surgeon Thomas Rees wrote in 1986 that African Americans were emulating him: 'patients are mightily impressed with the Caucasian-like transformation of the previously Negroid features of Michael Jackson, the noted entertainer' (quoted in Gilman, 1999: 117). Stanek continues

> we are looking at the same man, [a] few years later, who has had more surgery to his nose whereby the nose is slightly narrower. There's some suggestion that he may have had surgery to his cheeks which appear to be fuller. He still looks very attractive and the surgery has clearly done no harm to his appearance.

Stanek must be careful not to condemn all of Jackson's surgery: as I have shown, there is a 'correct' amount of surgery and knowing where to draw the line between proper and 'too much' is vital to being a successful cosmetic surgery recipient. Stanek traces the steps Jackson takes in creeping up to this line: 'he has a much narrower nose. His skin has become very much lighter. His chin has now developed a dimple. Again, surgery has achieved an improvement to his face, and certainly has caused no adverse effects' ... and then crossing it:

> the features are becoming a little more bizarre. The nose has become very pointed and grossly narrowed and certainly not in proportion with the rest of his face. The chin is much more pronounced and the skin has become considerably paler, but also what is noticeable is that the upper part of the face has become more effeminate than the lower part of the face.

At the exact moment Stanek deems Jackson's face to have become 'bizarre', 'effeminate' and 'not in proportion' his syntax changes dramatically. Previous commentary on the photos address Jackson as a person: 'he has a much narrower nose', but once the line is crossed his features become dissociated from him: they are 'the features', 'the nose' and 'the chin'. This effectively dehumanises Jackson by separating him from his own face. Calling his face by its separate parts also highlights the extent to which everyone *but* Jackson now owns it: it is ours to comment on and criticise. As one member of the paparazzi said, 'It got to a point in the late nineties, people wanted to see, what was the nose doing today?' (*Wacko Jacko* documentary, 2003)

In working to actually become a body that is neither black nor white Jackson invites hostility from all sides of racial debates. But what if his stated stance, 'it don't matter if you're black or white' (song lyrics to 'Black Or White', *Dangerous*, 1991) coupled with the aggressive intention to neutralise race on his own body, actually indicate an openness to kinds of identity where it *really* 'doesn't matter'?

Intergender

Jackson is not transgender – moving from one gender to the other – but rather intergender: incorporating both. Baudrillard speaks of a growing absence of difference between male and female bodies, bound up with what he sees as a decline in the display of sexual characteristics. In *America* he says 'the outer signs of masculinity are tending towards zero, but so are the signs of femininity' (1998: 35). He suggests that our 'new idols' have *undefined* gender. Jackson's feline body and remodelled face is a careful arrangement of 'masculine' and 'feminine' features: the jutting cleft chin is at gender-odds with the wide tattooed eyes and minuscule nose.

Once 'the face' is deemed to have changed from handsome to strange, Stanek stops focusing on the proper correction of unattractive (negro) features, and turns instead to gender, which he declares is 'unbalanced' in Jackson:

> We are looking at his latest picture and overall his face is aesthetically not pleasing. His nose has become Pinocchio-like with [a] very short pointed tip. It may not even be functioning because of the extreme narrowing... This chin is very wide, out of proportion with the nose. If you divide the face into two parts, the upper part of the face looks feminine, the lower part looks masculine. The two halves don't really fit together and therefore his face looks bizarre.

Alongside his appropriated whiteness, Jackson's nose is his most controversial cosmetic surgery feature. His multiple adjustments have made it, metaphorically, whiter than white – it is a narrower and pointier nose than white people have. In fact, only cartoon characters have noses like Michael Jackson. The link that Stanek makes to Pinocchio is a common one: it aligns Jackson with a quintessential liar, a boy whose nose grew longer and longer the more untruths he told. Of course the analogy is totally illogical because Jackson's nose is getting smaller and smaller, but the implication that he is a deceiver is what sticks: again, he is represented as deceitful. Just as female bodybuilders may be criticised for having 'misappropriated' masculine physical characteristics and are often deemed monstrous (Heywood, 1998: 49–56), Jackson is monstrous because he has adopted some of the signs and symbols of traditional femininity and claimed them as his own. His creation of an intergender body disturbs and upsets 'natural' gender dichotomies, and Stanek's most damning criticism of Jackson's face is that it is neither feminine nor masculine.

Making a body bigger is a way of making it more masculine, which is why the woman bodybuilder finds herself in a socially precarious situation: her body has become large and phallic and is therefore no longer 'feminine'. Michael Jackson suffers an inversion of her predicament. He has made himself metaphorically and – especially with certain features, particularly his nose and hair – literally smaller. Bodybuilders grow and set themselves on stage to be inspected and scrutinised as larger-than-life. Their monstrosity is writ large, borne on the surface of the body, completely externalised. In contrast, Michael Jackson shrinks with his annihilated nose, his flattened hair and his loose satin shirts and baggy black trousers that hide the contours of his body. His public demeanour – elegant, gentle, almost unfailingly polite – is reminiscent of a cute young girl, as is his high whispery public speaking voice. The surgical and other masks he wears in public with low-brimmed hats delete his face even further, reducing it to eyes, like a woman in a veil. This metaphoric smallness, traditionally associated with femininity, is another of his 'wrongful' appropriations – he is accused of trying to look like a white woman. But he does not look like a woman. Rather, his gender is neutralised by cosmetic surgery and he now resembles an androgynous anime that is almost all eyes. Jackson's self-fashioning of a cartoon face and his loose clothing partly eliminate traditional signs of adult sexuality, but then on stage he reappropriates masculinity by dramatically grabbing his crotch. His masculine posturing, like Lolo Ferrari's feminine posturing discussed in Chapter 6, is mere dress-ups: like Lolo, he has rendered himself sexless, adopting markers of heterosexual normativity (for her it is the massive breasts, for him it is the macho crotch-grab, lovingly quoted by Madonna and Justin Timberlake) as childlike dress-ups.

In justifying his cosmetic surgery (on the rare occasions he admits to it) he compares himself to women stars who have had cosmetic surgery. Interestingly, they are women from a bygone era so he oversteps historical barriers too: 'Judy Garland and Jean Harlow and many others have had their noses done. My problem is that as a child star people got used to seeing me look one way' (1988: 229). The lumps on Orlan's forehead work in a similar but more abstract way to join feminine and masculine. While they are meant to depict the Mona Lisa's lumpy forehead they are also reminiscent of breast implants (also made from silicone). However, they are the size and shape of testicles, and must be in part a commentary on the ongoing discussions about the Mona Lisa being a painted-over self-portrait of Da Vinci himself, thus being male and female. Both Jackson and Orlan bring overtly male and female characteristics together on their faces, conflating and juxtaposing gender differences.

The Child Within

Child-abuse allegations and investigations against Michael Jackson in 1993 were settled out of court.[7] He was tried on new charges in early 2005 and acquitted. The last thing I want to do here is somehow link his cosmetic surgery to his alleged paedophilia. This is often done in the popular press and results in further demonisations of radical cosmetic surgery practitioners. However, Jackson's fixation with children and childhood is compelling when thinking about how it might relate to his immersion in the world of cosmetic surgery. Indeed, I believe that the figure of the child is intimately connected with makeover culture and the notion of endless becoming.

Jackson passionately identifies with children and seems to believe that he is a child himself. One of the more extraordinary conversations with Martin Bashir in the infamous 2003 television documentary *Living with Michael Jackson*[8] is about Jackson's attachment to the novelised character Peter Pan. Jackson not only adores the fictional character but declares 'I am Peter Pan'. He says he loves him because he 'represents youth, childhood, never growing up, magic, flying', and he continues 'I just have never, ever grown out of loving that'. Peter Pan is not just any young boy, and he is also plainly not a younger version of Michael Jackson. He is a generic, fantastic überboy, representing boyhood as only a fictional character can do. Invented by Scottish author J. M. Barrie in 1902, he lives in Never-Never Land with fairies and his friends the Lost Boys. Life is a series of exciting adventures *sans* parents or the reality of one day having to become adult. Jackson's theme park-style ranch home in Santa Barbara is named Neverland (also a reference to Elvis Presley's Graceland home and Disneyland), and Jackson showed a preference for "Peter Pan collars" through 2002 (see Figure 15). For Jackson, who writes about an unhappy childhood and says that in some ways he missed out on childhood altogether (1988), the idea of such a boy must be hugely seductive. He told an audience at Oxford in March 2001 that 'all of us are products of our childhoods. But I am the product of a lack of a childhood, an absence of that precious and wondrous age where we frolic playfully without a care in the world' (quoted in Orth, 2004).

Children are visibly always in the process of becoming: childhood is a malleable form defined as not-yet-adult. 'Childhood' invokes potential, development, growth and transformation. Claudia Castañeda's book *Figurations: Child, Bodies, Worlds* (2002) looks at how childhood is constructed 'naturally', culturally and imaginatively, and how it is produced through history, science, medicine and theory. In discussing how theory, particularly poststructural theory, selects the figure of the child for use as a becoming-agent, she quotes Gilles Deleuze and Felix Guattari:

Figure 15 Cover of Australian *Woman's Day*, 1 April 2002. David Gest, Liza Minnelli, Michael Jackson and Elizabeth Taylor at Minnelli's wedding to Gest. Jackson is wearing a 'Peter Pan collar'.

'the girl and the child do not become; it is becoming itself that is ... a child. The child does not become an adult ... the child is the becoming-young of every age' (Deleuze and Guattari, *A Thousand Plateaus: Capitalism and Schizophrenia*, quoted in Castañeda, 2002: 144).

She interprets this cryptic statement with graceful ease, noting that Deleuze and Guattari see the child as a 'pure form to be inhabited' and as a *'form* of becoming' (2002: 147).

> [Deleuze and Guattari] figure the female ('girl') child and the generic 'child' not as persons with their own forms of embodiment, history, and location, but rather as the condition of becoming itself... To 'become young', in these terms, is to take the form of the child, which in turn is defined as a condition of becoming (rather than being). (2002: 146)

For Castañeda this kind of theorising is highly problematic because it is yet another way in which the figure of the child is adopted and exploited by the adult world. She describes postmodern and poststructuralist theorists using the figure of the child to disrupt the normative (adult) subject in order to throw light on adult concerns and as a tool to discuss adult modes of being. But the child itself is left with no form: it is 'contentless', and 'does not itself constitute an entity in its own right' (2002: 147). In the case of poststructural theory she explains that the child-figure lacks materiality, and instead 'takes the form of the experience of becoming, once again, where becoming is both a longed for and desired "bliss". The bliss of becoming, in other words, becomes attainable by taking on the form that is the child. To become a child is to inhabit becoming itself.' (2002: 147–8) Inhabiting or incorporating the figure of the child is a way of going back to being *all potentiality*: the child, in representing 'becoming itself', always has the capacity for transformation and development.

Jackson's shameless appropriation of the figure of the child to describe himself parallels the stance that Deleuze and Guattari adopt for their own theoretical ends. Through Castañeda's lens we see that Jackson's seizure of clichéd childhood characteristics like honesty, innocence and acceptance (while things like bullying and selfishness are never mentioned) in order to promote himself as a better, more pure and particularly as a 'becoming' person are an overt manifestation of a common cultural refrain. The bizarreness of his stance is perpetrated not because of his attitude to childhood, which is one reflected in Western society at large, but in its heart-on-sleeve honesty, his ability (because of wealth) to indulge it, and in his wholesale ingesting of the child – 'I am Peter Pan, I'm Peter Pan in my heart' (Bashir, 2003).

As with his cosmetic surgery, which takes the cultural logics of self-improvement, glossy surfaces, de-racialisation and the pursuit of normalised beauty to their logical ends, so too his starry-eyed attitude to childhood simply takes a set of commonly acceptable cultural ideas to their logical extreme. Paradoxically, in identifying with the boy who never grows up, Jackson hardens and partly negates the element of transformation that is inherent in children. Peter Pan is different from real children because he won't transform and he won't grow up. He is a tragic figure absurdly lacking the essence of childhood – finitude – and thus his failure to be a real boy is in fact close to the 'absent' childhood that Jackson experienced.

The Problem of Puberty

Jackson writes in *Moonwalk*: 'My appearance began to really change when I was about fourteen. I grew quite a bit in height. People who didn't know me would come into a room expecting to be introduced to cute little Michael Jackson and they'd walk right past me ... I was not the person they expected or even wanted to see.' (1988: 95–6) Serious acne and a dramatic growth spurt – which leave many teenagers underconfident – were worse for Jackson because the public loved his incredibly endearing pre-teen self. He describes moments of acute embarrassment when he is neither recognised nor accepted in his 'new' body. These were reverse Peter Pan moments, when other people wanted him to stay a child and had difficulty reconciling him as a gangly and spotty teen. In this way, the 'Panisation' of Michael Jackson cannot be seen as entirely his own doing: his life and his performances were so intertwined that his identity hinged on the public's opinion of him: 'You must remember that I had been a child star and when you grow up under that kind of scrutiny people don't want you to change, to get older and look different' (1988: 227).

Orlan was similarly distressed by puberty. She speaks of a revelation that came at puberty: the appearance of breasts and pubic hair. These changes were horrifying to her: 'I couldn't stop it, it was against my will' (Brand, 2000a: 301). Later, when she fell pregnant, the reality that her body was somewhat uncontrollable was terrible: '[it] was so unbelievable at first that I thought that my will alone would cause me to abort; but it didn't, nature kept it going' (Brand, 2000a: 301). Her horror parallels Jackson's dismay at the body's transformability. Both artists' negative preoccupation with puberty are compelling when considering their relationships with cosmetic surgery. Orlan's stance 'against' puberty is aggressive, conscious and feminist, embracing her adulthood and autonomy utterly, while Jackson's is passive-aggressive, subconscious and distressed, working towards the impossible recreation of an idealised and idyllic childhood. Both of them attempt to control the body: she declares it an envelope that can be modified according to the mind's desires, he declares repeatedly that the body doesn't matter: 'I was really the same person inside, even if you didn't recognize me' (Jackson, 1988: 275). I don't offer this analysis as a psychological diagnosis of troubled individuals but rather to show how these two artists have used their own experiences of common cultural anxieties in their subsequent artistic practices.

Performers in Sickness and in Health

Jackson and Orlan brought private pain, display and cosmetic surgery becomings into the public domain at least a decade before shows like *Extreme Makeover*. Unlike recipients of *Extreme Makeover*, their cosmetic surgeries do not happen in a bubble. For all its exposition of cosmetic surgery's processes, *Extreme Makeover* returns to the cosy idea of magical transformation at the end of each programme, comparing before and after bodies and glorying in the Reveal. Recipients of *Extreme Makeover* are expected to merge back into everyday life. In contrast, Orlan and Jackson's makeovers are never-ending. Their chosen aesthetics are constant reminders of the bloody surgeries they have endured; the way they look prevents them from blending into everyday life. Each of them is now a living work of art, often recognised as such by other artists. Orlan's self-body-portrait is deliberate and planned; Jackson's is a haphazard, accidental collage. He doesn't perform his operations publicly the way that she does but his face announces to the world all the work done – its paleness and peculiar features evoke pain and anaesthetic. Both artists bring the private to the public, turning the operating spaces of cosmetic surgery inside out.

Jackson has two modes of public presentation: as the powerful concert/video performer and as the ailing invalid. He will 'disable' himself one day, appearing in public hobbling on exoware such as pristine chrome crutches, only to emerge the following evening in concert sporting golden leg armour, looking like a cross between a fantasy of the posthuman cyborg and a medieval gallant knight. On stage and in film and video he represents himself as monarchic, god-like, and is made more mobile and more powerful via his sculptural prosthetics. This Michael Jackson is highly sexualised, grabbing at his crotch as he over-performs aspects of masculinity. His technological enhancements are metallic, reminiscent of robotic sci-fi or cyber-imagery.

In contrast Jackson has a 'sick' or 'disabled' public performance that he increasingly adopts when he is making a public appearance rather than a public performance. For example, arriving at airports where he knows there will be photographers he is likely to wear a surgical mask or walk on crutches. He has been photographed in slings, plaster, bandages, braces and even in wheelchairs. These accessories, whether 'medical' or not, are significant in the construction of his public persona.

Vanity Fair reporter Maureen Orth writes of seeing Jackson at court in 2002: 'He had only a sock on his left foot, but he was able to walk unassisted. As soon as it was time to enter the courtroom, however, Jackson fell onto a pair of crutches and started limping markedly. We were told he had been bitten by a spider.' (Orth, 2003) In surgery Orlan presents a temporarily disabled body, prone and somewhat immobile, subject to the power of others. And strikingly, Jackson, for all his secretiveness and even outright denial of his cosmetic surgery, does the same thing. He is entranced with presenting his body as hurt and as needing prosthetics. His presentation of his non-stage-performing self as weak and sick is a lateral and perhaps unconscious public acknowledgement of his continual surgeries. Orlan's display of the cosmetic surgery process is extroverted and central to her artistic practice. Jackson's display of the same process comes to us in code: he simply *presents* with symptoms of someone in a process of painful transformation, with no explanation of their cause. For both artists, the body as a work-in-progress is a concept with huge import, although Orlan's presentation of this concern is more consciously forthright than Jackson's.

Jackson oscillates between someone enjoying rude health, able to dance and sing energetically, and a person suffering from debilitating sickness. He displays cyborgian advantages and disadvantages, expressing the range of interpretations between paranoia and seduction that we all experience when considering technologies like cosmetic surgery that augment, repair, invade and enhance the body. His whole public image is about the blurring of these boundaries. Perhaps, as he asserts, his first nose job was really because of his hair catching fire during the filming of the Pepsi commercial. But a medical intervention led to many more cosmetic ones, and the two modes of surgery are intertwined. Jackson's surgeries are publicly 'performed' (although not overtly like Orlan's) through his surgical masks and other prosthetics.

In contrast, Kathy Davis places Orlan at a distance from her cosmetic surgery, viewing cosmetic surgery as an artistic tool and her body as a 'canvas'. Davis refutes suggestions that her own scholarly work on cosmetic surgery can be compared to Orlan's *Reincarnation*: 'Orlan's project is not about a real-life problem; it is about art... Her body is little more than a vehicle for her art and her personal feelings are entirely irrelevant' (Davis, 1997: 175–6, quoted in Ince, 2000: 126). Kate Ince strongly rejects this: 'it is hard to imagine a more wrongheaded approach to Orlan's work than this... Since she is a body artist, it is accurate to say that Orlan's body is her vehicle, but it is also still a material entity from which her personal identity is inseparable.' (Ince, 2000; 126–7) Certainly, there are two intertwined Orlans: firstly the artist who uses cosmetic surgery as her medium and secondly the woman who is dramatically altered by cosmetic surgery. Ince is critical of attempts to separate them and says that Davis 'can in fact only disable the comparison between Orlan and the majority of women who have cosmetic surgery by imposing a rigid binary opposition between art and reality, or art and life...' (Ince, 2000: 127). And of course art/reality is one of the binary oppositions that Orlan and Michael Jackson transgress. Orlan vividly re-created her body as a canvas in the name of art and became inescapably bound to living out the consequences of that choice: she suffers when the operations cause her pain, she has had to undergo corrective surgery, she endures misunderstandings and ridicule from the press, and she presumably also experiences joy (and financial gain) from her surgical results. Her art is her body: ordinary personal life and artistic practice could not be more knotted.

The life/art merge of Michael Jackson is an inversion of this: he is intensely private and secretive about his cosmetic surgery, intent on keeping it separate from his role as a public performer. This intent has patently failed: it floods out from private to public spectacularly and impacts on his public life and performances whether he wants it to or not. Doctor/patient confidentiality is all but lost, without the surgeon saying a word, because the proof is carved on Jackson's face. The side effect of Orlan's work is that she necessarily lives even mundane moments as a piece of living art. Conversely, the side effects of Jackson's private, deeply personal relationship with cosmetic surgery is that it forces its way into making a radical impact on his professional life.

Martyrs for our Time

> When he sings, it is with the voice of angels. When his feet move, you can see God dancing. (Bob Geldof, introducing Michael Jackson at the 1996 *Brit Awards*, http://news.bbc.co.uk/hi/english/static/events/brit_awards/jarvis.htm)

> Orlan not only produces photographs of her operations which show her lips exposed and wet with blood trickling down her cheek, alongside grapes, which play off Christian iconography, she also collects and juxtaposes samples of her blood and flesh from the operations in ways which resemble the medieval cult of relics. (Featherstone, 1999: 9)

Orlan and Jackson may be the high priest and priestess of makeover culture. Both have presented themselves at key career moments (perhaps with tongue in cheek, but probably not) as saintly or messianic, and as martyred. At the 1996 *Brit Awards* Jackson performed his 'Earth Song'. On stage he wore Messiah-like white robes and long flowing hair. Children and old people took turns to come and shelter beneath his outstretched arms. He appeared at once protective and almighty, and reminiscent of a persecuted Christ on the cross.[9]

Rather than analysing the possible psychological motives for the hagiographic imagery that each artist has played with, I suggest we take these performances at face value. We may engage with the possibility that these artists are martyrs for our time, embodying and displaying some key contemporary fears and horrors. By performing and experiencing the painful physical and social stigmas associated with extreme cosmetic surgery, Jackson and Orlan make the anxieties 'real' and in some way take the burden of extreme enactment away from the general populace. They push the contemporary alarm about seductive transformative technologies such as cosmetic surgery to its polar end, ingesting and evoking all of its horror.

This results in a confrontation of a sort, as the grisly artist delivers a painful reality to a tender audience. But it also means that the audience/congregation is able to unburden itself of some of the consternation connected with more mundane deployments of cosmetic surgery, or of other technologies that make us willing cyborgs like heart and liver transplants. The distaste that can come about because of technologised twenty-first-century bodies is removed from the body of the populace to the bodies of extreme practitioners. In a chapter published in 2002 about Stelarc and Orlan, Zoë Sofoulis and I argued in a similar vein that

> Each claims not to be religious – Orlan is specifically blasphemous, Stelarc rigorously atheist – yet by placing themselves as the ones prepared to suffer bodily in their critiques of collective secular ideals (whether of art, beauty or techno-evolution), they can be positioned alongside mystics of the Middle Ages who voluntarily suffered for the sake of holiness. (2002: 56–7)

Like martyrs, Jackson and Orlan are suffering for the sake of beliefs, ideals and for others: they become monstrous so that we don't have to. Performing an ethics of welcome they bear the strain of hospitality, opening themselves to future possibilities and playing the roles of host and hostess of makeover culture.

Cartoon Monsters

In her project *Self-Hybridations*, Orlan worked on a 'global survey' of notions of beauty from ancient non-Western cultures. The first instalment was a series of computer-generated self-portraits inspired by ancient Olmec and Mayan body modifications; the created heads have high elongated foreheads, asymmetric features, different skin colours and 'scarification' patterns. Later she used African and European modifications: Figure 16 shows a juxtaposition between lip stretching – something Western culture may consider barbaric – and the common practice of curling hair. For Orlan, morally and aesthetically, there is simply no difference between these two beauty technologies. In the *Hybridations* series Orlan uses digital imaging software instead of surgery, so is able to create unlimited variations on her theme, almost unhindered by time and place. *Reincarnation* was laborious – set firmly in the now – because although it was grounded in a computer-generated amalgamation, it could only be realised through real surgery.

The transformations required in *Self-Hybridations* are so varied that they can only be achieved digitally. Despite being digital, the portraits inspired by Mayan and Aztec beauty practices evoke pain and forced physical change; the skulls are altered to such a degree we can't imagine an undamaged brain. Elongated foreheads, deep scarification, twisted necks: these are asymmetries designated 'ugly'. Part of Orlan's purpose is to shock – to make us realise that what we think of as ugly is another culture's beauty – and importantly, she also shows that digital and virtual modes of transformation can be just as confronting as 'real' ones.

Ince makes an interesting distinction between modern and postmodern performance art. She says that in postmodernity

> the body had become digitally saturated, thoroughly and completely mediatized by the images and electronic signals transmitting the surgery to the world beyond the operating

Figure 16 Orlan (2002) *African Self-hybridization: Surmas Woman with Lip Plug and Face of Euro-Saint-Etienne Woman with Rollers*, digital photograph on colour photographic paper. Edition of 7. 49¼ × 61½ in. Courtesy Galerie Michel Rein, Paris

theatre. Orlan's 'omnipresence' [one of the operations in the *Reincarnation* series] was achieved via media technology, and was as such a prime example of postmodern media culture, in which physical reality has given way entirely to mediatized reality, and referents are subsumed in the continuous circulation of signs. (2000: 104)

Orlan's multiple VR metamorphoses demonstrate that the 'fantasy of desire' is not possible. Presented as a collage, the digital modifications are striking in their differences from 'normal' faces, and in their differences from each other. The colours are reminiscent of Warhol's Marilyn Monroe and Jackie O collages but where Warhol's faces are two-dimensional variations on a deliberately shallow, 'pretty' theme, Orlan's show her face twisted and turned inside out, the features distorted irrevocably.

Jackson was animated from an early age: *The Jackson Five* cartoon appeared on US television in 1971. He wrote in his autobiography *Moonwalk*, 'I loved being a cartoon. It was so much fun to get up on Saturday mornings to watch cartoons and look forward to seeing ourselves on the screen. It was like a fantasy come true for all of us' (1988: 99). As an adult Jackson has continued to represent himself via digitisation and animation and is especially interested in showing transformations. Lee analyses the *Thriller* video, concentrating on how Jackson metamorphoses into a monster (werewolf/zombie) and back again throughout the narrative:

> What is poignant is his desire for otherness, for metamorphosis, which enables him to transcend his othered humanity (his blackness, compulsive heterosexuality) while at the same time reinscribing him in another otherness, another monstrification, though the latter one is self-willed rather than conventionalized. (1994)

For Lee, Jackson's transformations, both in real life and on video, are a form of ironic resistance similar to Haraway's cyborgs, which 'blasphemize the boundary between the collective and individual through an infinite availability of appropriation and rearticulation' (1994). Particularly significant is Lee's interpretation of Jackson's final metamorphosis in *Thriller* into a zombie indistinguishable from a mass of other zombies, and his final metamorphosis in *Moonwalker* into a rabbit identical to a mass of other rabbits. After going from monster to human and back again in each video, the final scenes both show Jackson indistinguishable from the herd. Thus, the dichotomies that Jackson plays with include individual/collective and organic/digital, and show a desire for invisibility through sameness – precisely the opposite of what his cosmetic surgery has achieved.

Jackson's metaphoric smallness works on levels other than androgyny and femininity. He is a 'larger-than-life' performer who nevertheless works at invisibilising himself. His seeming desire for a lack of bodily presence manifests in increasing efforts to delete the body, particularly the sexual body. By whittling away his nose, bleaching his skin and becoming thinner, Jackson flattens himself into something like a two-dimensional cartoon drawing. It is as if the image of himself that he has lived with for so many years has finally taken over – image and identity have literally conjoined. This is hard to witness. One of the things that makes people wince when they see Jackson's pale, almost disappearing, visage is the beholding of a battle between two and three dimensions. If Jackson is trying to become a cartoon-self then he is working on yet another boundary: that between real and virtual. Mark Poster says that the struggle to reconcile 'reality' and virtuality is one of postmodernity's central concerns: the increase in simulations and representations results in a widening of earlier definitions of reality: '[the] effect of new media such as the Internet and virtual reality … is to multiply the kinds of "realities" one encounters in society' (Poster, 1995, reprinted in 2001: 620). He uses communities as an example:

> Just as virtual communities are understood as having the attributes of 'real' communities, so 'real' communities can be seen to depend on the imaginary: what makes a community vital to its members is their treatment of the communications as meaningful and important. Virtual and real communities mirror each other in chiasmic juxtaposition. (Poster, 2001: 621)

In the same way, we could argue that virtual people (cartoon characters, images of pop stars) operate in 'chiasmic juxtaposition' to real people. In postmodernity the two are no longer separated but have become intertwined. Jackson embodies both reality and virtuality, and shows that trying to separate them is no longer a fruitful task.

Becoming and Endlessness

The 'fantasy' operations that Orlan has mentioned and planned are announced with great seriousness and – I think – with every intention of completion.[10] Operation number ten of *Reincarnation* was meant to place a giant twisted nose stretching from mid forehead to the centre of Orlan's face (Griffin, 1996) but has still not happened, and Orlan seems to have moved on to other things. The Cronenberg script for *Painkillers* is completed but the film has not been made. Neither the 'opening and closing of the body' operation nor the one that would 'considerably alter [her] appearance, and enhance [her] physical faculties' have taken place. For Kate Ince, the incompleteness of *Reincarnation* has become integral to the open-endedness that is at the core the project:

> Saint Orlan's reincarnation (as?) will never be definitively complete: her surgical self-transformation is not work *on* identity, but a work *of* identity … [she] did not just set herself a model to emulate, a visual goal that she could achieve … What she did was to find in a controversial contemporary medical practice a kind of allegory for the way in which finite human subjectivity can continue to modify itself, materially and endlessly. (2000: 111)

Similarly, unfulfilled promise of further dramatic operations should not be read as failure to deliver but rather as testament to Orlan's intention to be endlessly transforming. She acts out makeover culture's promises for dramatic transformation whilst emphasising its demands for a never-ending dedication to becoming. Corporeal and logistical impediments may be to blame for the lack of realisation of these projects but the fact that they have not taken place becomes part of their impact. In an inversion of the in-your-face demonstrability of *Reincarnation*, these operations don't need to be seen. They express an open-endedness that is always present in Orlan's work and are part of the prosthetic ethics of welcome that she performs. At least two of the fantasy operations are about opening the body only for the sake of opening. She has said that for 'opening and closing of the body' she has chosen her armpit for locality and vision. The cut will be located close to her face, so her face can be filmed and photographed next to it. Visually the armpit has hairs: the deep slit will resemble a vulva.[11] 'Opening' is quite different from 'cutting'. By calling her operation 'opening' Orlan treats the body as a portal. Like the hidden doors of fairy tales that mysteriously appear and lead into other worlds only to magically disappear again, Orlan's sutured armpit will have scar tissue grow over it, the parted sides of flesh will meld, the hairs will cover over any trace that there was once an opening there. Like other magical doors it is temporary but will reveal hidden worlds before becoming impenetrable again. In this operation she enacts only the gash, the space between: there is no before or after.

So here Orlan performs makeover culture's quintessential action: *all between*, she enacts the essence of becoming but then takes even this a step further in the operation for Cronenberg's proposed film, where she would be, seemingly, completely opened from head to toe. These imagined operations are about making connections at a deep, primal level. Performance artist Rachel Rosenthal says: 'we are so isolated from the other, so lonely. Self-penetration, physical and violent, is a metaphysical response to this despair of ever connecting deeply. So we … pierce the separating membrane. We explode the integrity of form' (quoted in Dery, 1996: 167). The body is turned inside out, opened as much as possible without being destroyed. What *is* destroyed is containment – the body becomes hole, not whole – gaping with possibility, completely and consciously welcoming. Everyday cosmetic surgery recipients may be mere mortals of makeover culture compared to Orlan, but her work shows that they can also be figured as performing acts of inclusion, acts that open their bodies to networks of connections and possibilities for endless transformation.

Conclusion

Susan Stewart says that we know our bodies only in parts, and that therefore the self-image, that which is projected out and introjected back to us, is what constitutes the self. 'Others' tell us more about ourselves than themselves because they mirror our own image: 'Since we know our body only in parts, the image is what constitutes the self for us; it is what constitutes out subjectivity. By a process of projection and introjection of the image, the body comes to have the abstract "form", the abstract totality, by which we know it.' (1993: 125)

Orlan enacts both projection and introjection of the image: her carnal art projects, deeply connected with her image, are designed to be consumed. But the images she creates are also hospitable, creating metaphoric spaces for new kinds of meaning. She makes holes without end, recesses without solid form, pockets capable and incapable of holding anything. Thus she enacts the endless, idealised *becoming* of makeover culture and an ethics of welcome. In contrast, Jackson's body appears more two-dimensional and more metaphorically closed the more cosmetic surgery he has. He usually denies the slash between before/after, absurdly attempting to negate it by trying to pass himself off as someone who just happens to look the way he does. Against his flat smoothness Orlan is messy and open, her skin-casing undone as she celebrates, documents and performs the slash. They represent two poles of makeover culture. Hers is a three-dimensional leaky body, glorifying its own messiness. His is a two-dimensional stitched-up body working hard to be 'clean'.

These two artists perform a prosthetic identity that is monstrous in the sense of ushering in that which is not yet known, welcoming many futures, opening to alterity and being in a state of constant change. They operate as interfaces between present-bodies and future-bodies, whilst also demonstrating a kind of identity where agency is distributed and the ideal human is utterly connected with others.

They embody the prickly intertwining of private and public, professional and personal, high and low art, and reality and virtuality. These uncomfortable pairings are increasingly part of life in postmodernity. The preoccupation with how to live across multiple worlds is a common postmodern trope, and many of our contemporary cultural productions show that postmodern subjects can and must negotiate through many worlds concurrently in order to manage everyday life successfully. The quintessential postmodern subject is comfortable in virtual or real realms, and in multiple scapes, including mediascapes (Poster, 2001; Turkle, 1996). Both artists operate in multiple worlds – one of the ways they do this is via their extreme cosmetic surgery.[12]

Orlan and Jackson publicly present their bodies in the messy and painful stages of evolution at least as often as they present them in their 'finished' states. Thus periods of between/becoming are commodified: moments of development and change are (sometimes literally) placed centre stage and are glamorised by being attached to fame and controversy. Vivian Sobchack argues that in a heavily mediatised landscape 'the morph [is] this ideal object' (Muller, 'Interview with Vivian Sobchack', n.d.). In other words, the process of becoming is now a sought-after experience and mode-of-being in itself.

Jackson was considered by many to be the best pop singer-songwriter in the world, and one of the best performers: perhaps he is now the world's best cosmetic surgery recipient, taking the practice into new arenas, extending it to create an entirely new aesthetic. He is certainly a pioneer of a unique aesthetic, as acknowledged by his biographer Michael Toure who said:

> Well, he clearly in 'Thriller' does not look like he did with the Jackson 5... I'll tell you, I don't remember when it was. It had to be in the early '90s, I think. And I looked at him and I said, 'Wow, he can't look any weirder than this'... and two years later, I said the same thing... And two years after that, I said the same thing. 'This is it. You can't get any weirder than this'... And every year or so I look at him like, 'He topped me yet again.' (quoted in Mankiewicz, 2003)

The future that these monstrous figures are open to is not some techno-nightmare, nor a utopia where prostheticism is controlled in order to enhance and serve human mobility or cognition. Rather it is a future that is uncontrolled, prosthetic in the sense of being open to others, to experiment, to being penetrated and penetrating, to alterity.

–8–

Transit Lounges for the Self

Billboards in [a] fanciful future will exhort the motorist: KEEP AMERICA BEAUTIFUL, VISIT YOUR LOCAL PLASTIC SURGEON.

Aronsohn and Epstein, *The Miracle of Cosmetic Plastic Surgery*

As long as we are using disciplinary technologies within their own terms, we are bound to the dynamics of suffering that they induce.

Heyes, *Self-Transformations*

In this concluding chapter, following the mode of analysis begun in Chapter 2, I deploy architectural templates to consider cosmetic surgery aesthetics. Makeover culture is compared to Rem Koolhaas's 'Junkspace' theory and to Stewart Brand's 'evolutionary buildings'. Finally, an analysis of Melbourne's Federation Square is deployed to discuss alternative cosmetic surgeries.

Junkspace

Cosmetic surgery is a kind of architecture of the human body. It can create decorative changes to the surface and immediate sub-surface of the body like Botox® and dermabrasion, or more visceral renovations and restorations like implants and liposuction. The stretched middle age requires continual maintenance. In order for the appearance to be somewhat frozen in time there must be rigorous and even ritualistic 'behind the scenes' medico-beauty technologies at work. One journalist describes how 'devotees of cosmetic surgery observe their beauty regimens – the twice-weekly hair appointments, the weekly scorched-earth depilations, the bimonthly teeth whitening, the thrice-yearly cosmetic-surgery consultations, and the annual surgical procedures' can be compared to 'the self-scourging rigor of a medieval ascetic' (Mead, 2006: 90).

Architect and critic Rem Koolhaas, in an extraordinary essay (2001), which Fredric Jameson says combines 'revulsion and euphoria' and is a 'postmodern artefact in its own right' (2003: 73), constructs a theory of 'Junkspace'. He argues that contemporary architecture creates spaces that *depend* on being endlessly altered and upgraded: 'Junkspace is fanatically maintained...' (2001: 411). Koolhaas ponders the non-stop architectural restructuring and interior refurbishment of spaces such as airports and shopping malls and extends his observations to Western culture in general: 'restore, rearrange, reassemble, revamp, renovate, revise, recover, redesign, return – the Parthenon marbles – redo, respect, rent: verbs that start with *re-* produce Junkspace' (2001: 415).

In a set of remarks that complement my notion of makeover culture Koolhaas mourns the proliferation of Junkspace alongside people's increasing acceptance of inconvenient renovations and restorations as almost permanent facets of everyday life:

> Renovation and restoration were [once] procedures that took place in your absence; now you're a witness, a reluctant participant.... Seeing Junkspace in conversion is like inspecting an unmade bed, someone else's. Say an airport needs more space. In the past new terminals were added, each more or less characteristic of its own age, leaving the old ones as a readable record, evidence of progress. Since passengers have definitively demonstrated their infinite malleability, the idea of rebuilding on the spot has gained currency... (2001: 413)

Just as building renovations are no longer hidden but are now 'in the face' of the urbanite – who is confronted daily with all sorts of re/constructions from gaping holes to escalators that lead only to a sign telling us to turn back – images and narratives of the between/becoming stages of cosmetic surgery are now less proof of secret procedures that we hope nobody knows about. Visualisation and narrativisation of the *processes* of cosmetic surgery are no longer taboo but have become part of an everyday lexicon: demystified components of a 'lifestyle choice'. The stretched middle age requires constant upkeep and the performance of that upkeep is increasingly in the public eye. Through cosmetic surgery and related technologies such as hair dyeing and slimming, middle-aged bodies are seen as permanently in need of repair, ever-improvable and ideally in a constant process of change.

> Aging in Junkspace is nonexistent or catastrophic; sometimes an entire Junkspace – a department store, a nightclub, a bachelor pad – turns into a slum overnight without warning: wattage diminishes imperceptibly, letters drop out of signs, air conditioning units start dripping, cracks appear as if from otherwise unregistered earthquakes; sections rot, are no longer viable, but remain joined to the flesh of the main body via gangrenous passages. (Koolhaas, 2001: 413)

This evocative description of the rot that sets in immediately if Junkspace is not constantly attended to registers in the cosmetic surgery world where bodies with one 'renovation' demand another and then another: an 'S' lift may 'reveal' the need for an eye lift while many breast implants last only a decade before they need to be replaced. However, once the ageing body ceases to participate in restoration or renovation it inevitably slips into aesthetic decline and possibly even the horror! of unadorned old age. Following Koolhaas's logic the cosmetic surgery-altered body itself is an example of Junkspace, renovated or at least 'maintained' potentially into eternity, its surfaces falling into disrepair unless they are ceaselessly titillated, polished and re-done.

Learning Buildings

A counterpoint to *Junkspace* is Stewart Brand's *How Buildings Learn* (1994). While Koolhaas focuses on the contemporary moment, Brand looks at how structures evolve and grow over time: changing their 'skins', sprouting wings, fattening or slimming-down their porches and other surrounds, extending skywards, digging themselves into the earth or 'shrinking' as they become dwarfed by taller surrounding structures. He finds that 'Almost no buildings adapt well. They're *designed* not to adapt; also budgeted and financed not to, constructed not to, administered not to, maintained not to, regulated and taxed not to, even remodelled not to. But all buildings (except monuments) adapt anyway, however poorly, because the usages in and around them are changing constantly.' (1994: 2)

According to Brand, architects are deluded by the notion that 'good' buildings must stand the test of time and therefore not change. He argues instead that buildings should be built to 'know' they must inevitably change and alter. His 'knowing' buildings don't require 'the work of generations of space planners, repairmen and fixers, like in the Middle Ages' (Koolhaas, 2001: 408). Instead they use 'evolutionary design' and technologies such as 'aware' self-mending concrete (Brand, 1994: 221).

Brand's philosophy of building design advocates organic architecture that parallels the human body's ability to renew itself even as it ages, to grow and to mend, and to adapt around scar tissue. This largely speculative architecture mimics the body's ability to ingest products, to modify and augment itself with non-organic materials and to delete or adjust with surgery – this is an architecture that can offer the 'prosthetic ethics of welcome' I explained in the last chapter. Brand's adaptable buildings may go through a lifelong series of cosmetically enhanced façade changes, or they may update their interiors beneath seemingly deteriorating surfaces. They do not serve to imitate a form that is ideal, classical and unchanging – 'set in stone', or immortalised in bricks and mortar – rather they parallel the living, sprouting, but also degenerative, human body. They embrace the possibility – indeed the inevitability – of Junkspace as part of their evolution, but Junkspace is not their *raison d'être*.

Bodies in a state of makeover are aesthetically close to Junkspace, always in their gym gear or hospital gowns, rushing towards an unattainable Bonaventure-like state of perfection. In contrast, Brand's notion of versatile temporal architecture aligns with a mutable body that may be altered in multifarious ways. An alternative, even utopic, cosmetic surgery might be close to the architecture that he describes – it would be part of a series of active, vigorous body technologies that do not seek to hide themselves, their processes, or the corporeal histories of the bodies they

operate on. It would position the body as dying, healing, technologically augmented/
diminished and scarred. Such bodies might look quite different to the cosmetic
surgery bodies that we are used to. They might be decoratively scarred; they might
feature plastics and metals on their surfaces; they might have interchangeable parts;
they might be joined to each other and to their environments in as yet undreamed of
ways.

Other Worlds

Architecture in postmodernism is not restricted to tangible, real life structures.
There are also the computer architectures of cyberspace and virtual reality. In postmodernism we are presented with a range of real and simulated worlds across which
being, consciousness, souls and bodies may be located or divided. Postmodern city-
scapes, for example, are made up of many layered realities and modes of being. This
plurality and how to live in it is the *raison d'être* of cyberpunk and science fiction.
The film *The Matrix* (Warner Bros, 1999), where characters negotiate between a
horrifying machine-dominated reality and an utterly believable simulation of the late
twentieth century, and the novel *Neuromancer* (Gibson, 1984), where the protagonist
is desperately seeking 'upload' into the neural net (cyberspace) and wishes to leave
his 'meat' (body) behind, are typical of these genres.

I suggest that cosmetic surgery is also a way to cope with multiple worlds: an
attempt to locate the body meaningfully in environments that are hyper (Jameson,
2001), simulated (Baudrillard, 1994) and multiple (Turkle, 1996). This is precisely
why it lends itself so well to expression in fiction and to the fantasy-scapes of reality
television. As I showed in Chapter 7 it can be a symbolic juncture between real
and unreal worlds. However, in contrast to fantasies of leaving the 'meat' behind,
cosmetic surgery seeks to make earthly bodies perfect. New social identities created
in non-corporeal landscapes like cyberspace are complemented and paralleled by
purely physical technologies such as cosmetic surgery. The much-analysed modified
virtual self is complemented by a corresponding modified physical self: in this way
cosmetic surgery recipients are exemplary postmodern beings.

In Chapter 4 I suggested that the time-space that cosmetic surgery bodies inhabit
is 'other' because it refuses to accept traditional temporality and seeks to create its
own durée by *designing* ageing. Cosmetic surgery has the potential to work with
digital technologies to allow us to occupy multiple temporalities and durées and also
multiple spaces: real and imaginary, organic and artificial, human and non-human.
Perhaps our material and digital worlds will one day be so closely woven that
surgery per se won't be necessary – we'll be able to adopt digital skins like wrapping
paper. We might take on animal shapes or enter virtual places where bodies are made
of dust or wind. These musings are the stuff of science fiction – but remember, so
was 'cyberspace' when Gibson imagined it in 1984.

Federation Square

I showed in Chapter 2 how cosmetic surgery in its current form shares the constrained aesthetics, desires and aims of the Bonaventure. I suggested that following Jameson's logic we can picture bodies surgically altered in interesting, non-repressive ways. Feminist geographer Kathleen Kirby suggests that new kinds of postmodern space 'may offer precisely the material for building a new kind of subjectivity, one that will not leave non-dominant subjects at the theoretical and political margins' (1996: 46). It is this utopic notion that leads me to speculate on how a much more recent postmodern building, Federation Square in Melbourne, might work as a template for cosmetic surgery that is not bound by the tyrannies of 'femininity' and youth.

Federation Square is a complex of public buildings housing Australian art galleries, a centre for the moving image, alternative cinema space, cafes and restaurants. Put simply, its aesthetics and corporeal experiences invert the Bonaventure's. Both structures lack definite entry-points but while the Bonaventure's entrances are closed and almost indiscernible, Federation Square's edges blur into adjoining streets and the adjacent riverbank: it is 'open' like an origami slightly undone. Where the Bonaventure's mirrored surface is vertical and non-porous Federation Square's façades pulse with multihued angles and unpolished, fragmented stonework – this is a building with cellulite. And where the Bonaventure discourages walking in favour of grand spectacle via elevators, Federation Square's walls flow into its footways while unstructured pathways and ground level text-sculptures encourage wandering. It is dramatically different in conception and in terms of its usage to the Bonaventure and suggests ways that cosmetic surgery could move beyond its current glossy airbrushed aesthetic.

The Square is radically unsquare, comprising seemingly haphazard checks and intersecting triangles in its overall plan and patchworked surfaces (Figure 17). Architect Julian Raxworthy writes that the gradual incline of its plaza gives 'one's stride a peculiar but active sense of movement' (n.d.: 8). This is in marked contrast to the Bonaventure's focus on escalators and elevators. The 'peak' of the plaza offers winks to the nearby river and into the galleries. In terms of usage, architecture critic Leon Van Schaik describes the endless casual visitors who 'throng the space ... [enjoy] views in and out, and engage with this repository of their culture in a new-found civility' (2003:61). This is a building that from its inception both absorbed and extended the city's existing cultures. It is ambitiously *part* of the metropolis, not dumped in place like the Bonaventure but woven into the existing cityscape (see Figure 18). Raxworthy calls it a 'delicate and dense pedicure for the city, seen through lanes and gaps in blocks' (n.d.: 10). This is a highly planned environment where every piece of material is carefully placed while each stone retains its geological markers – nothing is homogenised. The organic is self-consciously married to the manufactured to create stimulating and sociable space. Intimacy is combined with enormity: for example, the zigzag edges of the immense desert-like plaza offer shade

Figure 17 Federation Square, Melbourne, paving detail, photo courtesy David Gabriel-Jones

Figure 18 Federation Square, Melbourne, looking towards St Paul's Cathedral, photo courtesy David Gabriel-Jones

and sanctuary. Human scale and pace are integral to the site's successful operation. Connectivity, non-uniformity and deliberate 'leftover' spaces result in continual interest and expressiveness.

For all its considerate interjections with the city though, Federation Square acknowledges its insertion as *wounding*. Its edges jut and shatter while its intimate textures are raised and dimpled, expressing their own scarification. Valerie Fournier has written about how wounds can increase connectivity between bodies and the world: 'injuring provides, by its massive opening of human bodies, a way of connecting disembodied beliefs or ideas with the force and power of the material world (the flesh)' (2002: 69). Federation Square recognises the violence of its own creation and in doing so makes muscular connections with the city in a way that the Bonaventure can't. In this way it is more closely aligned with body modification practices such as scarification and tattooing than with mainstream cosmetic surgery, which in trying to create seamlessly smooth bodies is secretive and in denial about its painful processes.

Sydney artist Yiorgios Zafiriou has undergone a series of cosmetic surgery operations including breast reduction, lipectomy,[1] nipple grafts and an abdominoplasty (tummy-tuck). He took great care to achieve a scar-result he was happy with and took sketches to the consultations (see Figure 19): 'to discuss with my surgeon what

Figure 19 Yiorgios Zafiriou, *Scar Patterns* (2004), image courtesy the artist

I wanted as scar residue inscribed on my chest' (2006: 60). This seemingly small act of control and the way that Zafiriou has shared his experiences at art shows and conferences is a way to both demystify cosmetic surgery procedures and take some control of the process.

In the 2005 exhibition *Somatechnics* at Macquarie University, staged as part of the Body Modification Conference Mark II, Zafiriou exhibited seven printed panels inspired by his original sketched diagrams. He says that his *Breast Surgery Scar Patterns* are 'pastel, soft and approachable. They conceal and reveal the bloody nature of surgery' (2006: 62).

After his operations he created soap and leather out of his own biological waste.[2] He says 'liposuction fat and skin excised during cosmetic surgery are actually very useful materials. The leather is an ideal trim for hats, bags and shoes' (email correspondence with the author, 2006). Deliberately provocative, his work highlights the very *material* nature of cosmetic surgery whilst aligning it with practices of sustainable recycling.

Private and public architectures are often likened to or consciously based upon the human form and psyche. In *The Architectural Uncanny*, Anthony Vidler documents in the work of postmodern architects such as Daniel Libeskind a return to the notion of architecture embodying and abstractly representing the human body – an idea that was seemingly abandoned along with the rise of Modernism (1992: 69–82). Tracing histories of body and architecture, Vidler finds distinctions and similarities between the referent or figurative body in Renaissance buildings and the rise of corporeal metaphors in postmodern architecture. He explains how the notion of a 'whole', perfect body was used as architectural analogy before Modernism: 'buildings were bodies, temples the most perfect of all ... Francesco di Giorgio showed a figure superimposed literally on the plan of a cathedral and of a city, while Filarete compared the building's cavities and functions to those of a body, its eyes, ears, nose, mouth, veins, and viscera.' (1992: 71)

In contrast, Vidler describes the body found in more recent architectural forms as '...a body in pieces, fragmented, if not deliberately torn apart and mutilated almost beyond recognition' (1992: 69). Federation Square fits his descriptions of architectures that express a disturbed and 'cut' or even dismembered body. However, it is also a space where bodies may manoeuvre softly, secure in their heterogeneity. Precisely because the environment acknowledges its own wounding capacity, folds itself into its surrounds, is constructed of diverse materials that are made to fit together without losing their individual histories, and creates a variety of nooks and pockets that cradle the body, it invites a body/architecture relation that is a postmodern version of di Giorgio's body-in-the-cathedral (Figure 20).

In Chapter 5 I explained Mary Russo's definition of the grotesque: 'the body of becoming, process, and change ... connected to the rest of the world' (1994: 62–3). The grotesque body acts out a carnivalesque and participatory symbiosis that sutures the gap between voyeur and exhibited artefact. This helps explain

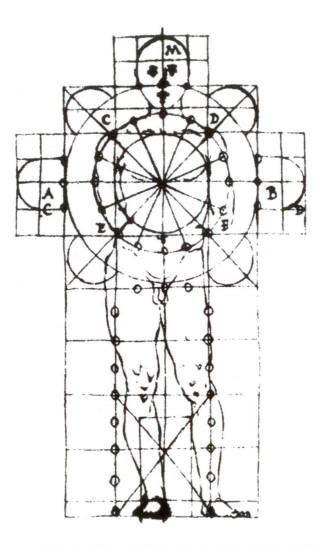

Figure 20 Francesco di Giorgio (1439–*c*.1501). Drawing inscribing the human body into a basilica plan, Trattati di Archittetura, Ingegeria e Arte militare, Siena, Italy

how Federation Square's aesthetics could be translated into cosmetic surgery. The Square is a 'grotesque' body intertwining with its environment, remarking upon its own otherness while maintaining closeness to the rest of the city. In contrast the Bonaventure is a (wilfully) 'freak' body-on-display, separate to its surrounds. The buildings are not just metaphors, they also affect the human bodies inside them: in the Bonaventure bodies are bound to be either spectacle or audience, but in Federation Square relations are much more mobile as distinctions between inside and outside are blurred and people range over and through its heterogeneous planes.

Conclusion

> 'It's going to be more complicated than that,' interpolated Lizzie. 'This old witch sees storms ahead, my girl. When I look to the future, I see through a glass, darkly. You improve your analysis, girl, and then we'll discuss it.' (Angela Carter, *Nights at the Circus*, quoted in Russo, 1994: 179)

Many of the extreme practitioners I have discussed in previous chapters are more 'freak' than 'grotesque'. But if a trajectory such as the one between the Bonaventure and Federation Square is drawn between mainstream cosmetic surgery and individuals who have 'gone too far' we see that while they may be 'freaks' now, they nevertheless point towards a moment when such modifications could in fact be near-mainstream. Russo argues that the body of the freak has the potential to embody all of the positive social significance that Bakhtin's idealised grotesque and carnivalesque body offered, and that it can act as a vital connection between all parts of contemporary society: 'As a radical model of sociality, the freak body is as capacious and extensive as the grotesque body in the model of Bakhtin. It reaches out and makes fantastical connections between and within genders, bodies, costumes, subcultures, architectures, landscapes, and temporalities.' (Russo, 1994: 106) Of course this is only *potential*, because as long as freak bodies are still belittled, punished and banished, as I have shown they often are, the side effects of freakishness outweigh the possibilities for social change. Lolo Ferrari chose freakishness utterly and fatally. She embraced makeover culture on literal and mythological levels and as a 'living corpse' highlighted its deathlike aspects. Farrah Fawcett and Cher have had 'one operation too many', pushing anti-ageing surgery to its limits and overstepping boundaries of 'graceful ageing'. Pamela Anderson's unstable breast implants show that all femininity is a movable mask, a performance, while Jocelyn Wildenstein's unusual and defiant idea of beauty simply challenges mainstream aesthetics. Michael Jackson now has a face unlike any other. He resembles a Japanese anime princess and pioneers a new aesthetic; Are Flågan describes him as a 'Posterchild for the Future' (2003). Orlan orchestrated a series of astonishing performances that highlighted how mainstream cosmetic surgery adheres to an incredibly narrow version of loveliness, and how it only takes a slight turn to reposition it as something artistically radical. These practitioners show that cosmetic surgery has the potential to move from its current meagre aesthetic to being a celebration of the grotesque becoming-body. Grotesque cosmetic surgery would display its assorted effects without embarrassment, embracing heterogeneity and its overlaps with prosthetics and other body modifications.

It is hard to imagine a place where there might be multifarious bodies altered in styles like Jackson's or Orlan's, or with wings or extra limbs or eyes, but we already live with pierced tongues, hair dyes and nail extensions and not so long ago the now-common eyebrow ring seemed radical. A structure like Federation

Square is akin to Rosen's wings and Morgan's scored-on wrinkles; while celebrating surface aesthetics, it also moves towards a mobile functionality that is adaptive to its environment and enhances its region. It actively denies homogeneity and bears its own 'scars' proudly. Forms like this, that attempt to express the intertwining of nature/culture and past/present in ways that augment and comment upon the existing city, could both accommodate and inspire such diverse bodies while also embracing ones that may be *unmodified* because, as I suggest below, choosing *not* to have cosmetic surgery may soon be radical.

Although contemporary cosmetic surgery – especially for its extreme practitioners – offers new ways of dealing with corporeality, space and time, it remains essentially unfriendly, emphasising a uniform of white, middle-class, feminine beauty (Haiken, 1997: 175–227; Negrin, 2002; Padmore, 1998). Perhaps its current manifestation is a stepping stone that will lead to techniques that will allow bodies greater aesthetic and functional freedoms. An embrace of the metaphorical possibilities of the practice allows for a more open notion of the body-in-space, one that is close to Francesco di Giorgio's body-in-a-cathedral where organism and built environment support each other. The architectural templates here point towards an imaginative redeployment of cosmetic surgery, opening it to the possibility of creating bodies that are layered with aesthetic richness, fully interactive with each other and their environments, and shamelessly grotesque.

There is one form of engagement with cosmetic surgery that I have deliberately largely ignored: not having any. Many feminists will choose this option. But I have little doubt it will be increasingly difficult – facelifts are now accepted practice for wealthy baby-boomers and may well be commonplace for generation Ys and Xs. The decision *not* to have cosmetic surgery may soon require its own fortitude and knowledge about why cosmetic surgery exists and how it operates in and through makeover culture. It will have to work alongside cosmetic surgery's powerful promises of transformation and offer its own, better, promises. Opposition to cosmetic surgery may soon be useless for feminist ends unless it can be explained and recognised *as resistance*. Otherwise, it will be interpreted as 'not looking after yourself' and will enforce the very norms it wishes to question. And of course this compulsory 'explaining' and 'resisting' is yet another part of makeover culture, where labour is ever-present.

Cosmetic surgery is a crucial part and quintessential example of makeover culture. The cultural logics of makeover culture emphasise continual performances of becoming: improving, growing and developing are all more valued than achieving a point of finality. Good citizens of makeover culture effect endless renovations, restorations and maintenance on themselves and their environments, stretching and designing their faces, their bodies, their ages and their connections with technologies and other bodies. In turn, nothing is ever complete or perfected: everything and everyone is always in need of a literal or metaphorical facelift.

Notes

Introduction

1. In 2005, 1,813,542 invasive cosmetic surgeries were recorded by members of the American Society of Plastic Surgeons (ASPS) and other similar professional bodies. Liposuction was the commonest procedure followed by rhinoplasty, breast augmentation, blepharoplasty and abdominoplasty. If we add non-surgical procedures such as dermabrasion, collagen and Botox® injections to the list, the number increases to more than ten million procedures in 2005. In the period between 1992 and 2005, the number of surgical and non-surgical procedures performed by ASPS members increased by 775%; the increase from 2004 to 2005 was 38% (http://www.plasticsurgery.org/public_education/Statistical-Trends. cfm). British statistics are smaller and less comprehensive but show similar trends. The British Association of Aesthetic Plastic Surgeons (BAAPS) reported a 35% increase in operations from 2004 to 2005, with the top procedures being, in order, breast augmentation, blepharoplasty, breast reduction, face/neck lift, rhinoplasty, abdominoplasty and liposuction (http://www.baaps.org.uk/content/ view/49/62/). While these statistics are significant, they do not indicate the total number of operations performed, as they omit procedures performed by non-certified practitioners in both countries.

2. In Chapter 3 I refer to surgeons as 'he' and recipients as 'she'. While there are certainly female (even perhaps feminist) cosmetic surgeons who deserve attention, as do male recipients of cosmetic surgery, my generalisations merely highlight the gendered state of contemporary cosmetic surgery. Most cosmetic surgeons are men (one in nine is a woman) and most cosmetic surgery recipients (91%) are women (Davis, 2003: 41). Suzanne Fraser says that in popular culture surgeons are nearly always presented as male and recipients as female. She argues that this is not merely indicative of how things are but that such discourse is also materially productive, helping to create the conditions that it represents: 'the representation of surgeons as male and recipients as female is both the "product and process" of cosmetic surgery as a technology of gender; here gender stereotypes emerge from and help produce asymmetrical patterns in surgical practice' (2003: 63).

Chapter 1 Before/After: From Heresy to Makeover Culture

1. *NW* and *New Idea* are popular Australian women's magazines at the cheaper end of the market.
2. *The Jerry Springer Show* is a US programme shown on daytime television in Australia. A live talk show based around members of the public making 'confessions' to each other, it includes topics like 'I love you both' and 'Surprise! Your wife is a man.'
3. Chris Noth played 'Mr Big' in the US television series *Sex and the City*.
4. The saline implants are fitted with a valve that can be accessed after a local anaesthetic and a small incision. The implants can be made smaller or larger by adding or reducing saline through the valve. This technology is mainly used when women's breasts swell due to pregnancy and/or shrink after breastfeeding, so rather than highlighting the manufactured nature of the implants it does the opposite – keeping the breasts a uniform size throughout hormonal fluctuations.

Chapter 2 Space and Place: Globalisation and Mediascapes

1. Ethnoscape describes the 'landscape of people' who shift around the world, including immigrants, refugees, tourists, etc. Technoscape refers to computational and mechanical flows of information and technology that easily cross national borders. Finanscape is a way to describe the multinational currency that flows through the world's stock markets 'at blinding speed' (Appadurai, 1990a: 298).
2. In 2005 in the USA, non-whites had 2.3 million cosmetic surgery procedures – a 65% increase in twelve months, accounting for 20% of all cosmetic surgeries. Asian Americans had 437,000 surgeries, a rise of 58% from 2004. Latinos underwent more than 921,000 procedures, the largest number for any ethnic group, followed by African Americans, with 769,000. Cosmetic surgery for these two groups grew by 67% each in 2004. And while the most popular procedures overall were liposuction and breast augmentation, for the Asian community (whose cosmetic surgery rose 58%) they were rhinoplasty and double eyelid surgery (American Society of Plastic Surgeons, http://www.plasticsurgery.org/news_room/PST-06–04.cfm).
3. The Jamiah is 'a common community-based fund-raising system in Saudi Arabia where a number of members agree to pay a specific amount of cash into a common pool every month; the total sum is then given to one of the participants each month, providing a lump sum that he or she would not otherwise have to cover large personal expenses' (Hatrash, 2006).
4. Per capita rates of plástica are second only to the USA (and were higher in 2003). Brazil has about 4,000 registered cosmetic surgeons compared to the USA's 5,000. The average age of a plástica patient dropped from 55 in 1980 to 35 in 2000, and 21% of patients in 2004 were under 19 (Edmunds, unpublished).

5. Architect Cassandra Fahey's name for the work is 'White Noise'.
6. The 'open mouth' may be a comment on Anderson's pornographic status. In 1996 she and her then-husband Mötley Crüe drummer Tommy Lee starred in a sex video that they said had been stolen from their home and distributed on the Internet. The garage door is also acknowledgement of another St Kilda icon, Luna Park, a fun-park entered through a huge grinning mouth.
7. The glowing, concentric rings are similar to those that surround Maria, the robot that stars in Fritz Lang's 1927 silent film *Metropolis*. Significantly, they appear around her in the scene where she is created.

Chapter 3 Morphing Industries: Surgeons, Patients and Consumers

1. Actor-network theory (ANT) has been developed by Bruno Latour (1987, 1993), Michel Callon (1986) and John Law (1992) as a sociological approach for the examination of cultures, artefacts and processes. One of its most useful characteristics is that it states any 'actor-network' contains vital *objects* or *things* and people. These 'non-human' actors play key roles in determining power and establishing 'truths'. Its origins are in social studies of science and technology *in the making*. One of its main aims has been to explore the processes by which 'facts' and scientific 'truths' emerge over time. Its focus on methods of becoming and the ways that norms are produced aligns it nicely with makeover culture.
2. *Buyer of Beauty, Beware* (2006) (http://www.abc.net.au/4corners/special_eds/20061023/) shows breast augmentation and liposuction operations. The hour-long documentary also discusses differences between cosmetic and plastic surgeons in Australia.
3. The connection between art and science is the subject of an important body of psychoanalytic theory. It argues that 'pure art' and 'pure science' share similar psychic processes of projection and introjection and are two sides of the same coin: 'complementary ... surfaces of one truth' (Sharpe, 1935: 201). Further study of cosmetic surgeons using this body of knowledge might yield important insights. However, my concern here is not with the psychoanalytic processes of surgeons-as-artists but with their ongoing negotiations of a secure position within makeover culture.
4. See Dr. Francis R. Palmer III at http://www.beverlyhillsplasticsur.com/art.html
5. See Dr. Michael Evan Sachs at http://www.michaelevansachs.com/artgallery.htm
6. See Dr. A. Chasby Sacks at http://www.azcossurg.com/aboutus.htm
7. See Dr. Tony Prochazka at http://www.finecosmeticsurgery.com/our_doctor.htm
8. Because Botox® is a living substance a vial – which holds enough for several injections – must be used within four hours of opening. Sometimes patients have to pay for an entire vial whether they use it all or not. Botox® parties are a way to share the cost and so reduce each recipient's bill.

9. This is a line from Emily Dickinson's poem 'Because I could not stop for Death'.
10. Botox® costs between AU$300 and AU$500 per treatment and needs to be repeated every three to six months.
11. Bruno Latour glosses blackboxing as 'the way scientific and technical work is made invisible by its own success. When a machine runs efficiently, when a matter or fact is settled, one need focus only on its inputs and outputs and not on its internal complexity. Thus, paradoxically, the more science and technology succeed, the more opaque and obscure they become' (1999: 304).

Chapter 4 Stretched Middle Age: Mothers, Daughters and Fairy Tales

1. Covino says that 'in 2000, *Modern Maturity* was the most widely circulated magazine in America, having long held that distinction' (2004: 98).
2. In fact stretched middle age is beginning earlier and earlier. One of my students in 2005 told the class she used Botox® regularly. Her face was extremely smooth and when she smiled and spoke the skin on her forehead and around her eyes didn't move. She did indeed appear 'ageless' but throughout semester I assumed she was in her forties. She told me in the last class she was twenty-six.
3. Sociologist Abigail Brooks argues that cosmetic surgery creates 'cold, still' bodies by creating numbness and restricting muscle movement (2004: 228–9).
4. For reproductions of the images discussed here, see Jones, 2004a.

Chapter 5 Makeover Misdemeanours: Magazines and Monstrous Celebrities

1. While it is not uncommon to encounter two unrelated pieces on cosmetic surgery within one magazine, and find them completely at odds on questions of cosmetic surgery's legitimacy or desirability, they may share other, more far-reading perspectives on things like the meaning of 'nature', or the location of agency (Fraser, 2003: 62).

Chapter 6 Sleeping Beauties: Lolo Ferrari and Anaesthesia

1. At the time of writing a trial has not taken place. The charges may have been dropped, as online searches in English and French reveal nothing further.
2. Bronfen analyses many representations of feminine death including the anatomical wax casts of cadavers – mainly women – that were popular in the eighteenth century. She also looks at Richardson's 1747 novel *Clarissa* wherein a man

wishes to embalm the heroine's corpse, remove her heart and keep it in spirits so he can look at it forever.

3. Anaesthetic and aesthetic have the same etymological root, the Greek *aesthēsia*: perceptive or sensible.

4. Many pornographic websites still include pictures of Ferrari and make no mention of her death.

5. (*)(*) is sometimes used to represent Ferrari by her fans on websites.

6. One reading of the change from a full-figured body to the lean one we know today is in terms of women's move into public life. Full bodies can be understood to be domestic, wholesome and mothering while slim ones appear more 'masculine' and therefore have a better 'cultural fit' in the public domain, so are more acceptable as women enter the workforce and the professions.

7. All but one of the cosmetic surgery recipients I interviewed were what I call 'lifetime dieters': they had dieted and exercised all of their adult lives and were very much invested in being slim and slimmer. One murmured as we drove past an overweight woman, 'I would kill myself if I was that fat' (Kelly).

8. This cultural paradox is exemplified and the whole tension between 'hardbodies' and breasts is intensified in bodybuilding culture. The bodybuilding arena is perhaps the site in Western culture where women's bodies are seen to be the most masculine, particularly during competition where bodies must display maximum muscle and minimum fat/softness. In bodybuilding, breast implants are almost standard. Writing in 1998, Heywood stated that at least 80% of A-grade competitive women body builders in America have breast implants, and all women featured on the coveted cover of *Flex* have had implants (1998: 35–6).

9. 'Tszuj' is a word popularised by the television show *Queer Eye for the Straight Guy*. It means 'taking something and tweaking it, fluffing it, nudging it or finessing it to be a little more fabulous and a lot more fun' (Allen, Douglas, Filicia, Kressley, Rodriguez, 2004: 9). In the case of interior decorating it might mean adding a 'final touch' like a scented candle, in fashion it might mean a stylish rolling of the sleeves or addition of a scarf.

Chapter 7 Makeover Artists: Orlan and Michael Jackson

1. When I approached her to seek permission to use her images in this book Orlan generously consented, but wrote 'One thing I would like is to make sure of is that there is no mention in the book the idea that I am trying to "look like" Mona Lisa, or Venus ... this has very often been said about me, but is not my intention at all. I try to clarify this as much as possible' (email to the author, February 2007).

2. 'Viscera' usually means guts, or the inner abdomen, but can also mean 'the soft interior organs in the cavities of the body' (*Macquarie Dictionary*, 1997). I believe Orlan simply means to cut as deep as she can.

3. 'Mona Lisa's famous smile is a thin mouth receding into shadow. Her expression, like her puffy eyes, is hooded. The egglike head with its enormous plucked brow seems to pillow on the abundant, self-embraced Italian bosom. What is Mona Lisa thinking? Nothing, of course. Her blankness is her menace and our fear' (Paglia, 1990: 154).

4. Orlan's performances could have been particularly disturbing for New York and European Jews who may have associated them with Nazi medical experiments during the Second World War. Paul Virilio has made the connection between her work – which he calls 'Baroque surgical mutilations' – and Nazi experiments (Virilio, 2003: 43).

5. Orlan told Peggy Zeglin Brand 'I don't want the imitation; I don't want to be the model. Fashion has caught up with me' (2000: 298).

6. The 'one drop rule' (or 'one drop theory') says that it only takes one drop of African blood to make a person African American in the United States. 'The nation's answer to the question "Who is black?" has long been that a black is any person with **any** known African black ancestry' (Davis, F. J., 1991).

7. Stephen Hinerman, a cultural theorist who writes about popular music, gives a thoughtful and in-depth media analysis of the tabloid narratives that surrounded the 1993 child-abuse scandal that engulfed Jackson and was eventually settled out of court for a much-speculated-upon 'undisclosed sum'. The 1993 scandal included genuine police charges and a court case, and showed Jackson to be a '"perfect polysemic figure" in that anyone's interpretation could never be completely wrong' (Hinerman, 1997: 159). As Hinerman says, the tabloid discourses around the 1993 scandal were not concerned with finding or presenting a 'truth' or coming to a conclusive finding. Rather, the sales interests of the tabloids were best served by perpetuating a continuation of the questions: 'Even if they were ultimately unable to find a truth, the Jackson story gave them a profitable, lengthy narrative to focus on. The "Did he or didn't he?" question did not have to be answered so much as asked – and asked, and asked, and asked' (1997: 159–60).

8. In February of 2003 a documentary about Michael Jackson, *Living with Michael Jackson*, was aired in countries across the world. It was made by British journalist Martin Bashir, who was already famous for having conducted a controversial interview with Princess Diana. Bashir spent eight months – on and off – with Jackson, and the documentary contained scenes that audiences found bizarre. A shopping scene showed Jackson on a spree, randomly spending hundreds of thousands of dollars (at least) on Egyptian artefacts in a glitzy Las Vegas shopping mall. Another scene showed Jackson with two of his children – both wearing veils – visiting the Berlin Zoo. But the most controversial scene showed an adolescent boy and Jackson holding hands and telling Bashir of sleepovers where the boy stayed in Jackson's bed. Jackson told Bashir he didn't see anything wrong with sharing his bed with children, describing the practice as 'charming' and 'innocent'. The 2005 court case where Jackson faced charges of child molestation was brought by a boy who featured in the documentary.

9. The lead singer of English band *Pulp*, Jarvis Cocker, stormed the stage and bared his buttocks to the cameras in protest, incensed by what he saw as an absurd and arrogant performance.

10. In a strange parallel, Jackson is reported as releasing a 'never-ending string of press releases' promising elaborate projects such as theme parks in Zimbabwe and Warsaw, purchase of The Royal Yacht *Britannia*, and a business partnership with a Saudi prince (Orth, 2004: *Vanity Fair*, http://www.vanityfair.com/commentary/content/articles/050207roc002d)

11. During the operation she plans to speak and breathe into the hole, giving it life and voice. The juxtaposition of the faux-vulva with the mouth (the activities Orlan plans are all to do with her mouth: reading aloud, laughing, talking) is horrifying and comic – a visual vagina dentata.

12. Notably though, the cosmetic surgery of Orlan and Jackson makes it impossible for them to operate in the mundane or suburban world. Orlan says 'in my normal life – in the bus, in the subway, in the street – it ends up being very difficult for me. All types of people want to speak with me, look at me' (quoted in Brand, 2000: 295).

Chapter 8 Transit Lounges for the Self

1. Lipectomy, like liposuction, removes fat. However lipectomy is purely surgical – skin is lifted and the fat is cut away – while liposuction uses suction. Liposuction is sometimes known as 'suction assisted lipectomy'.

2. In the movie *Fightclub* (1999) the protagonists steal bags of human fat from the dumpster of a liposuction clinic and turn it into soap, which they then sell to department stores to be purchased by the same women who had it sucked out in the first place. References to soap and leather made from human skin should also, always, evoke memories of the Holocaust.

References

Adams, A. (1997) 'Molding Women's Bodies: The Surgeon as Sculptor', *Bodily Discursions: Genders, Representations, Technologies*, State University of New York Press, Albany, NY, pp. 59–80.

Adams, P. (1996) 'Operation Orlan', *The Emptiness of the Image: Psychoanalysis and Sexual Differences*, Routledge, London and New York, pp. 141–59.

Alexander, I. (2002) 'Requirements, Myths, & Magic', *Requirenautics Quarterly*, http://easyweb.easynet.co.uk/~iany/consultancy/papers.htm (accessed 27 August 2005).

Allen, T., Douglas, K., Filicia, T., Kressley, C. and Rodriguez, J. (2004) *Queer Eye For The Straight Guy*, Bantam, Sydney, Auckland, Toronto, New York and London.

American Academy of Facial Plastic and Reconstructive Surgery (2004), *2003 Membership survey: Trends in Facial Plastic Surgery*, http://www.facial-plastic-surgery.org (accessed 27 August 2005).

American Board of Plastic Surgery, http://www.abplsurg.org/index.htm (accessed 27 August 2005).

American Society of Plastic Surgeons, http://www.plasticsurgery.org (accessed 25 November 2006).

Appadurai, A. (1990) 'Disjuncture and Difference in the Global Cultural Economy' (long version), *Public Culture* 2(2): 1–24.

Appadurai, A. (1990a) 'Disjuncture and Difference in the Global Cultural Economy' (short version), *Theory, Culture & Society* 7: 295–310.

Appadurai, A. (2001) 'Grassroots Globalisation and the Research Imagination', in Arjun Appadurai (ed.), *Globalisation*, Duke University Press, Durham, NC and London, pp. 1–22.

Aronsohn, R. and Epstein, R. (1970) *The Miracle of Cosmetic Plastic Surgery*, Sherbourne Press Inc., Los Angeles.

Ashikari, M. (2005) 'Cultivating Japanese Whiteness: The 'Whitening' Cosmetics Boom and the Japanese Identity' *Journal of Material Culture* 10(1): 73–91.

Awful Plastic Surgery, http://www.awfulplasticsurgery.com/ (accessed 20 November 2006).

Awkward, M. (1995) '"A Slave to the Rhythm": Essential(ist) Transmutations; or, The Curious Case of Michael Jackson', *Negotiating Difference: Race, Gender, and the Politics of Positionality*, The University of Chicago Press, Chicago and London, pp. 175–192.

Baird, J. (2004) *Media Tarts: How the Australian Press Frames Female Politicians*, Scribe Publications, Australia.

Balsamo, A. (1996) *Technologies of the Gendered Body: Reading Cyborg Women*, Duke University Press, Durham, NC, New York and London.

Bankard, B. (April 13, 2004) 'Ugly Women', *Phillyburbs Insider*, http://www.phillyburbs.com/pb-dyn/news/212–04132004–281113.html (accessed 27 August 2005).

Bashir, M. (2003) *Living with Michael Jackson* (television documentary), Granada Television, first shown on ITV (UK), 3 February 2003.

Baudrillard, J. (1994) *Simulacra and Simulation* (trans. Sheila Glaser), University of Michigan Press, Michigan.

Baudrillard, J. (1995) 'Plastic Surgery for the Other', *ctheory* No. 41 (trans. F. Debrix), http://www.ctheory.com (accessed 27 August 2005).

Baudrillard, J. (1998) *America* (trans. C. Turner) Verso, London and New York.

Bergson, H. (1955) *An Introduction to Metaphysics* (trans. T. E. Hulme), New York, The Liberal Arts Press.

Biggs, H. (2002) 'The Ageing Body', in M. Evans and E. Lee (eds), *Real Bodies: A Sociological Introduction*, Palgrave Macmillan, London and New York, pp. 167–84.

Biggs, S. (1999) *The Mature Imagination: Dynamics of Identity In Midlife and Beyond*, Open University Press, Philadelphia.

Blistene, B. (2004) *Orlan: Carnal Art*, Editions Flammarion, Paris.

Blum, V. (2003) *Flesh Wounds: The Culture of Cosmetic Surgery*, University of California Press, Berkeley, Los Angeles, London.

Boland, Y. (1998) 'Skin Rejuvenators', *Good Medicine Handbook: The Complete Guide to Cosmetic Surgery and Anti-Ageing*, ACP Publishing, Australia, pp. 28–33.

Bonner, F. (2003) *Ordinary Television: Analysing Popular TV*, Sage Publications, London, Thousand Oaks, New Delhi.

Bordo, S. (1990) 'Reading the Slender Body', in M. Jacobus, E. Fox Keller and S. Shuttleworth (eds), *Body/Politics: Women and the Discourses of Science*, Routledge, New York and London.

Bordo, S. (1993) *Unbearable Weight: Feminism, Western Culture, and the Body*, University of California Press, Los Angeles.

Bordo, S. (1997) *Twilight Zones: The Hidden Life of Cultural Images From Plato to O.J.*, University of California Press, Los Angeles.

Bordo, S. (1998) 'Braveheart, Babe, and the Contemporary Body', in E. Parens (ed.), *Enhancing Human Traits*, Georgetown University Press, Washington, DC, pp. 189–221.

Bordo, S. (2000) 'Beauty (Re)Discovers the Male Body', in P. Z. Brand (ed.), *Beauty Matters*, Indiana University Press, Bloomington and Indianapolis, pp. 112–54.

Borges, J. L. (1978) *'The Aleph' and Other Stories, 1933–1969* (trans. N. T. Di Giovanni), E. P. Dutton, New York.

Braidotti, R. (1994) *Nomadic Subjects: Embodiment and Sexual Difference in Contemporary Feminist Theory*, Columbia University Press, New York.

Braidotti, R. (1996) 'Signs of Wonder and Traces of Doubt: On Teratology and Embodied Differences', in N. Lykke and R. Braidotti (eds), *Between Monsters, Goddesses and Cyborgs: Feminist Confrontations with Science, Medicine and Cyberspace*, Zed Books, London and New Jersey, pp. 135–52.

Brand, P. Z. (2000) 'Introduction: How Beauty Matters', in P. Z. Brand (ed.), *Beauty Matters*, Indiana University Press, Bloomington, pp. 1–23.

Brand, P. Z. (2000a) 'Bound to Beauty: An Interview with Orlan', in P. Z. Brand (ed.), *Beauty Matters*, Indiana University Press, Bloomington, pp. 289–313.

Brand, S. (1994) *How Buildings Learn: What Happens After they're Built*, Penguin Books, New York.

British Association of Aesthetic Plastic Surgeons, http://www.baaps.org.uk/ (accessed 25 November 2006).

Broadbent, L. (2002) 'Age Old Problem', *NW*, Australian Consolidated Press, Australia, 21 January, pp. 22–5.

Bromley, M. and Vokes-Dudgeon, S., (2004) 'Keeping up with the toy boys', *New Idea*, Australian Consolidated Press, Australia, 28 February, pp. 4–7.

Bronfen, E. (1992) *Over Her Dead Body: Death, Femininity and the Aesthetic*, Manchester University Press, Manchester.

Brooks A. (2004) ' 'Under the Knife and Proud of It:' An Analysis of the Normalization of Cosmetic Surgery', *Critical Sociology* 30(2): 207–39.

Brown, S. D. (1999) 'Electronic Networks and Subjectivity', in Á. J. Gordo-López and I. Parker (eds), *Cyberpsychology*, Macmillan Press Ltd, London, pp. 146–65.

Brownell, S. (2005) 'China Reconstructs: Cosmetic Surgery and Nationalism in the Reform Era', in Joseph S. Alter (ed), *Asian Medicine* and *Globalisation*, University of Pennsylvania Press, Philadelphia, pp. 132–50.

Brunsdon, C. (2003) 'Lifestyling Britain: The 8–9 Slot on British Television', *International Journal Of Cultural Studies* 6(1): 5–23.

Brush, P. (1998) 'Metaphors of Inscription: Discipline, Plasticity, and the Rhetoric of Choice', *Feminist Review* 58: 22–44.

Butler, J. (1990) *Gender Trouble: Feminism and the Subversion of Identity*, Routledge, London and New York.

Buyer of Beauty, Beware (2006) Television Documentary, Australian Broadcasting Corporation *Four Corners*, aired 23 October. Available on broadband at http://www.abc.net.au/4corners/special_eds/20061023/ (accessed 7 November 2006).

Bytheway, B. (1995) *Ageism*, Open University Press, Buckingham.

Cadigan, P. (1991) *Synners*, Bantam Books, New York.

Callon, M. (1986) 'Some elements of a sociology of translation: domestication of the scallops and the fishermen of St Brieuc Bay', in J. Law (ed.), *Power, Action and Belief*, Routledge and Kegan, London, pp. 196–233.

Callon, M. (1991) 'Techno-economic networks and irreversibility', in J. Law (ed.), *A Sociology of Monsters: Essays on Power, Technology and Domination*, Routledge, London and New York, pp. 132–61.

Canguilhem, G. (1978 [1966]) *On the Normal and the Pathological*, D. Riedel Publishing Company, Dordrecht, Boston, London.

Castañeda, C. (2002) *Figurations: Child, Bodies, Worlds*, Duke University Press, Durham, NC and London.

Chaney, D. (1995) 'Creating Memories: Some Images of Aging in Mass Tourism' in M. Featherstone and A. Wernick (eds), *Images of Aging: Cultural Representations of Later Life*, Routledge, London and New York, p. 209–24.

Charles, C. A. D. (2003) 'Skin Bleaching, Self-Hate, and Black Identity in Jamaica', *Journal of Black Studies* 33(6): 711–28.

Chernin, K. (1994) *The Obsession: Reflections on the Tyranny of Slenderness*, Harper Perennial, USA and Canada.

Cindy Jackson official website, http://www.cindyjackson.com (accessed 27 August 2005).

Cosmetic Institute of Australia, http://breastimplantsaustralia.com (accessed 27 August 2005).

Cosmetic Surgery Report (1999), New South Wales Select Committee Report to the NSW Minister for Health, NSW Health Care Complaints Commission.

Collins, H. and Yearley, S. (1992) 'Epistemological Chicken', in A. Pickering (ed.), *Science as Practice and Culture*, University of Chicago Press, Chicago and London, pp. 301–26.

Couldry, N. (2003) 'Actor Network Theory and Media: Do They Connect and on What Terms?' http://www.lse.ac.uk/collections/media@lse/pdf/Couldry_ActorNetworkTheoryMedia.pdf (accessed 19 November 2006).

Covino, D. C. (2001) 'Outside-In: Body, Mind, and Self in the Advertisement of Aesthetic Surgery', *Journal of Popular Culture* 35(3): 91–102.

Covino, D. C. (2004) *Amending the Abject Body: Aesthetic Makeovers in Medicine and Culture*, State University of New York Press, Albany.

Crandall, J. (1997) 'Bodies on the Circuit', *ctheory*, http://www.ctheory.com (accessed 27 August 2005).

Darling-Wolf, F. (2003) 'Media, Class. And Western Influence in Japanese Women's Conceptions of Attractiveness', *Feminist Media Studies* 3(2): 153–70.

Davies, B. (2000) *(in)scribing body/landscape relations*, AltaMira Press, New York and Oxford.

Davis, F. J. (1991) 'The One-Drop Rule Defined', *Who is Black? One Nation's Definition*, Pennsylvania State University Press, Pennsylvania (excerpt) http://www.pbs.org/wgbh/pages/frontline/shows/jefferson/mixed/onedrop.html (accessed 27 August 2005).

Davis, K. (1991) 'Remaking the She-Devil: A Critical Look at Feminist Approaches to Beauty', *Hypatia* 6(2): 21–43.

Davis, K. (1995) *Reshaping the Female Body: the Dilemma of Cosmetic Surgery*, Routledge, New York.

Davis, K. (1996) 'From Objectified Body To Embodied Subject: A Biological Approach To Cosmetic Surgery', in S. Wilkinson (ed.), *Feminist Social Psychologies: International Perspectives*, Open University Press, Buckingham and Philadelphia, pp. 104–18.

Davis, K. (1997) '"My Body is My Art": Cosmetic Surgery as Feminist Utopia?' in K. Davis (ed.), *Embodied Practices: Feminist Perspectives on the Body*, Sage, London, pp.186–81.

Davis, K. (1998) 'The Rhetoric of Cosmetic Surgery: Luxury or Welfare?' in E. Parens (ed.), *Enhancing Human Traits: Ethical and Social Implications*, Georgetown University Press, Washington DC, pp. 124–34.

Davis, K. (2003) *Dubious Equalities and Embodied Differences: Cultural Studies on Cosmetic Surgery*, Rowman and Littlefield Publishers, Inc, Oxford.

De Beauvoir, S. (1970) *Old Age*, Penguin, Harmondsworth, England.

Delves Broughton, P. (1999) 'Divorce for Bride of Wildenstein', *Zimbabwe Sunday Times*, 25 April, http://www.suntimes.co.za/1999/04/25/news/news20.htm (accessed 27 August 2005).

Depraz, N. (2002) 'Confronting death before death: Between imminence and unpredictability', *Phenomenology and the Cognitive Sciences* 1(2): 83–95.

Dery, M. (1996) *Escape Velocity: Cyberculture at the End of the Century*, Grove Press, New York.

Doane, M. (1982) 'Film and Masquerade: Theorizing the Female Spectator', *Screen* 23, Nos 3/4, pp. 74–87.

Douglas, M. (1979) *Purity and Danger*, Routledge and Kegan Paul, London.

Dr 90210 (n.d.) http://www.ienhance.com/dr90210/dr90210-premiere.asp (accessed 27 August 2005).

Duckett, V. (2000) 'Beyond the Body: Orlan and the Material Morph', in V. Sobchack (ed.), *Meta Morphing: Visual Transformation and the Culture of Quick-Change*, University of Minnesota Press, Minneapolis and London, pp. 208–23.

Edmunds, A. '"Engineering the Erotic": Aesthetic medicine and modernization in Brazil' (unpublished paper).

Extreme Makeover official website (n.d.) http://abc.go.com/primetime/extrememakeover (accessed 27 August 2005).

Featherstone, M. (1995) *Undoing Culture: Globalisation, Postmodernism and Identity*, Sage, London, Thousand Oaks, New Delhi.

Featherstone, M. (1999) 'Body Modification: An Introduction', *Body & Society* 5(2): 1–13.

Featherstone, M. and Wernick, A. (1995) 'Introduction' in M. Featherstone and A. Wernick (eds), *Images of Aging: Cultural Representations of Later Life*, Routledge, London and New York, pp. 1–15.

Fischer, D. (1978) *Growing Old in America*, Oxford University Press, Oxford.

Flågan, A. (2003) 'Posterchild for the Future: Living with Michael Jackson', *ctheory*, http://www.ctheory.net/text_file.asp?pick=370 (accessed 27 August 2005).

Foucault, M. (1973) *The Birth of the Clinic: An Archaeology of Medical Perception* (trans. A. Sheridan), Tavistock Publications, London.

Foucault, M. (1977) *Discipline and Punish: The Birth of the Prison* (trans. A. Sheridan), Vintage, New York.

Fournier, V. (2002) 'Fleshing out Gender: Crafting Gender Identity on Women's Bodies', *Body & Society* 8(2): 55–77.

Fraser, S. (2003) *Cosmetic Surgery, Gender and Culture*, Palgrave Macmillan, London and New York.

Fraser, S. (2003a) 'The agent within: agency repertoires in medical discourse on cosmetic surgery', *Australian Feminist Studies* 18(40): 27–44.

Freuh, J. (1996) 'Polymorphous Perversities: Female Pleasures and the Post-menopausal Artist', *Erotic Faculties*, University of California Press, Berkeley, London, pp. 81–112.

Friedan, B. (1994) *The Fountain of Age*, Vintage, London.

Fuller, G. (1997) 'Generation Airbag' (exhibition review), *Globe e Journal of Contemporary Art*, Issue 5 http://www.arts.monash.edu.au/visarts/globe/issue5/sbtxt.html (accessed 27 August 2005).

Gagné, P. and McGaughey, D. (2002) 'Designing Women: Cultural Hegemony and the Exercise of Power among Women Who Have Undergone Elective Mammoplasty', *Gender and Society* 16(6): 814–38.

Gatens, M. (1996) *Imaginary Bodies: Ethics, Power and Corporeality*, Routledge, London and New York.

Gibson, P. C. (2000) '"No-One Expects Me Anywhere": Invisible Women, Ageing and the Fashion Industry', in S. Bruzzi and P. Church Gibson (eds), *Fashion Cultures: Theories, Explorations and Analysis*, Routledge, London and New York, pp. 79–89.

Gibson, W. (1984) *Neuromancer*, Ace Books, New York.

Gilleard, C. and Higgs, P. (2000) *Cultures of Ageing: Self, Citizen and the Body*, Prentice Hall, Harlow.

Gillespie, R. (1996) 'Women, the Body and Brand Extension in Medicine: Cosmetic Surgery and the Paradox of Choice', *Women and Health* 24: 69–83.

Gillis, J. R. (1975) *Youth and History: Tradition and Change in European Age Relations, 1770 to the Present*, Academic Press, New York.

Gillis, J. R. (1993) 'Vanishing youth: The uncertain place of the young in a global age', *YOUNG: Nordic Journal of Youth Research* 1(1), http://www.alli.fi/nyri/young/1993–1/y931gill.htm (accessed 27 August 2005).

Gilman, S. L. (1999) *Making the Body Beautiful: A Cultural History of Aesthetic Surgery*, Princeton University Press, Princeton, New Jersey.

Gilman, S. L. (2005) 'The Astonishing History of Aesthetic Surgery', in Angelika Taschen (ed.), *Aesthetic Surgery*, Taschen, Köln, London, Los Angeles, Madrid, Paris, Tokyo, pp. 62–111.

Gilman, S. L. (2005a) 'Ethnicity and Aesthetic Surgery', in Angelika Taschen (ed.), *Aesthetic Surgery*, Taschen, Köln, London, Los Angeles, Madrid, Paris, Tokyo, pp. 112–35.

Gimlin, D. (2000) 'Cosmetic Surgery: Beauty as Commodity', *Qualitative Sociology* 23(1): 77–98.

Goin, J. and Goin, M. (1981) *Changing the Body: Psychological Effects of Plastic Surgery*, Williams & Wilkins, Baltimore.

Gold, T. (April 2002) 'Meg Ryan', *Marie Claire* No. 80, pp. 82–6.

Goodbyemag (n.d.) 'Lolo Ferrari', www.goodbyemag.com (accessed 27 August 2005).

Goodman, M. (1994) 'Social, Psychological, and Developmental Factors in Women's Receptivity to Cosmetic Surgery', *Journal of Aging Studies* 8(4): 375–96.

Greer, G. (1999) *The Whole Woman*, Doubleday, London.

Greer, G. (2000) 'Gluttons for Porn', *The Observer*, Sunday 24 September, http://observer.guardian.co.uk/review/story/0,6903,372210,00.html (accessed 27 August 2005).

Griffin, A. (1996) 'Facial Figurations', *New Statesman & Society*, 12 April, p. 30.

Griffin, K. (2003) 'A Changed Woman: Kathy Griffin', *People Magazine*, 14 July, www.ienhance.com (accessed 27 August 2005).

Grimm Brothers (1898) *Grimm's Fairy Tales* (trans. L. L. Weedon) Ernest Nister, London, http://www.scils.rutgers.edu/~kvander/snowwhitetext.html (accessed 27 August 2005).

Grimm Brothers (1973) 'Snow-White and the Seven Dwarfs', in L. Segal and M. Sendak (eds), *The Juniper Tree and Other Tales from Grimm, 2*, The Bodley Head, London, pp. 256–74.

Grimm Brothers (1987) *The Complete Fairy Tales of the Brothers Grimm: Volume I. Tales 1–100* (trans. J. Zipes), Bantam, New York.

Grosz, E. (1994) *Volatile Bodies: Towards a Corporeal Feminism*, Allen & Unwin, Sydney.

Gullette, M. (1997) *Declining to Decline*, The University Press of Virginia, Charlottesville and London.

Gullette, M. (2004) *Aged by Culture*, The University of Chicago Press, London.

Haiken, E. (1997) *Venus Envy: A History of Cosmetic Surgery*, The Johns Hopkins University Press, Baltimore, Maryland.

Haiken, E. (2000) 'The Making of the Modern Face: Cosmetic Surgery', *Social Research* 67(1): 81–97.

Halberstam, J. (1995) *Skin Shows: Gothic Horror and the Technology of Monsters*, Duke University Press, Durham, NC.

Hambleton-Jones N. (2005) *10 Years Younger*, Transworld Publishers, London.

Hareven, T. K. (1995) 'Changing Images of Aging and the Social Construction of the Life Course' in M. Featherstone and A. Wernick (eds), *Images of Aging: Cultural Representations of Later Life*, Routledge, London and New York, pp. 119–34.

Hari, J. (2002) 'Winging it not just a flight of fancy', *The Sydney Morning Herald*, 16–17 March, World Section, p. 23.

Harkness, L. (2004) *The Australian Guide to Cosmetic Surgery*, Coulomb Communications, Port Melbourne Australia.

Hartley, P. (n.d.) *Project Façade*, http://www.projectfacade.com (accessed 20 November 2006).

Hatrash, H. (2006) 'Demand for Plastic Surgery On the Rise, Says Specialist', *Arab News*, Sunday 7 May, http://www.arabnews.com (accessed 21 August 2006).

Heath, S. (1986) 'Joan Riviere and the Masquerade', in V. Burgin (ed.), *Formations of Fantasy*, Methuen & Co. Ltd, London, pp. 45–61.

Henley, J. (2000) 'Larger than Life', *The Guardian Archive*, http://www.guardian.co.uk (accessed 27 August 2005).

Henley, J. (2002) 'Husband arrested for Lolo Ferrari's Murder', *The International Guardian*, http://www.guardian.co.uk/international/story/0,3604,660564,00.html (accessed 27 August 2005).

Henley, J. (2002a) 'Doing Lolo Justice', *Guardian Unlimited*, http://www.guardian.co.uk/elsewhere/journalist/story/0,7792,840235,00.htm (accessed 27 August 2005).

Hernandez-Perez, E. and Khawaja, H. A. (2003) 'Praise for Cosmetic Surgery', *International Journal of Cosmetic Surgery and Aesthetic Dermatology* 5(2): 207–11.

Hesse-Biber, S. (1996) *Am I Thin Enough Yet?: The Cult of Thinness and the Commercialization of Identity*, Oxford University Press, Oxford and New York.

Heyes, C. J. (2007) *Self-Transformations: Foucault, Ethics, and Normalized Bodies*, Oxford University Press, New York and Oxford.

Heyes, C. J. (2007a) 'Cosmetic Surgery and the Televisual Makeover: A Foucauldian Feminist Reading', *Australian Feminist Media Studies* 7(1): 17–32.

Heywood, L. (1998) *Bodymakers: A Cultural Anatomy of Women's Body Building*, Rutgers University Press, New Brunswick.

Hine, T. (1999) *The Rise and Fall of the American Teenager*, Harper Collins, New York.

Hinerman, S. (1997) '(Don't) Leave Me Alone: Tabloid Narrative and the Michael Jackson Child-Abuse Scandal', in J. Lull and S. Hinerman (eds), *Media Scandals: Morality and Desire in the Popular Culture Marketplace*, Columbia University Press, New York, pp. 143–63.

Hirsch, M. (1989) *The Mother/Daughter Plot: Narrative, Psychoanalysis, Feminism*, Indiana University Press, Bloomington and Indianapolis.

Hirschhorn, M. (1996) 'Orlan: Artist in the Post-human age of mechanical re-incarnation', in G. Pollock (ed.), *Generations and Geographies*, Routledge, London, pp. 110–34.

Hodge, R. and Kress, G. (1988) *Social Semiotics*, Polity Press in association with Basil Blackwell, Cambridge, UK.

Hodgkinson, D. (1998) 'Are These Stars Cheating Their Genes?' *Gloss: The Essential Anti-Ageing Magazine*, Atlantic and Pacific Publishing, Sydney, October/November, pp. 24–6.

Humphreys, L. (2002) *Michael Jackson's Face* (Television Documentary) RDF Media, London.

Huss-Ashmore, R. (2000) '"The Real Me": Therapeutic Narrative in Cosmetic Surgery', *Expedition* 42(3): 26–38.

Ince, K. (2000) *Orlan: Millennial Female*, Berg Publishers, Oxford.

Irigaray, L. (1985) *The Sex Which is Not One* (trans. C. Porter), Cornell University Press, Ithaca, New York.

Jackson, M. (1988) *Moonwalk*, William Heinemann Ltd, London, Melbourne and Auckland.

Jacobson, N. (2000) *Cleavage: Technology, Controversy, and the Ironies of the Man-made Breast*, Rutgers University Press, New Brunswick, NJ.

Jameson, F. (2001) 'Postmodernism, or the Cultural Logic of Late Capitalism', in M. G. Durham. and D. M. Kellner (eds), *Media and Cultural Studies: Keyworks*, Blackwell, Oxford, pp. 550–87 (originally published in *New Left Review* 146 (1984): 53–92).

Jameson, F. (2003) 'Future City', *New Left Review* 21: 65–79.

Jeffreys, S. (2000) '"Body Art" and Social Status: Cutting, Tattooing and Piercing from a Feminist Perspective', *Feminism and Psychology* 10(4): 409–29.

Jones, M. (2004) 'Architecture of the Body: Cosmetic Surgery and Postmodern Space', *Space and Culture: International Journal of Social Spaces* 7(1): 90–101.

Jones, M. (2004a) 'Mutton Cut Up as Lamb: Mothers, Daughters and Cosmetic Surgery', *Continuum: Journal of Media and Cultural Studies* 18(4): 525–39.

Jones, M. and Sofoulis, Z. (2002) 'Orlan and Stelarc in the Middle Ages', in Joanna Zylinska (ed.), *The Cyborg Experiments: the Extensions of the Body in the Media Age*, Continuum, London p. 56–72.

Jordan, J. W. (2004) 'The Rhetorical Limits of the "Plastic Body"', *Quarterly Journal of Speech* 90(3): 327–58.

Kamel, Y. (2004) 'Taking looking good that extra step', *Middle East Times*, http://yomnakamel.blogspot.com/2004_05_01_yomnakamel_archive.html (accessed 21 August 2006).

Kaplan, E. A. (1999) 'Trauma and Aging: Marlene Dietrich, Melanie Klein, and Marguerite Duras', in K. Woodward (ed.), *Figuring Age: Women, Bodies, Generations*, Indiana University Press, Bloomington and Indianapolis, pp. 171–94.

Karash, J, and Smith Knight, J. (2000) 'Family Finds Price of Beauty Worth Results', Dayton Daily News, 6 June, http://www.personalsurgeon.com/library/familyfindsprice.asp (accessed 27 August 2005).

Karcher, E. (2005) 'The Michelangelo of the Scalpel: Ivo Pitanguy', in Angelika Taschen (ed.), *Aesthetic Surgery*, Taschen, Köln, London, Los Angeles, Madrid, Paris, Tokyo, pp. 170–6.

Katz, S. (1995) 'Imagining the Life-span: From Premodern Miracles to Postmodern Fantasies', in M. Featherstone and A. Wernick (eds), *Images of Aging: Cultural Representations of Later Life*, Routledge, London and New York, pp. 61–75.

Kaw, E. (1993) 'Medicalization of Racial Features: Asian American Women and Cosmetic Surgery', *Medical Anthropology Quarterly*, New Series 7(1): 74–89.

Kim, L. S. (2004) 'Race and Reality … TV', *Flow: A Critical Forum on Television and Media Culture* 1(4), idg.communication.utexas.edu/flow (accessed 27 August 2005).

Kirby, K. M. (1996) 'Re: Mapping Subjectivity: cartographic vision and the limits of politics', in N. Duncan (ed.), *BodySpace: Destabilizing Geographies of Gender and Sexuality*, Routledge, London and New York, pp. 45–55.

Kirkland, A. and Tong, R. (1996) 'Working within Contradiction: The Possibility of Feminist Cosmetic Surgery', *Journal of Clinical Ethics* 7(2): 151–9.

Koolhaas, R. (2001) 'Junkspace: The Debris of Modernization', *Project on the City 2: Harvard Design School Guide to Shopping*, Taschen, Koln and Tokyo, pp. 408–21.

Kristeva, J. (1982 [1974]) *Powers of Horror: An Essay on Abjection* (trans. L. S. Roudiez), Colombia University Press, New York.

L'Image Cosmetic Surgery, http://www.limage.com.au/home.asp (accessed 27 August 2005).

Laforteza, E. (2007) 'The Whitening of Brown Skins and the Darkening of Whiteness', *Reconstruction: Studies in Contemporary Culture 7(1)*, http://reconstruction.eserver.org/

Lakoff, R. T. and Scherr, R. L. (1984) *Face Value: The Politics of Beauty*, Routledge & Kegan Paul, Boston, MA.

Lang (2004) 'Heather and Jane take to the Knife', *Woman's Day*, ACP Publishing Ltd, Sydney, p. 16.

Latour, B. (1987) *Science in Action: How to Follow Scientists and Engineers through Society*, Harvard University Press, Cambridge, MA.

Latour, B. (1993) *We Have Never Been Modern* (trans. Catherine Porter), Harvard University Press, MA.

Latour, B. (1994) 'On Technical Mediation – Philosophy, Sociology, Genealogy', *Common Knowledge* 3(2): 29–64.

Latour, B. (1997) 'On Recalling ANT', Keynote Speech made at the 'Actor Network and After' Workshop, Keele University, www.comp.lancs.ac.uk/sociology/stslatour1 (accessed 28 August 2007).

Latour, B. (1999) *Pandora's Hope: Essays on the Reality of Science Studies*, Harvard University Press, Cambridge, London.

Law, J. (1992) 'Notes on the Theory of the Actor-Network: Ordering, Strategy, and Heterogeneity', *Systems Practice* 5(4): 379–93.

Lee, Q. (1994) 'cyborg identity/metamorphosis/skin', *Hitting Critical Mass: A Journal of Asian American Cultural Criticism* 1(2), http://socrates.berkeley.edu/~critmass/v1n2/leeprint.html (accessed 30 September 2003).

Lerche Davis, J. (2003) '10 tips for a successful face lift', http://www.msnbc.msn.
com/id/3076544/ (accessed 19 November 2006).

Levy, M. (2000) 'Cosmetic Surgery Brought Us Closer', *Daily Mail*, London, 25
April, www.personalsurgeon.com/library/broughtuscloser.asp (accessed 6 July
2007).

Lovelace, C. (1995) 'Orlan: Offensive Acts', *Performing Arts Journal* 49: 13–25.

Lyons, A. S. and Petrucelli, R. J. (1978) *Medicine: An Illustrated History*, Abradale
Press, New York.

MacDonald, B. (2001) *Look Me in the Eye: Old Women, Aging, and Ageism*,
Spinsters Ink, Denver, Colorado.

MacDonald, M. (1999) 'The Dark Side of Humanity: The Work of Robert Hertz and
Its Legacy' (book review), *The Australian Journal of Anthropology*, http://www.
findarticles.com/p/articles/mi_m2472/is_1_10/ai_55007538 (accessed 24 August
2007).

Mankiewicz, J. (2003) 'Two Plastic Surgeries?' *MSNBC News*, http://www.msnbc.
com/news/873876.asp?cp1=1 (accessed 6 July 2007).

Manley, J. H. (n.d.) 'The Man in the Mirror', http://www.swmed.edu/home_pages/
publish/magazine/mirror.html (accessed 6 July 2007).

Marianne (n.d.) 'About Me', *YesThey'reFake*, www.yestheyrefake.net/about
(accessed 6 July 2007).

Marshall, P. D. (1997) *Celebrity and Power: Fame in Contemporary Culture*, University of Minnesota Press, Minneapolis.

Mayer, V. (2005) 'Extreme Health Care', *Flow: A Critical Forum on Television and
Media Culture* 2(6), idg.communication.utexas.edu/flow (accessed 6 July 2007).

McCarthy, A. (2005) 'The Republic of Tyra', *Flow: A Critical Forum on Television
and Media Culture* 2(5), idg.communication.utexas.edu/flow (accessed 6 July
2007).

McCorquodale, D. (1996) (ed.), *Orlan: This Is My Body – This Is My Software*,
Black Dog, London.

McGeogh, P. (2006) 'The Changing Face of Iran', *Sydney Morning Herald*, 19–20
August, pp. 23 & 30.

McPherson, T. (2005) 'Transform Me, Please…', *Flow: A Critical Forum on Television and Media Culture* 1(9), idg.communication.utexas.edu/flow (accessed
6 July 2007).

Mead, R. (2006) 'Proud Flesh', *The New Yorker*, 13 November, pp. 90–2.

Mercer, K. (1986) 'Monster Metaphors: Notes on Michael Jackson's *Thriller*',
Screen 26(1): 26–43.

Meronk Eyelid Plastic Surgery, http://www.drmeronk.com/asian/asian-overview.
html (accessed 6 September 2006).

Miller, L. (2003) 'Mammary Mania in Japan', *Positions* 11(2): 271–300.

Moos, D. (1996) 'Memories of Being: Orlan's Theater of the Self' *Art + Text* 54:
67–72.

Morgan, K. (1991) 'Women and the Knife: Cosmetic Surgery and the Colonization of Women's Bodies', *Hypatia* 6(3): 25–53.

Muller, N. (n.d.) 'Interview with Anne Balsamo', http://users.skynet.be/nattyweb (accessed 6 July 2007).

Muller, N. (n.d.) 'Interview with Vivian Sobchack', http://users.skynet.be/nattyweb (accessed 6 July 2007).

Mulvey, L. (1989) 'Visual Pleasure and Narrative Cinema', *Visual and Other Pleasures*, Indiana University Press, Bloomington, pp. 14–26.

Negrin, L. (2002) 'Cosmetic Surgery and the Eclipse of Identity', *Body & Society* 8(4): 21–42.

Nip/Tuck, (2003) 'Nanette Babcock,' FX Networks, US, Series 1, Episode 3.

NW (30 September 2002) 'Designer Doubles', Australian Consolidated Press, Australia, pp. 22–3.

NW (28 July 2003) 'Plastic Surgery Disasters', Australian Consolidated Press, Australia, pp. 12–15.

O'Beirne, N. (1999) 'The "Docile/Useful" Body of the Older Woman', in J. Onyx, R. Leonard and R. Reed (eds), *Revisioning Aging: Empowerment of Older Women*, Peter Lang, New York, pp. 109–22.

O'Bryan, C. J. (2005) *Carnal Art: Orlan's Refacing*, University of Minnesota Press, Minnesota.

Ormrod, S. (1995) 'Feminist Sociology and Methodology: Leaky Black Boxes in Gender/Technology Relations', in K. Grint and R. Gill (eds), *The Gender-Technology Relation: Contemporary Theory and Research*, Taylor & Francis, London and Bristol, pp. 31–47.

Orth, M. (2003) 'Losing His Grip', *Vanity Fair*, http://www.vanityfair.com/commentary/content/articles/050207roc002c (accessed 10 July 2007).

Orth, M. (2004) 'Neverland's Lost Boys', *Vanity Fair*, http://www.vanityfair.com/commentary/content/articles/050207roc002d (accessed 10 July 2007).

Ovid (2004) *Metamorphoses*, Book X (ed. H. Günther), http://www.latein-pagina.de/ovid/ovid_m10.htm#5 (accessed 10 July 2007).

Padmore, C. (1998) 'Significant Flesh: Cosmetic Surgery, Physiognomy, and the Erasure of Visual Difference(s)', *Lateral: A Journal of Textual and Cultural Studies* 1, http://www.latrobe.edu.au/english/lateral (accessed 10 July 2007).

Paglia, C. (1990) *Sexual Personae: Art and Decadence from Nefertiti to Emily Dickinson*, Yale University Press, London and New Haven.

Peterson, R. (2005) 'A Place of Sensuous Resort: Buildings of St Kilda and Their People', St Kilda Historical Society, (e-book) http://www.skhs.org.au (accessed 10 July 2007).

Phillips, T. (2006) 'Changing the face of cosmetic surgery, Brazil leads the plástica revolution', *The Guardian*, Monday 7 August, http://www.guardian.co.uk/brazil/story/0,,1838805,00.html (accessed 19 November 2006).

Pile, S. and Thrift, N. (1995) 'Mapping the Subject', in S. Pile and N. Thrift (eds), *Mapping the Subject: Geographies of Cultural Transformation*, Routledge, London and New York, pp. 13–51.

Poster, M. (2001 [1995]) 'Postmodern Virtualities', in M. G. Durham. and D. M. Kellner (eds), *Media and Cultural Studies: Keyworks*, Oxford, Blackwell, pp. 611–25.

PM Archive (2001) 'Plastic surgery while on safari', 21 May, http://www.abc.net. au/pm/stories/s300362.htm (accessed 5 September 2006).

Prime Time Live (1995) Interview with Michael Jackson and Lisa Marie Presley, http://www.allmichaeljackson.com/interviews/primetimeliveinterview/html (accessed 6 July 2007).

Rackham, A. (1920), *The Sleeping Beauty*, William Heinemann Ltd, London.

Radner, H. (1995) *Shopping Around: Feminine Culture and the Pursuit of Pleasure*, Routledge, New York.

Raxworthy, J. (n.d.) 'Grid Games and Interpretation Machines: A Critique of the Landscape of Federation Square, Melbourne, Australia', unpublished paper.

Ray, R. E. (2003) 'The uninvited guest: mother/daughter conflict in feminist gerontology', *Journal of Aging Studies* 17(1): 113–28.

Renahan, A. (1999) 'Facing extinction: The Lebanese nose', *The Daily Star*, Beirut, 22 February, http://almashriq.hiof.no/lebanon/600/610/617/lebanese_nose.html (accessed 19 November 2006).

Renshaw, H. (2002) 'Celebrity Plastic Surgery Disasters', *NW*, Australian Consolidated Press, Australia, 21 January, pp. 16–19.

Reuters, 'Hitler returns to Berlin – in wax', *China Daily Online*, http://www. chinadaily.com.cn/english/doc/2004–03/18/content_315863.htm (accessed 6 July 2007).

Ring, A. (1998) 'The countdown to new heights of sexist ageism in the media of the new world order', in M. Alexander (ed.), *Refashioning Sociology: Responses to a New World Order*, The Australian Sociological Association 1998 Conference Proceedings, QUT Publications & Printing, Brisbane, pp. 87–96.

Ring, A. (1999) 'Anti-ageing in the era of the older person', *Everybody* (VicHealth) 5, March, pp. 10–12.

Ring, A. (1999a) 'Cosmetic surgery magazines: mass mediating the new face of medical practice', *Australian Studies in Journalism* 8: 118–38.

Ring, A. (1999b) 'The Marketing of cosmetic surgery: doctors and the beauty trade', *The Australian Health Consumer* No. 2: 20–2.

Ring, A. (2002) 'Using "anti-ageing" to market cosmetic surgery: just good business, or another wrinkle on the face of medical practice?' *Medical Journal of Australia* 176(12): 597–9.

Riviere, J. (1986) 'Womanliness As a Masquerade', in V. Burgin (ed.), *Formations of Fantasy*, Methuen & Co. Ltd, London, pp. 35–44 (first published in *The International Journal of Psychoanalysis* (IJPA) 10, 1929).

Robinson, K. (2004) 'Skin bleaching in independent Ghana: the visuality of self-commodification', *Gender and Visuality Conference Proceedings*, University of the Western Cape, Cape Town, South Africa, 26–29 August 2004, http://www.uwc.ac.za/arts/gendervisuality/robinson.doc (accessed 27 August 2005).

Rose, N. (1996) *Inventing Ourselves: Psychology, Power and Personhood*, Cambridge University Press, Cambridge, New York, Melbourne.

Rose, N. (1999) *Powers of Freedom: Reframing Political Thought*, Cambridge University Press, Cambridge.

Rosen, C. (2004) 'The Democratization of Beauty', *The New Atlantis: A Journal of Technology and Society*, Spring, www.thenewatlantis.com/archive/5/rosen (accessed 27 August 2005).

Russell, D. (2004) 'The Tumescent Citizen: The Legend of Ron Jeremy', *M/C Journal* 7(4), http://www.media- culture.org.au/0410/01_citizen.php (accessed 27 August 2005).

Russo, M. J. (1994) *The Female Grotesque: Risk, Excess and Modernity*, Routledge, New York.

Shabazz Steward, N. *I'm Juxtaposing* (blog) http://www.8bm.com/diatribes/Volume01/diatribes016/diatribes313–333/diatribes315.htm (accessed 27 August 2005).

Sharpe, E. F. (1935) 'Similar and Divergent Unconscious Determinants Underlying the Sublimations of Pure Art and Pure Science', *IJP* 16: 186–202.

Shaviro (2003) 'The Pinocchio Theory: Michael Jackson Unmasked' http://www.shaviro.com/Blog/archives/000042.html (accessed 27 August 2005).

Sheldon Lloyd, M. (2005) 'An elective with a top plastic surgeon in Brazil', BMJCareers.com, http://careerfocus.bmjjournals.com/cgi/content/full/330/7499/190 (accessed 8 September 2006).

Sheldon, S. and Wilkinson, S. (1998) 'Female genital mutilation and cosmetic surgery: Regulating non-therapeutic body modification', *Bioethics* 12n(4): 263–86.

Shelley, M. (1985 [1818]) *Frankenstein or, The Modern Prometheus* (ed. M. Hindle), Penguin Books Ltd, Harmondsworth, England.

Shildrick, M. (2002) *Embodying the Monster: Encounters with the Vulnerable Self*, Sage, London.

Sofoulis, Z. (1998) 'Cyborgs and Other Hybrids: Latour's Nonmodernity', paper presented at *Encore Le Corps: Embodiment Now and Then Conference*, Gender Studies Centre, University of Sydney, 8 December 1998 (later published in modified form in German as 'Post- Non- And Para- Human: Toward a Theory of Sociotechnical Personhood' (trans. G. Gehlen) in M. Angerer, K. Peters and Z. Sofoulis (eds), *Future Bodies: Zur Visualisierung von Körpern in Science und Fiction*, Springer-Verlag, Wein and New York, pp. 273–300.

Soja, E.W. (1994) 'Postmodern Geographies: Taking Los Angeles Apart', in R. Freidland and D. Boden (eds), *NowHere: Space, Time and Modernity*, University of California Press, Berkeley, Los Angeles, London, pp. 127–62.

Spitzack, C. (1988) 'The Confession Mirror: Plastic Images for Surgery', *Canadian Journal of Political and Social Theory* 12(1–2): 38–50.

Stewart, S. (1993) *On Longing: Narratives of the Miniature, the Gigantic, the Souvenir, the Collection*, Duke University Press, Durham, NC and London.

Stratton, J. (1996) *The Desirable Body: Cultural Fetishism and the Erotics of Consumption*, Manchester University Press, Manchester and New York.

Talwar, P. K. (2002) 'Scalpel Pretty', http://femina.indiatimes.com/articleshow/26169121.cms (accessed 27 August 2005).

Taschen, A. (ed.) (2005) *Aesthetic Surgery*, Taschen, Köln, London, Los Angeles, Madrid, Paris, Tokyo.

The Gillies Archive, http://www.nzedge.com/heroes/archive (accessed 27 August 2005).

The Royal College of Surgeons, England (n.d.) 'What is the difference between a cosmetic surgeon and a plastic surgeon?' http://www.rcseng.ac.uk/ (accessed 27 August 2005).

Tseëlon, E. (1995) *The Masque of Femininity, The Presentation of Woman in Everyday Life*, Sage Publications, London, Thousand Oaks, New Delhi.

Tulloch, L. (2004) 'Facing the Future', *The Australian Women's Weekly*, ACP Publishing Pty Ltd, Sydney, Australia, November, pp. 137–8.

Turkle, S. (1996) *Life on the Screen: Identity in the Age of the Internet*, Weidenfeld & Nicholson, London.

Van Schaik, L. (2003) 'School of Melbourne: Federation Square', *Monument* 54: 61.

Vasaga, J. (9 May, 2003) 'The doctor and his doll', *The Guardian*, http://www.guardian.co.uk/g2/story/0,3604,952099,00.html (accessed 27 August 2005).

Vidler, A. (1992) *The Architectural Uncanny: Essays in the Modern Unhomely*, MIT Press, Cambridge, MA and London.

Virilio, P. (2003) *Art and Fear* (trans. J. Rose), Continuum, London and New York.

Waldby, C. (2000) *The Visible Human Project: Informatic Bodies and Posthuman Medicine*, Routledge, London.

Walz, T. (2002) 'Crones, Dirty Old Men, Sexy Seniors: Representations of the Sexuality of Older Persons', *Journal of Aging and Identity* 7(2): 99–112.

Warner, M. (1994) *From the Beast to the Blonde*, Chatto & Windus, London, pp. 218–40.

Watts, J. (2003) 'A tall order', *The Guardian*, Monday 15 December, http://www.guardian.co.uk/china/story/0,7369,1107283,00.html (accessed 9 September 2006).

Weaver. L. (2003) 'Cosmetic surgery booming in China', *CNN.com*, http://www.cnn.com/2003/WORLD/asiapcf/east/11/06/china.cosmetic.surgery/ (accessed 9 September 2006).

Weil Davis, S. (2002) 'Loose Lips Sink Ships', *Feminist Studies* 28(1): 7–35.

Weiss, G. (1999) 'The Durée of the Techno-Body', in E. Grosz (ed.), *Becomings: Explorations in Time, Memory, and Futures*, Cornell University Press, Ithaca and London, pp. 161–75.

Who Weekly 10th Anniversary edition (2002) 'Pammy's World', Time Inc., Sydney, 4 March, pp. 110–11.

Wilentz, A (2006) 'To Keep or Not to Keep Your Nose', *Los Angeles Times*, 9 July, http://www.latimes.com (accessed 5 September 2006).

Winter, B., Thompson, D. and Jeffreys, S. (2002) 'The UN Approach to Harmful Traditional Practices: Some Conceptual Problems', *International Feminist Journal of Politics* 4(1): 72–94.

Wolf, N. (1991) *The Beauty Myth*, William Morrow, New York.

Woodward, K. (1991) *Aging and Its Discontents: Freud and Other Fictions*, Indiana University Press, Bloomington and Indianapolis.

Woodward, K. (1995) 'Tribute to the Older Woman: Psychoanalysis, Feminism and Ageism' in M. Featherstone and A. Wernick (eds), *Images of Aging: Cultural Representations of Later Life*, Routledge, London & New York, pp. 79–96.

Young, I. M. (1990) 'Breasted Experience' in *Throwing Like a Girl and Other Essays in Feminist Philosophy and Social Theory*, Indiana University Press, Bloomington, pp. 189–209.

Zafiriou, Y. (2006) *Extreme Art: the Invention of Identity in Performance Art through Ritual, Pain, Body Modification and Surgery*, unpublished Master of Visual Arts Dissertation, Sydney College of the Arts, Sydney University..

Zimmerman, S. M. (1998) *Silicone Survivors: Women's Experiences with Breast Implants*, Temple University Press, Philadelphia.

Zylinska, J. (2002) 'Prosthetics as Ethics', in J. Zylinska (ed.), *The Cyborg Experiments: the Extensions of the Body in the Media Age*, Continuum, London, New York, pp. 214–36.

Index